RENTAL PROPERTY INVESTING

QuickStart Guide®

RENTAL PROPERTY INVESTING

QuickStart Guide®

The Simplified Beginner's Guide to
Finding and Financing Winning Deals,
Stress-Free Property Management,
and Generating True Passive Income

Symon He, MBA

Editors: Bryan Basamanowicz, Marilyn Burkley
Cover Illustration and Design: Katie Poorman, Copyright © 2021 by ClydeBank Media LLC
Interior Design & Illustrations: Katie Poorman, Brittney Duquette, Copyright © 2021 by ClydeBank Media LLC

First Edition – Last updated: May 25, 2021

ISBN-13: 9781636100081 (paperback) | 9781636100098 (hardcover) | 9781636100104 (eBook) | 9781636100111 (audiobook)

Publisher's Cataloging-In-Publication Data
(Prepared by The Donohue Group, Inc.)

Names: He, Symon, author.
Title: Rental property investing QuickStart Guide : the simplified beginner's guide to finding and financing winning deals, stress-free property management, and generating true passive income / Symon He.
Other Titles: Rental property investing Quick Start Guide
Description: [Albany, New York] : ClydeBank Finance, [2021] | Series: QuickStart Guide | Includes bibliographical references and index.
Identifiers: ISBN 9781636100081 (paperback) | ISBN 9781636100098 (hardcover) | ISBN 9781636100258 (spiral bound) | ISBN 9781636100104 (ePub)
Subjects: LCSH: Real estate investment. | Rental housing--Finance.
Classification: LCC HD1382.5 .H4 2021 (print) | LCC HD1382.5 (ebook) | DDC 332.6324--dc23

Library of Congress Control Number: 2021932841

Author ISNI: 0000 000 48306 9096

For bulk sales inquiries, please visit www.clydebankmedia.com/orders, email us at orders@clydebankmedia.com, or call 888-208-6826.
Special discounts are available on quantity purchases by corporations, associations, and others.

ClydeBank Media LLC
69 State Street, Suite 1300A
Albany, NY 12207

Contents

PART I – PLANNING TO WIN AT THE RIGHT PRICE

PART II – PLANNING TO WIN WITH THE RIGHT PROPERTY

BEFORE YOU START READING, DOWNLOAD YOUR FREE DIGITAL ASSETS!

 Tenant Templates

 Various Types of Rental Calculators

 Rental Comparison Worksheet

 Market Analysis Tool

TWO WAYS TO ACCESS YOUR FREE DIGITAL ASSETS

Use the camera app on your mobile phone to take a picture of the QR code or visit the link below and instantly access your digital assets.

or www.clydebankmedia.com/rental-assets

 SCAN ME   **VISIT URL**

A Special Note from the Author

I am writing this book in the midst of the COVID-19 global pandemic, a disruptive event of a scale the world has not seen for more than one hundred years. The effect on real estate markets worldwide is undeniable. Many of you, despite your interest in this space, are sure to question the extent to which rental property investing remains a viable endeavor.

While the effects and implications of the pandemic may have shocked and shuffled the markets, opportunities in rental property, in my judgment, are not destined to fade away, but rather to transform. Some of the rental property markets that have seen their values plummet will see a robust and vigorous recovery, similar to that of the last recession—the great financial crisis of 2008—where countless real estate investors enjoyed lavish capital gains over the decade that followed. In fact, if you're interested in navigating the downturn skillfully, then you've chosen the perfect time to educate yourself on this topic. Throughout the book I'll address some of the pandemic-related challenges, changes, and opportunities presented by these unprecedented times.

Big, disruptive, unforeseen events do more than just damage markets. They also naturally create shifts in behavior. Your challenge as a rental property investor is to learn how to spot those shifts and match them with emerging opportunities both now and in the future. It is my sincere hope that you will use the lessons of this book to equip yourself with the tools you need to survive and thrive in the coming years, aided by a strong portfolio of income-generating properties. You can do it. I'll show you how.

Introduction

This book is for the answer-seekers, those who are curious, skeptical, or admittedly ignorant about rental property investing. Maybe you're unsure of how much money you need to get started or whether you're ready to be someone's landlord. Maybe you're not sure whether you have the chops for negotiating great real estate deals and managing properties. There are many competing and often contradictory voices out there, shouting their opinions as to what you should think about rental property investing. From reality TV shows to news stories to the personal and hearsay accounts of family members and friends, I've found that such anecdotal accounts are more apt to obscure than to illuminate the essential truths of rental property investing. The way a property is acquired and made rent-ready, when depicted on television, rarely lines up with reality. News stories and personal accounts tend to focus on the most extreme, atypical, and negative situations, often involving the "nightmare tenant" or the "evil slumlord." Again, such dramatizations are removed from the day-to-day realities of rental property investing and management. My aim in writing this book is to provide a reliable and realistic source of information on the subject, one based on my own fifteen years of experience in owning and operating rental properties. This type of investing and wealth-building through rental properties is a subject I'm fiercely passionate about, and I gain enormous personal fulfillment from bringing my knowledge and experience to others. Over the last seven years I've engaged and tutored over 350,000 students in 180 countries on this subject. With this book, I aim to expand my reach to an ever-wider class of real estate entrepreneurs.

You should commend yourself for taking interest in such an exceptional entrepreneurial pursuit, one that has the potential to transform your life. Unlike many other wealth-building endeavors, success in rental property investing can be achieved irrespective of a person's education level or how much money they currently have in the bank. Many of the concepts I present in this book are meant to take you from zero knowledge to your first investment. That's where the hardest challenge lies. And when you have your first investment, the fun part is imagining, dreaming, and planning what it will take to go from one property to a whole portfolio of ten properties and more. If you're willing to work hard and stay focused, then you'll find this business has a way of taking good care of you. If you don't quit easily and you know how to roll with the punches as they come, then you'll discover that there are invaluable lessons behind every setback and that each obstacle and hardship you encounter is in fact a crucial stepping-stone on your road to success. I'm looking forward to sharing my knowledge with you in the pages that follow, but first, allow me to share some of the highlights of my own journey in rental property investing.

An Unexpected Path to Real Estate Expertise

I earned my MBA at Stanford after receiving degrees in both computer engineering and economics from UC Irvine. After school, I was hired by a private equity firm to work on commercial real estate acquisitions without any prior background in real estate (we all start with no experience once, even me!). This was a baptism by fire for me, as I was quickly immersed in a new and unfamiliar world, one with its own rhythms and rules, and even its own language. Terms like *asset class*, rental yield, and internal rate of return soon became part of my ever-growing lexicon. After participating in more than $500 million worth of commercial real estate investments over five years, I jumped at the chance to move back to my hometown of Los Angeles to join the Panda Restaurant Group (PRG) in a supporting role for new store openings and market expansions. There, I continued to build upon my real estate investing experience, ultimately becoming responsible for the evaluation and acquisition of commercial properties for the various subsidiaries of PRG, such as Panda Express, Panda Inn, and Hibachi-San.

It was during my tenure at PRG that I was approached by a few of my colleagues and asked to join a group of like-minded investors. The group included several other Panda employees as well as several associates from outside our organization. Because we all worked full time, we called this ragtag bunch "the Weekend Fund." Seeing as I had experience in locating and analyzing commercial properties, I was tasked with building the framework of our investment process. I became the analyst, the trusted member of the group who searched the markets, evaluated risk, and determined our potential profits. Although we all worked to locate potential investment deals, it fell to me to assess those deals and give the ultimate green light for the investment. If I said yes, we would invest.

In just a few years, we located and invested in over thirty rental properties throughout Texas, California, Arizona, and Nevada. My professional experience up to that point in my career had been primarily in *commercial properties*—those intended for business use—but the Weekend Fund venture turned my attention toward single-family home rental properties. I learned the ropes of the *residential property* investment universe, and I loved it. I even decided to begin building my own personal portfolio, outside of the pooled resources of the Weekend Fund. Fast forward to today: I have invested in more than 150 properties, many in pooled investment funds, while several others are traditional direct investments that I continue to operate on my own.

In my quest for higher investment returns, my interest in residential properties naturally opened my eyes to the brave new world of short-term rentals. Over the last several years, these rental opportunities, often found on platforms like Vrbo or Airbnb, have captivated the imagination of the real estate investing community. In response to the budding interest in the topic, I started one of the earliest blogs on the subject, www.learnbnb.com. I also coauthored *Airbnb For Dummies* to help other investors explore the fascinating world of short-term rentals—more on this topic in chapter 6.

From Expertise to "Expert"?

Amid all the analyses I was conducting for my investments, I was also analyzing potential deals for friends and acquaintances seeking advice regarding their investing endeavors. I was happy to respond to these requests for a time, but once word spread that I was an "expert" in the field, those requests flooded in. Was I an expert? Did I have wisdom that people wanted to hear? Maybe. To test the waters, I launched an online course, designed to educate anyone about the field of real estate investing. This course, I reckoned, could become a new venture, a business opportunity I could develop alongside my greater investing journey.

As I began to develop more course material and acquire more and more students, I noticed that two distinct questions were on the minds of most prospective rental property investors:

1. Can I do this?
2. If yes, then how?

Answering the first question is easy. Yes. Property investors come in all shapes and sizes and hail from vastly diverse backgrounds; personality-wise as well, they are not all cut from the same cloth. Common perceptions of the investor, that he is a member of an exclusive club, ranking among society's elite—all of this is nonsense. Being a coach and tutor, I've had successful students of many different stripes who have achieved success in this field, often taking very different approaches. In fact, you'll hear from several of them directly as you proceed through these pages.

If you apply yourself and remain committed to the process, the results will come. Mine is not a get-rich-quick scheme. The process I teach is easy to understand in theory and can be learned and repeated. It doesn't involve complex mathematics or exotic data analysis. It does, however, require commitment, persistence, and hard work. My successful students are those who intrepidly embrace new challenges, trust in themselves, and never quit. If you can work through the frustrations and failures—better still, if you can learn from them—then you are going to succeed in the end.

The answer to the second common question—how do I invest in rental property?—is more nuanced. It's this very question that led me to write this book. In the pages that follow, I will attempt to provide you with my best answer. I will present the principles and processes involved in locating, purchasing, and operating a rental property investment. As with all QuickStart Guide™ titles, the teaching approach I take in this book is suitable for a pure beginner. Many of the concepts and terms presented here may be new to you. Moreover, I might contradict some of the opinions you've previously formed about this topic. All I ask is that you keep an open mind. Stay with me. Follow the examples I provide. By the end of this book, I will have answered the second question and provided a path for you to reap the returns of your first healthy, profitable rental property. After that initial goal is accomplished, the sky's the limit.

Rental Property? In This Economy?

As I'm writing this book, we are in the midst of a global pandemic that has registered nearly 65 million confirmed cases and claimed 1.5 million lives. Unfortunately, it appears we're still only at the start of a major winter wave in the Northern Hemisphere. Schools are closed. Travel is restricted. Thousands of businesses have closed their doors for good. Millions have lost jobs and are unsure if unemployment benefits will be extended. Our world has changed. Our lives have changed. As a caregiver to my immunocompromised mother, I understand firsthand what that means.

Although it is difficult, we must look beyond the immediate impact and examine the long-term implications of this massive disruption. The job market may take several years to recover, and as incomes get stretched and people worry about having enough to pay their bills, this uncertainty spills over into the real estate arena. Despite these troubled times, I continue to see rental property investing as a powerful investing and wealth-building tool. In fact, there are other factors, beyond even the reach of the pandemic and its ensuing economic fallout, that make rental property investing more relevant now than it's ever been before. Here are two reasons that the demand for rentals is increasing and should continue to increase: (1) the persistent urbanization of the country's population and (2) the lifestyle choices of the millennial generation.

In the 1970s, around 70 percent of the population of the United States lived in high-density cities. In recent times, that number has climbed to over 80 percent. The trend of migrating away from rural areas into urban ones is not slowing down, as you can clearly see in figure 1. People want to live in the city. They want access to more vibrant job opportunities, increased local amenities and attractions, and a lifestyle on the vanguard of the hip and modern. To achieve their dreams of living in the city, people rent out of necessity, because buying property is prohibitively expensive.

fig. 1

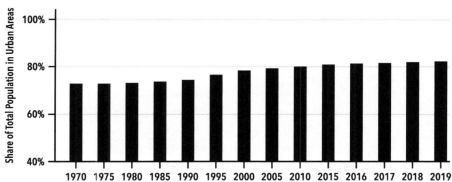

The steady increase of the urban American population

In addition to greater rental demand resulting from urbanization trends, the lifestyle choices of the millennial generation also push rental demand higher. Millennials have radically shifted away from the trends of previous generations. They are delaying marriage. They are choosing to wait longer to have kids. And they are forgoing the tradition of buying their own home. In 2016, when the median age of millennials was approximately twenty-eight, only one third of millennials owned their own homes. Compare this trend with that of the previous two generations: half of all baby boomers and Gen Xers owned their own homes by age twenty-eight. While economic factors such as mounting student debt and increased property values undoubtedly influence the decisions made by millennials, there's more to the story. Beyond economics, the millennial generation is expressing a profound cultural shift in values and norms. They reject the traditions of the past in favor of new lifestyles, which often do not involve getting married and owning a home in the suburbs. They are more transient, shifting jobs four times, on average, in their first decade out of college. The bottom line is that fewer and fewer homeowners means more and more renters.

This optimistic take on the rental market's growth prospects may contravene the stories you've heard. In the wake of the COVID-19 pandemic, the media is rife with overly pessimistic perspectives on the real estate market and its near-term outlook. My advice: don't despair. We've been through economic crises and downturns in the past and the market reliably recovers. The 2008 recession (and subsequent recovery) provides us with lessons on how to navigate these difficult times.

After the great financial crisis of 2008 and the ensuing recession, there's no doubt the real estate market changed. No longer were lending institutions willing to offer mortgages without significant down payments supplied by the borrower. Minimum credit scores and solid employment requirements replaced the "No Income, No Asset" (NINA) loans that once were so easy to find. But even though the real estate market was radically altered, the rental market improved. From 2008 to 2018, the average rental price in the US jumped from $824 to $1,012 per month, a nearly 23 percent bump. And the phenomenon is not restrained to this country. Canada's average rental price increased similarly, from $802 to $1,002 CAD.

fig. 2

AVERAGE RENT

2008	2018
$802 CAD	$1,002 CAD
$824 USD	$1,012 USD

EVOLUTION OF NET AMOUNTS

The ten-year rental market recovery after the 2008 recession

The numbers cited in figure 2 reflect the average rent across the specified country at large. Certain specific markets experienced much quicker recoveries in their rental markets. For example, look at Manhattan, where it's not uncommon for renters to pay upwards of $4,000 per month for their apartments. Rental property owners across all tiers of pricing saw a tremendously quick recovery, with prices bouncing back to pre-recession levels within just three years (figure 3).

fig. 3

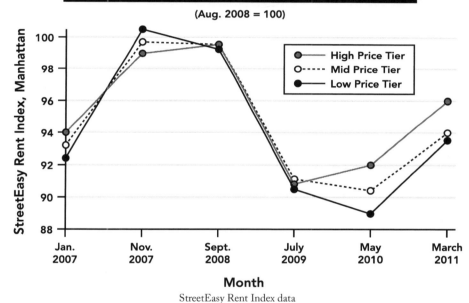

The speedy three-year recovery of rent prices in Manhattan was consistent across multiple price tiers.

Knowing what we do about the fallout of the 2008 real estate market, we can consider it likely that the pandemic will have an effect, even a profound effect, on the future real estate market. But history assures us that rental prices will continue to do what they've always done: recover and thrive. It's important for investors to understand real estate cycles, to expect them and not fear them. I'll teach you how to do this in chapter 3.

Rental Property Offers Security in the Storms

Sudden economic downturns, such as those experienced during the 2008 recession and the COVID-19 pandemic, can leave a serious crack in your financial foundation—your salary may be at risk due to the threat of layoff, and your savings may be at risk due to market volatility. Many economists anticipate that a significant proportion of pandemic-related layoffs, maybe upwards of 40 percent, will be permanent. And even the jobs that do return may not do so for some time.

NOTE

Not to be overly alarmist, but some epidemiologists predict that we will see one or two global pandemics on the same scale as COVID-19 within the next fifty years. That may sound bleak, but it should serve as a reminder that in addition to protecting our health, we also need to find a way to protect our income and investments.

One of the advantages of rental property investing is that it enables you to invest in a resilient asset that reliably appreciates in value over long time horizons and can be less reactive to adverse market conditions and major economic shocks. Mind you, this is especially true if you are able to pick the right markets and properties. Some experts claim that the stock market, despite being more volatile, does outperform real estate in terms of appreciation. If we look at historical returns of the S&P 500—an index that includes 500 different companies—over the last ninety years, the average return is almost 10 percent, 9.8 percent to be precise. In that same period of time, the median housing market in the US appreciated by just 3.5 percent. At a glance, investing in real estate doesn't look like the most solid investment plan. But if we take a closer look, we'll find this comparison to be disingenuous in several ways; it's not exactly apples-to-apples.

First, that magic 10 percent figure for *equities* is an *average* and not indicative of what you can expect every year. Imagine that you had $10,000 invested in a stock market. In year one, you make 100 percent returns, and your portfolio is now worth $20,000. The next year, it loses 50 percent, and your portfolio's worth returns to $10,000. In year three, you make another 100 percent return. And in year four, it loses 50 percent of its value again. Though the average return of this stock market is 25 percent over those four years, what is your actual return? Zero. After four years of riding this wave, you still have only $10,000. Though this is an exaggerated example of the more volatile nature of investing in the stock market, the "average return" metric hides a larger issue, which is the actual return that you can expect in any given year. If you look at the S&P 500 Index, you can find several instances where the annual returns were minus 10 percent or even worse (figure 4). During the crash of 2008, the S&P 500 Index fell by more than 40 percent from its 2007 highs. What would you do if you caught an unlucky streak just as you were about to enter retirement?

fig. 4

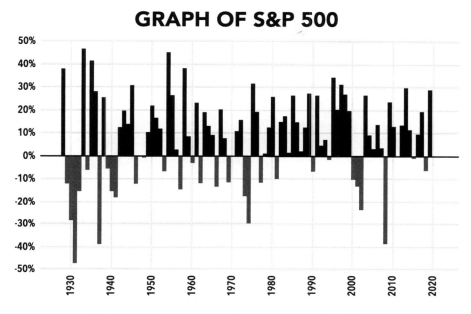

The S&P 500 year-to-year performance over the last 90 years

The advantage of owning a rental property investment is that you have control over your appreciation. When you invest in stocks, you pay your money and hold on for the ride. You have no say in how the company operates. You simply have to trust it will make responsible decisions that lead to an improved value over time. In rental properties, however, your hand is on the steering wheel. If you can buy your property at a market discount (I'll show you how to do that in chapter 4), then you can make renovations and improvements to force an increased appreciation sooner. You're not at the mercy of some unknowable force with a rental property. You have full control over how well your property appreciates.

The second problem in comparing rental property investing to investing in equities is the income, or *yield*. Rental properties can provide a remarkably reliable source of income, especially if you have a diversified portfolio of rentals. Every month, you collect rent from your *tenants*, a factor that is not considered in many investment comparisons. These rental returns will make up the bulk of your total gains. When you factor in rental income as well as the average appreciation value of a property, your rental property investments may outperform equity investments. What about dividend-paying stocks?

Do they not count as income-producing assets? Of course they do, but even still, they can't compare with rental returns.

The returns gained by rental property investors purely through rents collected (irrespective of asset appreciation) are more noteworthy than you might think. Using data that examined real estate returns since 1870, *The Quarterly Journal of Economics* published a study of the proportion of rental income to asset appreciation for several countries. This study also looked at the dividend income from equities, just to be certain that comparisons were made equitably, on an apples-to-apples basis. The results were clear and definitive. For most countries, rental income outperformed the dividend income from equity markets, and that rental income accounted for the bulk of all returns made from an investment property. In the US in particular, the potency of rental income is nothing short of staggering (figure 5).

THE RATE OF RETURN ON HOUSING AND EQUITIES

	HOUSING		EQUITIES	
	Capital Gain Share of Total Return	Rental Income Share of Total Return	Capital Gain Share of Total Return	Dividend Income Share of Total Return
Australia	53.0%	47.0%	59.0%	41.0%
Belgium	40.4%	59.6%	62.3%	37.7%
Denmark	38.5%	61.5%	55.9%	44.1%
Finland	57.9%	42.1%	69.8%	30.2%
France	58.8%	41.2%	56.5%	43.5%
Germany	36.6%	63.4%	52.7%	47.3%
Italy	67.6%	32.4%	72.0%	28.0%
Japan	42.5%	57.5%	71.8%	28.2%
Netherlands	40.2%	59.8%	52.6%	47.4%
Norway	36.6%	63.4%	59.8%	40.2%
Portugal	61.6%	38.4%	80.4%	19.6%
Spain	62.3%	37.7%	57.6%	42.4%
Sweden	37.0%	63.0%	62.8%	37.2%
Switzerland	45.7%	54.3%	58.0%	42.0%
UK	58.6%	41.4%	58.2%	41.8%
USA	31.8%	68.2%	60.5%	39.5%

GRAPHIC

fig. 5

Source: data from Jordà et al., 1879-2015
Comparison between housing and equities markets, income returns included

In the US, *more than two thirds* of your total gains from a property investment are found in your rental income. If you leave that figure out of your comparison (financial experts, I'm looking at you), you are only showing half the picture. Even amid a major market disruption (which I will cover in chapter 13), your rental income can be a resilient and powerful force to build your cash flow and net worth.

Preparing to Win in the Rental Market

There are dozens of practical guides for operating rental properties. Most of them walk you through the minutiae of landlording, dealing with tenants, and determining rents. But that's like teaching you how to parallel park without first covering basic vehicle operation. Before we do anything else, we have to spend some time planning and preparing.

Most outsiders look in on the practice of rental property investing and see a cycle of actions. First, you buy a property. Then you operate it, putting in tenants and collecting rent for a period of time. Finally, you earn enough profit from the property to buy the next property (figure 6).

fig. 6

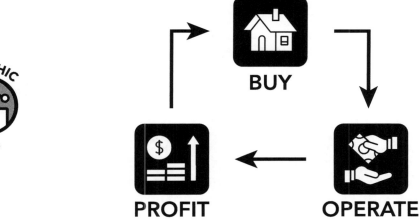

How most people view the cycle of rental property investing

You might be tempted to think that if you simply buy the first property you find, you'll achieve the same results you would have achieved by waiting for the next property, or the next after that. But that's like saying if you just get yourself to the starting blocks of a 100-meter sprint in the Olympics, you'll cross the finish line and get the medal. Does Usain Bolt win his 100-meter races just because he happens to sign up? No. It's the hours of preparation in the gym that you don't see that enable him to win. It's the same with rental property investing. There is a popular aphorism in this business that says "you make your money when you buy." Essentially, this means that if you can prepare to win ahead of time, you set yourself up for success. In my years of being the "go-to analyst" for our Weekend Fund investing venture, I've learned that success is mostly determined by the amount of time spent *preparing* to win.

Let me be your personal trainer, walking you through the steps to prepare to succeed in rental property investing. You'll discover that every stage of the journey requires preparation. Laying the groundwork to buy your rental property at the right price ensures you can collect higher rents and earn more money from your eventual sale of the property. When you educate yourself on how to locate and analyze the best possible investment property, then you'll see significantly higher returns from your investment.

Shall we begin?

Chapter by Chapter

» **Part I: Planning to Win at the Right Price**

» Chapter 1, "Investment Ideas," begins our journey by introducing different strategies for rental property investing. This chapter explains the pros and cons associated with the age (older or newer) of the property chosen for your first investment. We will also explore some creative rebuttals to the argument that investing in rental properties is an overcrowded, overly competitive, and therefore unwinnable endeavor.

» Chapter 2, "How to Finance Your Investment," is the money chapter. We discuss the advantages of using debt to finance your property and how to find the right kind of debt to match your specific need. We'll also cover the creative solutions that can be used when traditional financing options become a challenge.

» Chapter 3, "Understanding Real Estate Cycles," delves into the typical patterns that can be observed in real estate markets. Once you can identify the current conditions of your market, you can make better decisions about when and where to buy.

» Chapter 4, "Building Resilient Cash Flow," talks about how to analyze your property's profit potential so you can earn the maximum rental returns.

» Chapter 5, "Exits and Exchanges," shows you how to identify the right time to sell. Though 90 percent of an investor's strategy involves holding on to their properties for long-term appreciation, this chapter explains when it makes sense to sell off and trade up in order to procure greater income.

» **Part II: Planning to Win with the Right Property**

» Chapter 6, "Rental Property Types," demonstrates the benefits of each type of property you can buy. We'll discuss traditional properties such as single-family homes, condos, and townhouses. We'll also learn about some exciting, uncharted property types— short-term rentals and mobile home parks—that can become lucrative investments for you.

» Chapter 7, "Market Analysis," is where we learn about the tools and measurements that serious investors use to locate and analyze potential deals. We cover how to reject the "good" deals in favor of the great. We'll also show you how to (and why you need to) widen your search to markets all over the country in search of the best deals out there.

» Chapter 8, "Where to Find Property Deals," answers the question of how to find the best potential properties. Good market analysis depends on finding a large number of properties from a wide range of sources. We'll go beyond traditional listings to expose some unexpected ways to find the most lucrative opportunities.

» **Part III: Planning to Win with the Right People**

» Chapter 9, "Building Your Team," introduces you to the people you need on your side. An investor is not alone, and this chapter covers the personal and professional relationships that will prove essential on your journey to success.

» Chapter 10, "The Basics of Landlording," is a practical chapter showing you what it takes to operate your property. We'll work through how to find the right tenant and how to handle the ongoing upkeep.

» Chapter 11, "Buyers and Sellers," shows you how to navigate the negotiations between buyers and sellers. This chapter will cover marketing your property to the right seller as well as presenting yourself as the best buyer for your next investment property.

» **Part IV: Plotting Long-Term Success**

» Chapter 12, "Ongoing Management," discusses the specifics of structuring your investments so that you can continue building and operating a profitable portfolio for years to come. We'll provide tips for selecting the right property management company and the right legal entity for your rental property investing venture.

» Chapter 13, "Long-Term Rental Income," addresses what it takes to create and sustain a stable income in an unstable world. We talk about how to prepare and diversify your portfolio to withstand the inevitable economic downturns.

PART I

PLANNING TO WIN AT THE RIGHT PRICE

| 1 |
Investment Ideas

Hope is not a strategy.

−JAMES CAMERON

There is a maxim in real estate that I have seen to be true, and it's this: You make your money when you buy. Contrary to popular belief, most of your profits are determined by your work at the beginning of the deal. Good rental *returns*, a consistent appreciation of value, and great exits will make you money, but only if you put in the effort at the beginning of the process. I could tell you all about renovations, attracting better tenants, the best time to raise your rents, and so on, but what good would it do if you did not already have in your possession a profitable, sustainable, carefully selected property? Attracting reputable tenants, for instance, is a great skill to have, but if you have no chance of covering your expenses and debt service costs, then your excellent tenants will, at best, mitigate your losses. The same is true for all the minutiae of being a landlord. I can tell you what to do and how to do it well, but everything is secondary to getting a good property at the right price. If you take the time to prepare your first step, then every step that follows is going to be easier and more rewarding.

When little children are learning about the world, they are always asking *why*. When people want to learn about building wealth through rental properties, they always ask *how*. But I think the best question to ask before anything else is *what*. What strategy will you pursue? What investment option suits your desires and your *risk tolerance*? What plan will take you down the road you want to travel?

People decide to invest in rental properties for different reasons. Perhaps you want to create a second income stream for your household. It might be that you want to replace your income entirely. Maybe you're looking to build equity in a property to supplement your retirement plan. Or maybe you're chasing an alternative to the more traditional investments in stocks, mutual funds, and bonds. Rental property will allow you to diversify. Regardless of your ultimate objective, the immediate goal of your very first rental property investment should be to secure your path toward a second investment. Accumulating rental properties, when done well, should be a game of profitable returns. When you do it right the first time, your experience makes it easier to scale your efforts into additional properties. Throughout this chapter, we'll explore a number of strategies as you begin your journey into real estate. But no matter which option seems best to you, remember that your immediate goal is to find a strategy that gets you to the next property.

One of the common misconceptions I hear from my students is that real estate investing essentially requires you to make a gamble. You spend your life savings on a down payment, hope that everything works out, and pray that you don't lose your shirt along the way. That is just not true. You can and should begin with small investments. I will work as hard as I can to give you the knowledge to succeed, but I won't be there to hold your hand on your first deal. There is a steep learning curve that only comes with experience. Try as you may, there will be bumps along the way, such as having long unplanned vacancies or underperforming on your expected rental returns. Although it's rare, you may even fail completely on your first try and lose the whole property to an "act of God," along with your investment. But even if such a worst-case scenario comes to pass, it doesn't have to be the end of your journey. One failure should not be allowed to demolish your resolve or set you back so far financially that you will never try again. Failure is, in fact, an excellent teacher. We all acknowledge Michael Jordan as one of the best basketball players of all time. His records are impressive, with six NBA championship rings, five MVP awards, and more. But not many remember his failures. He claims that he's lost over three hundred games in his professional career, and that on no fewer than twenty-six occasions he was trusted with the game-winning basket only to miss the shot. The key to success is not letting the failures prevent you from trying again.

NOTE

As a benchmark, I would suggest looking for a rental property worth $150,000 that, based on a traditional 20 percent down payment, requires only a $30,000 investment from you. Even if you live in one of the most expensive and inflated areas of the country, it is possible to begin at this level.

There is no "better" strategy. There is only the strategy that works for you and fits with your risk tolerance. Many first-time investors choose properties that are not labor-intensive. These investments, also known as core investments, are stable and reliable. They don't require major renovations in order to be habitable or profitable. The peril here is that these core investments tend to have lower return potential than other, less "turnkey" ready options. Nonetheless, if owning a core property provides the new investor with valuable experience, then the investment is a success. Define your terms this way, and any strategy you choose can work for you.

I will expand on some of the traditional models that rental property investors choose, each with its own pros and cons. I would also like to open your eyes to some fascinating new models that, in my opinion, can provide new investors with solid returns in less crowded *markets*.

The Only Strategy You'll Ever Need

Most newcomers to rental property investing encounter a plethora of investment gurus who claim to possess miracle strategies sure to result in sky-high returns. All you have to do is purchase their "secret" and you'll laugh all the way to the bank. Their hype is fraught with claims and expectations. If I took the time here to articulate my personal viewpoint on these "experts," it would threaten to swallow the entirety of this book. But what I will do is offer some positive commentary on the phenomenon of the real estate investing guru. They are all, at the end of the day, selling the same thing and making the same claim, and they are essentially right! Their strategies, which "work every time," are just variations on the age-old idea of buying low and selling high. The phrase "buy low, sell high" originates in the stock investing world. The real estate equivalent of that phrase is to spend less and make more. Spend less on your purchase price, your rehabs, your ongoing costs, and make more with your rental returns and an excellent exit price. Spend less and make more, and you'll come out ahead.

Though you can dress it up and put it in lights, buying low and selling high is a boring strategy; it's as boring as it is effective. Since it's not sexy to talk about the tried-and-true fundamentals of rental property investing, the "experts" adorn their products with hype and showy language, all in a ploy to sell you what amounts to a boring and unoriginal (albeit effective) strategy. They could save a lot of time and energy by simply reminding you of the old truth. If you buy at a low price and sell at a high price—either through collecting rents that more than cover your mortgage and other costs or through selling to a buyer in a final sale—then you will succeed. Everything else is just window dressing.

Throughout this section, keep in mind that you must always accept an essential trade-off between risks and rewards. The higher the potential reward you desire, the higher the risk you must be willing to accept. Higher risk strategies offer larger financial incentives but come with an increased possibility of losses. Lower risk investments generally aren't as lucrative but offer investors a greater assurance of basic profitability. This trade-off dynamic asserts itself across all strategies and asset types; it is one of the persistent truths of real estate.

Same Strategies, Different Names

The easiest way to think about all the different investment strategies is to simplify the whole transaction into two parts: money coming in and money going out. We call this the *cash flow schedule* and it is measured in both directions (figure 7). The "buy low, sell high" strategy is best thought of as limiting your cash flow out (buying low) and maximizing your cash flow in (selling high).

fig. 7

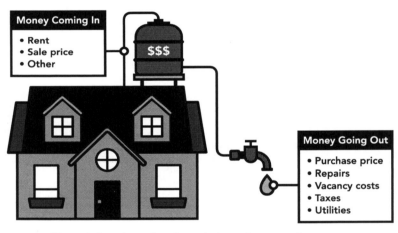

The cash flow dynamics of a typical rental property investment

Cash flow in is all the money that comes to you through the life of your rental property investment. This is likely going to be the rents you collect while operating the property and the final sale profits you make once you sell the property. But there could be other cash flow income as well, for example, charging tenants to use the backyard shed for storage. Investors in commercial properties, like office buildings or multifamily apartments, often have laundry facilities or parking that brings in extra income as well. You can also procure tax savings as a rental property owner through financial vehicles such as a *1031 exchange*. Maximizing your cash inflows will keep more money in your pocket.

Cash flow out, or "outflows," refers to the costs you will incur during your ownership of your rental property. Likely, the largest cash flow out will be the purchase price of the property. You may also see outflows in the form of repair and renovation costs that occur before you bring in your first tenant. You have debt service costs: all the interest and fees the lender is charging you for the loan you have on the property. You will have ongoing repair costs, *vacancy* costs, utilities on the property, taxes, and legal fees/closing costs on both the purchase and the sale. Everything that costs you or prevents your property from collecting its full income potential can be considered cash flow out.

If you are minimizing the cash flow out and maximizing the cash flow in, then you are essentially buying low and selling high and therefore succeeding. For example, let's imagine that you have two friends with rental properties, each trying to sway you to their own brand of operating that investment. Friend number one, we'll call him Andy, prefers to buy older homes in aging communities, but they are located in close proximity to newer neighborhoods. Because of the condition of the homes he buys, he has excellent potential value and pays less at the sale. He typically budgets an additional 10-20 percent of his purchase price to renovate the property and make it more appealing. He then attracts tenants who can't afford the rent in the higher-priced neighborhoods nearby but still want access to the amenities and schools of those neighborhoods. The rent he charges is significantly higher than the next-door neighbor's but attractively lower than those nicer homes in the upscale communities. As a result, his margins are quite high for the area.

Friend number two, we'll call him Graham, prefers a different approach. He chooses newer homes to rent out, one to three years old, and carefully selects properties that are in excellent shape. He rarely does any type of renovations, except maybe some cosmetic upgrades, and often takes over a property with an existing tenant that wants to remain in the home. If he does ever need to find a tenant, he chooses applicants who come with excellent recommendations and are less risky in the long run. His rental returns offer a lower yield for his purchase costs, but that newer home appreciates well over time, and the rent the tenant pays aggressively attacks the *principal* of the loan on the property, building Graham's equity quickly over time.

If some of the terms used in this comparative analysis are foreign, don't worry about it right now. All that matters is the cash flow schedules of each strategy, which are identical to one another. Both Andy and Graham are telling you the same thing—that they have a lock on the best rental property strategy. But you now know they are each employing the same "buy low, sell high" method, just expressed in different ways. In Graham's case, his properties cost more because they are newer, but he has no initial maintenance costs before he begins collecting rent from his tenants. His appreciation is consistent over time, but his exit price isn't dramatically higher than his purchase price. The home should appreciate well, with much of the loan paid down by the time Graham wants to exit the investment. In Andy's case, his purchase costs are lower, but he has significantly higher repair costs and maintenance bills. With three months of vacancy between the purchase and receipt of the first tenant's rent check, he has to wait longer than Graham before receiving any cash flow in, but when it does come, the yield on his investment is higher than that of other rental property investors in the area. And when he's ready to sell, his remodeling will force a new valuation at a higher price.

fig. 8

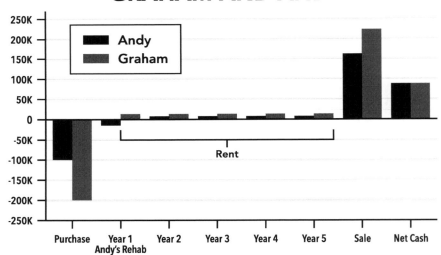

A simplified cash flow schedule for Graham and Andy
over the lifetime of their rental investments

In figure 8, you can see that Andy is paying less of a purchase price, as well as collecting lower rents. But his remodeling efforts give the home a higher valuation at the exit—Andy walks away with $80,000 in profit. Graham, on the other hand, pays double the purchase price for a nicer home and collects higher rents without any rehab costs, but the appreciation level on his home is more conservative. His strategy also nets $80,000 in profits. Each of them ultimately comes out on top because they both abide by a "buy low, sell high" strategy.

Q: Is one strategy better than the other?

Objectively, no. But subjectively, the strategy they each choose works for them. Andy has the expertise and time to remodel older properties where the risk of failure is higher. He chooses to enlist the help of contractors, which adds to his costs. Andy's initial investment is half of Graham's, but the $80,000 profit is equal. We'll cover this metric later, but Andy's yield is much higher, a better payoff from his investment. Graham, on the other hand, works full time and doesn't want operating a rental property to become another full-time gig. He also tends to be risk-averse, preferring safer investments. Although Graham can afford double the initial investment price, his return is the same as Andy's, a natural consequence of accepting less risk.

Should I Buy Old or New Properties?

When investors begin to look through the ads for their first rental property, they are torn between two options. Is it wise to purchase a new home? Or should I save money and buy an older property? And for most first-timers, choosing an older property seems like the financially prudent decision because they are often less expensive. Savvy investors, however, understand it's not the age of the property (or even the price) that matters—it's the value. If you can determine the value of a property, then you will know how to contextualize all the other variables.

You make your profits when you buy, not when you sell.

To buy profitably, you must value accurately. In chapter 4, I will introduce some common measures that will help you expand on this idea of valuation. But for now, as we talk more about investment ideas, I want to introduce a sliding scale for the types of investments that are out there on the market. They can generally be categorized into three groups: core, value-added, and opportunistic investments. *Core investments* are typically newer properties with no major upgrades needed. Core properties have easily projected returns for rent and appreciation. You might think of a recently built single-family home with a long-standing tenant as a typical core investment option. Core investments are found in stable markets with a strong focus on families, the most stable of all tenant types. They are low-risk, low-return investments.

On the opposite end of the spectrum are opportunistic investments, where you need to provide a lot of "sweat equity" to bring the property up to comparable standards. **Opportunistic investments** are a higher risk but in turn provide higher returns. An example of an opportunistic investment would be purchasing a dilapidated home for the raw land's value, tearing it down, and building a new property.

Anywhere between the two poles of core and opportunistic, you have **value-added investments**. You accept some risk of higher repair costs and unforeseen problems with the property in return for a potentially larger return on your investment. An example of this would be buying an older home in an established neighborhood. You redo the kitchen, bathroom, and flooring throughout the home as well as making some minor repairs. In return for your work, you charge higher rent than the properties in that same neighborhood.

Most first-time rental property investors stick with core or, occasionally, value-added investments. These groups present less risk to the investor's *capital* and they offer a stable, consistent (although not extravagant) return in the long term.

For a deeper dive into the core/value-added/opportunistic spectrum, check out my previous ClydeBank Media title, *Real Estate Investing QuickStart Guide*.

Not all new homes fall in the core investment category, and not all older properties require a value-added or opportunistic label. Let's take a glance at the general benefits and drawbacks of newer and older properties.

Buying New Properties

Everyone loves the word "new." Moving into a new home feels different than moving into a home that has endured the wear and tear of time and several different owners. For many homeowners, the ultimate dream is to finally move into a brand-new property of their very own. But does that same new-home appeal logically carry over into the rental property market?

GRAPHIC

fig. 9

Pros of Buying New Homes

» **Deferred maintenance**. As an investor in a new home, you should not need to figure repair costs into your purchase, which should keep your yearly maintenance bills to an absolute minimum. In general, avoid considering a new home with any added repair or maintenance costs.

» **Strong tenant selection**. The types of renters who want to live in a new property tend to be stable, reliable tenants. They want long-term lease agreements and are generally committed to maintaining the property's integrity.

» **Quick occupancy**. If you don't need to spend time renovating the property before installing your first paying tenant, it's much easier to begin covering your expenses. You may not even have to attract tenants if the home's existing tenant wants to remain there, making the transition between owners smooth and simple.

» **Less risk and more stability**. For investors, the option to buy a property that has less risk and promises a stable return over time is incredibly attractive. New homes face less risk of depreciation from disrepair and the wear of time.

Cons of Buying New Homes

» **Homeowner competition.** Who wants to live in a new home? Homeowners. New rental properties face stiff competition from the homeowner market, decreasing your bargaining power with potential tenants. Not to mention that neighborhoods with new homes are predominantly inhabited by people who live in their own properties.

» **Higher sales prices.** Although you always focus on value rather than price, a new rental property might not be cheap. Newer homes are significantly more expensive than older properties, so unless you have the capital to buy a new home, it might not be your best primary investment play.

» **Slow to scale.** The goal of your first investment is to get you to your second. If you buy a new property, it can take longer to get to a position where you are financially able to scale up to owning a second, third, or fourth property.

Buying Older Properties

In my opinion, the best choice for a first-time investor is to begin with an older property. I love the fact that "gently used" properties have a history of performance data that I can analyze to make my decision. On the other hand, there are considerably more unknown costs when buying older properties, which could scare away new investors who lack a high risk tolerance.

If this is your first rental property, a good rule of thumb is to avoid anything that would require you to get a permit. You can paint, repair siding, fix creaky doors, replace flooring, install new appliances, modernize the fixtures in the home, and much more. But if you take on anything structural, such as replacing the plumbing or tearing out walls, the risk level, at least for a beginner, is prohibitively high.

Pros of Buying Older Homes

» **Lower costs**. If you live in a high-priced metropolitan area like Los Angeles or New York, you might want to skip over the next line to avoid getting upset, but in many parts of the country you can buy homes for as little as $25,000. Even in pricier markets, older homes needing repairs can be acquired for pennies on the dollar. This maximizes the value you can get from the property, which is the real advantage of low sales prices.

» **Better returns**. For the price you pay at the sale, and even including repair costs, you can often get better returns from an older property relative to the capital you invest. While the monthly rent you collect may be lower than what you could get with a newer home, the *yield*—defined as the percentage of money you make compared to the money you invest—is much higher.

Cons of Buying Older Homes

» **Higher maintenance costs**. You will pay more than just the purchase price for an older home. Even if you only need to make minor repairs or cosmetic alterations, there will be steeper ongoing maintenance throughout the time of your ownership. Pay attention to the last known installation dates of major components like the roof, hot water unit, and plumbing. The costs of replacing these expensive items will add up quickly when they inevitably fail at some point.

» **Necessity of upgrades.** To draw tenants to your property and charge the rent you want—in other words, to remain competitive—you'll need to include upgrades. There might be nothing functionally wrong with the kitchen appliances, but that burnt-orange '70s color scheme could turn off prospective tenants.

» **Possibility of undesirable location.** You can fix the elements of a property, but you can't fix its location. Newer homes are more likely to be in upscale, stable neighborhoods, whereas older properties often aren't.

» **Smaller property size.** The average home size in 1970 was 1,576 square feet. In 2010, it was 2,430 square feet. Not only are people choosing to build bigger homes, but they want to rent bigger as well. Older properties with small square footages reduce your ability to subdivide or rent out individual rooms, thereby limiting your income.

» **Less energy efficient.** Because most older homes aren't built according to today's standards in building and materials, they are often more expensive to heat and cool. If a tenant can save $100 a month on utilities by renting a newer property, they will.

The BRRR(R) Strategy

An approach that has been rising in popularity is the BRRR(R) strategy. It stands for buy, rehab, rent, refinance (and repeat). One of the key features of a method like this is that you can scale to multiple properties by using a basic process. And that process is infinitely repeatable, making it a solid option for investors who want to rapidly grow their investments to include multiple properties.

The goal is to buy a property for less than its market value, make improvements and renovations, and use that forced appreciation to *refinance* a larger loan. That way, you are increasing *equity*—the dollar value of your ownership in a property—and increasing your rental income at the same time. The cumulative and desired effect is that you generate enough cash to finance the next property you want to buy. If it sounds a lot like a fix-and-flip, the type of deal you would see on popular reality TV shows, it's very close. The only difference is that you are not selling the property to another buyer immediately after the renovation. Instead, you are holding it and renting it out to tenants. Fix-and-flippers buy one property and sell one property, often working with just one home at a time. BRRR(R) operators buy one property, improve it, finance it, and then buy a second one without selling the first. They repeat the process again and again, quickly adding homes to their portfolio and cash to their income (figure 11).

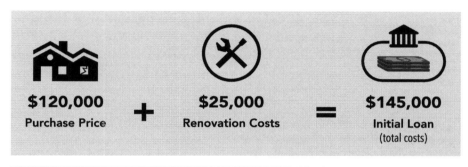

fig. 11

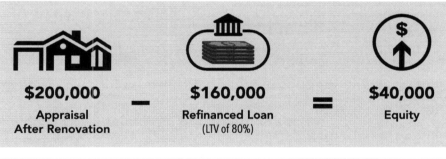

 **Original Home** Rents for $1200 → 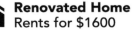 **Renovated Home** Rents for $1600

A very basic BRRR(R) investment strategy layout

Conceptually, the BRRR(R) method is simple to work out. At each stage of the process, you assume a level of risk. But as you gain experience over time, the strategy becomes less risky. Overall, you build up equity in each property you own while using the proceeds of your refinanced value to buy bigger and better properties.

There are risks associated with this strategy. A BRRR(R) practitioner must understand the potential value of a home, negotiate a purchase price lower than the potential value, understand how to renovate the property to reach that potential, and refinance the property at a high enough appraisal that they can pay off the loans for the purchase and remodeling costs. They also have to do all this while juggling other pressing concerns, such as advertising the property, screening prospective tenants, and determining appropriate rents. Get it right, and you can fast-track your way to your next deal. Get it wrong, and you're stuck with a property that underperforms in rental yield and doesn't leave you with enough capital to scale up any time soon.

NOTE

I have included an entire BRRR(R) case study in the appendix to provide a practical example of how this works.

Alternate Ideas

Rental property investors are not the rarity they once were. Now, you'll find dozens of competitors all vying for the same rental property investment, especially in hot markets. That level of competition can be daunting and even off-putting for new investors. To counter the fear of competition, many investors look to alternative, more creative solutions to get their feet wet. My goal, as I open your eyes to these new rental property investing ideas, is that you'll replace the old "I can't" language with a mentality that says, "I will."

MY TAKE

Creative approaches to rental investing let you stay ahead of the curve and remain profitable, no matter where you live or how many investors are competing with you.

Living in Your Own Rental

When you own your own home as well as a separate rental property, you have two mortgages in your name. The bank doesn't care if your tenants fail to pay their rent. All they care about is the fact that your name is on the mortgage. To avoid paying two mortgages (and as a method of saving up money for another property), many landlords prefer living in the property they are renting.

In some situations, this means that you will live in one of the rooms in the property. You may live in a basement suite or a spare add-on room. If the property is a duplex, then you can occupy one of the two standard living units and rent out the second. While not ideal for many investors over long periods of time, this approach has enabled many first-time buyers to quickly save up capital for a new investment.

Be sure to clearly lay out the expectations for shared costs such as utilities, internet, or upkeep of the property. Shared costs can be included in the monthly rent to save the hassle of splitting bills as they come in.

Subdividing Properties

If you ever went to college, you might already be familiar with what I'm about to propose. The idea of subdividing a property to create multiple spaces to rent within the same property is an idea similar to the dorm lifestyle. Only now, the idea is no longer bound just to colleges.

The concept of co-working has already taken root in the minds of many urban professionals as a viable alternative to working in an office space. Co-living is the natural extension of that idea and is a growing market. In cities, especially where space is at a premium, the practice of co-living solves many concerns about affordable living. Co-living facilities offer private rooms with shared spaces like kitchens, dining areas, entertainment zones, and laundry facilities. Tenants love the idea because these arrangements may often be leased on a six-month term or even a month-to-month basis, freeing tenants from the commitment of long-term lease agreements. Moreover, for city dwellers, a co-living arrangement can offer an attractive alternative to renting a single bedroom or studio downtown.

From an investor's perspective, co-living spaces can be marketed with great success to millennials and zoomers (Generation Z), since they are actively turning away from or delaying home ownership. As they pursue careers in the city, the expense of city housing leads them to consider options for co-living spaces.

Your strategy to provide a subdivided living space must include some thoughts on communal aspects of the home, such as amenities that attract younger generations. Alternatively, you could market a subdivided property for those of older generations who want to downsize and live a simpler life.

It's a wise practice to rent out different rooms at different rates depending on their amenities and square footage. People will pay 20-30 percent more per month if they have an adjoining bathroom or a larger bedroom. Also, consider renting out storage space in the garage to make extra income from the property. I have heard of investors charging upwards of $200 per month just for the use of an attached garage.

Geographic Arbitrage

You don't have to invest where you live. I will expand on this idea in chapter 7, but don't feel limited to the rental properties in your market. In fact, once you explore the idea that you can live and invest in markets of your choice, it opens up a whole new world of opportunities.

Arbitrage is the concept of using the advantages of one market to make money in another market. I like to use the phrase *geographic arbitrage* as a way to explain how this idea can be applied to rental property investing.

As I write this in the midst of a global lockdown, employers have been forced to acknowledge that remote working can be efficient and may be preferable to renting expensive office space. Your physical location might not affect your working career at all, which opens you up to the world of geographic arbitrage. What if you could live where the cost of living was cheaper, saving on taxes, rent, and cost of goods, all while still earning the same salary you do right now?

As you explore the different markets around the country, you'll find some that perform much better than your own. These markets can earn you some tidy profits, but only if you have the capital to make an investment. To understand how geographic arbitrage works, let's look at Terry, who works as a systems administrator for a thriving security company in San Francisco. Terry's salary is fantastic, but his rent takes a huge chunk out of his paycheck every month. Living in the Bay Area is incredibly expensive. Terry wants to invest in real estate in San Francisco, but at his current savings rate, it will take him years to come up with enough of a down payment for his initial property. Because Terry can work remotely, he decides to move closer to family in Provo, Utah. Terry now earns a San Francisco salary while paying rent in Utah dollars. But, in a twist, Terry finds some great deals in Austin, Texas—properties that show potentially rewarding returns but aren't nearly as expensive as those in

San Francisco. At his quadrupled savings rate, Terry will be investing in Austin properties in just eight months. Looking forward to seeing you out there, Terry!

Chapter Recap

» The goal of your first rental property is to facilitate your investment in a second rental property.

» Every investment play has its basis in the "buy low, sell high" strategy. Investing decisions can thus be simplified into the pursuit of minimizing expenses and maximizing income.

» New properties are attractive to tenants, but older properties are more accessible options for the first-time investor.

» To scale your portfolio to include many rental properties, the BRRR(R) strategy, with its repeatable process, offers strong advantages.

» Creative alternatives, like living in your own rental or subdividing a property, offer newcomers to rental property investing a way into the game.

| 2 |
How to Finance Your Investment

Chapter Overview
- » Getting the Capital You Need
- » Using Debt to Make More Profit
- » Conventional Loans vs. Creative Financing Ideas

I made my money the old-fashioned way. I was very nice to a wealthy relative right before he died.

– MALCOLM FORBES

When talking about rental property investing, I regularly mention numbers in the tens or even hundreds of thousands. To many first-time investors, that can be a chilling reminder that it takes money to make money—money they may not have. There are many investment properties that are affordable, and, sure, acquiring some takes a lot of money. But if you find the right deal, the price tag alone should not dissuade you—instead, to determine investment attractiveness you should always look at the income potential versus the cost. There's an entire market of financiers out there, eager to hand their money over to you so long as you can convince them that you're on track for a profitable endeavor. If you truly want to build a second income with a portfolio of rental properties, the task of locating the necessary *financing* should not stop you from reaching your goal.

Australian economist Joshua Gans wrote an informative and very entertaining book called *Parentonomics: An Economist Dad Looks at Parenting*. In the book, he talks about trying to bring the economics lessons he teaches in the classroom to his kids at home. In one memorable story, Gans talks about the challenge of using incentives to potty train their oldest daughter. As many parents do, they offered her a reward of a chocolate every time she went to the bathroom to do her business. After a successful event, she would receive her reward. The daughter quickly discovered she could simply sit on the little potty for hours at a time, eventually producing a result that earned her a chocolate treat.

In an attempt to counter his daughter's cleverness, Gans instituted a rule that she wasn't allowed to stay seated for longer than thirty minutes. The devious daughter, however, designed a new plan in which she simply split up one bathroom trip into two or three trips, thereby earning additional treats. Her shrewdness continued when her baby brother was going through potty training a few years later. Gans offered his daughter a reward if she would help by taking him to the bathroom when he needed to go. They both received a treat each time she did this. Once again, her resolve to eat more chocolate enabled her to find a loophole. In order to encourage her brother to take more trips, she force-fed the two-year-old cup after cup of water throughout the day, drastically increasing the number of bathroom breaks, and treats, they both received.

I tell this story because I admire this child's resolve, and I believe there is a lesson to be learned from her behavior. If you want something bad enough, you will find a way to get it. It's the same with financing your property. The prospect of raising thousands of dollars can be daunting; it keeps many people from trying to finance the rental property they want so much. In this chapter, I will show you several ways to generate the capital needed to finance your deal.

The Power of Leverage

Often called "debt financing," *leverage* is the most common way to think about debt in real estate. We call it leverage because the principle is similar to what you learned about levers in your high school physics class. A lever is a tool that allows one to lift heavy objects with less force. But here, instead of using a plank of wood to lift more physical weight, we are using leveraged money to exert more purchasing power, which, when done correctly, will result in more profitable rental properties (figure 12).

Using leverage allows you to build your rental income at a quicker pace. By using debt, you can buy larger, more profitable properties than you could otherwise afford, accelerating your growth from one investment to the next. Let's look at how this works.

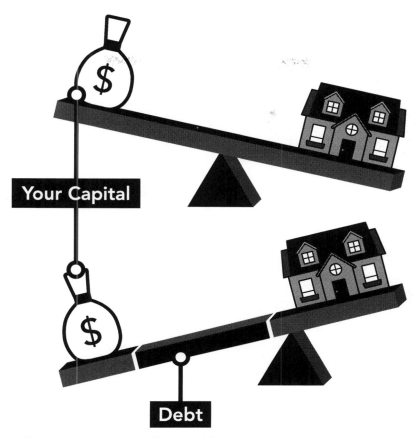

GRAPHIC

fig. 12

Your Capital

Debt

The strategic application of debt amplifies the power of your available capital.

NOTE

This is one of the big advantages of investing in real estate rather than traditional asset classes like stocks: access to low-interest debt. Following the pandemic lockdown of 2020, it is likely those rates will stay at or near record lows for years as the Federal Reserve Bank looks to do everything within its power to support the hobbled economy.

Imagine that you have $50,000 to invest in a rental property. If you wanted to buy a property using only your cash on hand, then you would have to limit your budget to a modest property that costs, at most, $50,000, which would produce only modest returns. Maybe after a few years you could sell the home and buy a slightly better property with a larger yield potential. True, this approach would keep you out of debt, but the time frame to a sustainable income that could replace your salary would be years away.

Another option would be to use that $50,000 as a down payment on a larger home. You could put a 50 percent deposit down on a $100,000 property in a market that could provide higher rental returns. You would have to pay the debt service costs, or the loan repayments (principal + interest) made to your lender, but the rents you earned would offset the extra costs.

A third option would be to spread out the same $50,000 in capital over two $100,000 properties, with a 25 percent down payment on each. Your debt service costs would be higher, but you'd now have two rental properties producing an adequate income as well as appreciating in value over time. As long as you had a rental return that covered your debt service costs, you'd have a significant advantage over the first cash-only option, as illustrated in figure 13.

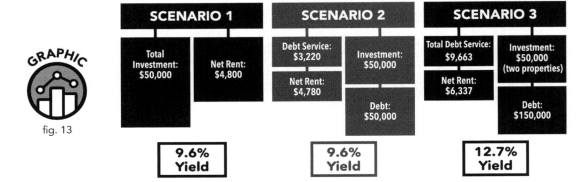

GRAPHIC

fig. 13

Hazards of Using Debt

It's clear that by using debt leverage you can finance bigger deals. When used correctly, debt can accelerate your profits. In light of this realization, it can be tempting to think that more debt is better. This brings me to one of the pitfalls of using debt: becoming overleveraged. Imagine the chaos of juggling a ton of debt when the housing market starts to slide, even by just a bit. During the housing bubble of the mid-2000s, this is exactly what happened when banks chose to put aside all logic and reason, offering incredibly attractive loan terms at minimal down payments. Often, these irresponsible lenders would offer loans to people who had no business accepting any kind of debt and clearly had no ability to repay the loan. Many of them were investors looking to take out mortgages on their third or fourth property but having no means to service all these new debt obligations. There were also plenty of everyday homeowners who put up their own properties as collateral so they could secure six- or seven-figure loans that they should never have qualified for. As soon as the housing market dropped, their homes were worth less than what they had financed, putting them underwater and unable to recoup their losses. To make matters worse, the banks rolled up and resold this bad debt to unwitting investors in the form of mortgage-backed securities. We don't have to imagine the chaos; we all watched it happen.

This is the first pitfall of using debt—using too much of it, which is also known as **overleverage**. Leverage is a balancing act. Just enough and it can magnify your profits. Too much and it can lead to significant losses. Having too much debt to service means having less equity in the property and higher monthly debt payments, which can break your investment's profit potential if you face unexpected vacancies or big expenses. You can become overleveraged if the cost of the debt payments is higher than the cash flow coming into the property. In such a scenario, where you find yourself paying *into* an investment on an ongoing basis, you have what's called a "negative cash flow" investment. You can also become overleveraged if you have no equity in the property, also known as being underwater. In such a scenario your financier's (or financiers') claim on the asset(s) has overwhelmed your own. Whatever money the asset(s) makes goes to them, not you. You can be overleveraged on a single property or on your portfolio as a whole.

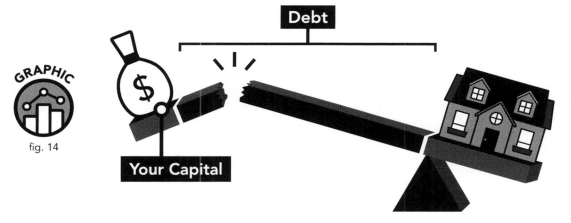

Too much leverage can break the whole deal.

A second common pitfall is to have **negative leverage**, meaning that using leverage to finance your property is costing you money; while you may not be technically overleveraged, your use of leverage has created a net negative cash flow. The opposite of negative leverage is **positive leverage**, which, when achieved, will improve your overall returns.

Let's walk through a few simple scenarios involving no leverage, positive leverage, and negative leverage:

Scenario A – No Leverage

You have $100 to invest. You make an investment using all your cash, and every year, you get $30 back from your investment. A 30 percent return on your money is nothing to sneeze at. Nice job.

$30 return / $100 investment = 30 percent return on investment of $100

Scenario B – Positive Leverage

Let's say you used debt to make the same $100 investment. Instead of spending all your cash, you take out a loan of $70, and you put in only $30. The debt service costs $15 every year. Therefore, your net return is $15 ($30 return minus $15 debt service cost). Though your total return in this scenario is $15 less than that of Scenario A, your yield is actually higher, a 50 percent return compared to Scenario A's 30 percent return. That is positive leverage. It increases your dollar-for-dollar returns compared to an all-cash scenario.

$15 return / $30 investment = 50 percent return on investment of $30

Scenario C – Negative Leverage

To be precise, negative leverage refers to your returns with leverage after you subtract what your returns would have been had no leverage been used. Imagine you take out the same $70 loan and receive the same $30 return on the property, but instead of a $15 annual cost to service the debt, you pay $25 because interest rates are too high. In this scenario you only make $5 in net returns ($30 return from the property minus $25 debt service cost). You can still afford to keep up with your debt costs (you're not overleveraged), but the leverage is hurting your overall return, not helping it.

$5 return / $30 investment = 16.7 percent return on investment

Had you stuck with the all-cash investment (30 percent return on investment), you would have done better than if you had taken on the expensive debt (16.7 percent return on investment). In this case, the expensive debt created negative leverage of 16.7 minus 30, or -13.3 percent.

Beyond your diminished returns, negative leverage may also presage greater financial turmoil. What if the cash flows you expected from the property don't materialize? Underperforming assets can heighten the risk of negative leverage and may even leave you overleveraged if the debt costs exceed the returns. In our scenario, you predicted you would make $30 every year from the property. But what if a bad turn of events dropped that return down to $15? In scenario A, you just make less money since you have no debt. Bad, but not catastrophic. In scenario B, that drop suddenly means that your debt expense is eating up all of your returns, leaving you with a return on investment (ROI) of exactly nothing. In scenario C, you end up overleveraged and losing money when your debt expense exceeds your returns, a negative ROI of -33.3 percent. Yikes!

MY TAKE

This is not just a 2008 problem. I see overleveraged properties right now in 2020. Many investors like using Airbnb and similar short-term rental platforms instead of leasing out to traditional long-term tenants. As I write this, the Great Lockdown has reduced some once-hot tourist destinations to figurative ghost towns. Along with many others, it's the overleveraged Airbnb owners who are suffering, with no guests to generate rental cash flow to cover their high mortgage payments. As a result, I am now seeing an influx of these units on the market as aggressive Airbnb owners scramble to unload the properties that have caused them to become overleveraged. According to AllTheRooms.com, a leading short-term rental data provider, the available supply of short-term rental listings has decreased in many major cities. Los Angeles' listings numbers have fallen 30 percent, from nearly 19,000 options in July 2019 to fewer than 13,000 listings one year later.

Conventional Mortgages

A ***conventional mortgage*** is what most rental property investors use to finance their deals. These loans are typically offered by banks or other lending institutions. Almost 75 percent of all mortgages are done through a conventional loan, and most of these are underwritten in accordance with the stringent guidelines of the two major government-backed financiers, Freddie Mac and Fannie Mae. These two organizations buy mortgages from banks, instantly replenishing capital so the banks and other lenders can offer more loans. Given the importance of selling off the loans and replenishing capital, banks are generally very cautious about adhering to Fannie and Freddie's guidelines before they issue a conventional loan.

In the early 2000s, banks made it simpler to secure loans. Lenders didn't require much to qualify borrowers, at least compared to today's standards. This easy lending strategy was a big cause of the massive housing bubble of that time, as banks were offering loans to people who should never have been approved. Those unwise decisions came back to bite them when the borrowers (surprise, surprise!) defaulted on their loans and all the financial institutions caught holding financial instruments backed by those subprime mortgages lost billions or went bankrupt, including major banks like Bear Stearns, Lehman Brothers, Washington Mutual, and Wachovia.

And now we live in an era where the banks have an understandably cautious approach to lending out money. It used to be possible to borrow hundreds of thousands of dollars without any demonstrated income or assets, even without a down payment. Now, those no-money-down mortgages are gone. Banks have raised the bar on what they will offer to low-credit-score borrowers. Loans are safer for lenders, but they are harder to come by. Nevertheless, despite there being more hoops to jump through and more barriers to entry, the savvy investor will find ways to secure needed financing. Remember, banks and lenders are in the business of lending. They want to lend you money to make money. An investor with a solid path to success poses a very attractive business opportunity.

There is a difference in how you approach a lender for a rental property than, say, how you'd go about procuring a personal loan for your home or car. The typical homeowner relies on a salary to pay off a mortgage. For that reason, lenders considering issuing a home loan will want to verify and inspect the borrower's pay stubs. With a rental property, it's a little different. You're not paying off the mortgage—your tenants are. With your first rental investment property, banks will look at your credit scores and employment history. But as you develop a larger portfolio, and especially if you're operating as an entity (see chapter 12), banks will factor the history of your investments and the strength of your portfolio into their decision to approve financing. As a rental investor operating twenty successful properties, you pose less risk of defaulting on your loans than a single-property owner.

MY TAKE

Shop around when looking for a conventional mortgage. Different lenders offer different products. You might start with your own bank, especially if you have trusted relationships there. You can also consult with a broker who collates all the options for you and can help you determine the best fit for your property. Just be sure to shop around and take in the lay of the land.

As I mentioned, conventional loans done through a bank must often conform to stringent government guidelines. But what if a borrower is worried they can't meet the standards set by a lender? Perhaps they have a low credit score, or perhaps they're pursuing a higher-risk, opportunistic rental property play. Such an investor may then turn to *portfolio lenders*. These are lenders who, rather than sell their loans, keep them in-house, in their own portfolios. Since these lenders do not have to answer to an outside party, they are free to evaluate using whichever lending criteria they choose, loosening the standards to accommodate borrowers who have no alternatives. Often, these portfolio lenders compensate for looser guidelines with high interest rates to offset the risk.

The higher rates portfolio lenders charge can drastically reduce your cash flow on an otherwise profitable property. Consider this type of lender only if you have no other traditional options.

Guiding Lenders to "Yes"

Essentially, lending institutions, whether banks, credit unions, or private lenders, all want to know that you can repay what you borrow. To succeed in securing a loan, you need to convince them that lending to you poses minimal risk to their capital. Even if you have lending experience from buying your own home, a rental investment loan requires that you present different metrics. To a lender, this means you have a useful debt service coverage ratio, or DSCR. The DSCR is a measurement of the total income you will make, divided by the total debt costs for the project.

$$DSCR = \frac{\text{NET OPERATING INCOME}}{\text{TOTAL DEBT SERVICE}}$$

fig. 15

Lenders want to know that your cash flow will adequately cover the costs of servicing your loan. A DSCR of 1 would technically cover the costs, but that's not enough. Lenders want to find DSCR numbers at least at 1.3, which shows your income exceeding debt costs by 30 percent, in order to consider the loan. In weaker economies, such as those in a recession or a recovery phase (see chapter 3), lenders will increase their minimum DSCR requirements, to 1.4 or 1.5, to account for the higher risk of defaults.

The Loan-to-Value (LTV) Ratio

Lenders will often use a metric they refer to as LTV (loan to value) to measure the risks of your loan and decide whether to approve financing. The LTV metric typically incorporates the appraised value of the property rather than the total cost of the project (figure 16).

$$\text{LOAN TO VALUE} = \frac{\text{LOAN AMOUNT}}{\text{APPRAISED VALUE}}$$

The rate that lenders use to determine their maximum loan amount is not fixed, but depends on many factors. Owner-occupied properties can often get financed with higher LTVs than investment properties. This is because lenders view investment properties as inherently riskier than those used as a primary residence. The theory is that you're more likely to pay your mortgage on time and in full if losing your home hangs in the balance.

EXAMPLE

A traditional lender might offer 80 percent LTV to someone buying their own home, but offer only 65 percent to an investor wanting to use the exact same property as a rental investment. For a $200,000 property, that's a difference of a $40,000 down payment or a $70,000 down payment.

PROPERTY VALUE = $200,000

MAX LTV	LOAN AMOUNT	DOWN PAYMENT
97%	$194,000	$6,000
95%	$190,000	$10,000
90%	$180,000	$20,000
85%	$170,000	$30,000
80%	$160,000	$40,000
75%	$150,000	$50,000
70%	$140,000	$60,000
65%	$130,000	$70,000
60%	$120,000	$80,000
55%	$110,000	$90,000

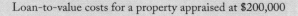

Loan-to-value costs for a property appraised at $200,000

As you can see in figure 17, the lower the LTV rate offered by a lender, the more it will cost you out of pocket.

For an investor in search of a great deal on a property, the LTV metric can come in handy. If you can buy a property below market value, you can open up new financing opportunities. Remember, the lender doesn't care about the price you paid, only about the appraised value of the property. It is the appraised value that determines their LTV rates.

Best Bank offers a 75 percent LTV for loans on rental investments. Carrie, a savvy rental property investor, has her eye on a property with an appraised value of $200,000. The owner needs to make a quick sale and is willing to sell it to Carrie for $170,000. Because Best Bank's LTV is based on the appraised property value and not the purchase price, Carrie can borrow as much as $150,000 (75 percent of $200,000) and make just a $20,000 down payment for the purchase of the property.

For investors, LTV is a key metric because it determines how much cash they will have to put down to secure financing. Since lenders use lower LTV rates for investment properties, investors should plan on coughing up 20-35 percent in down payments unless they're able to buy at below-market value. For many first-time investors, 20-35 percent can be expensive, even out of reach. If that's where you find yourself, don't give up hope. Perhaps it's time to get creative about getting financing for your investment deal.

Bottom line, most lenders typically offer 65-75 percent maximum LTV on loans for investment properties. Loans secured by Fannie Mae or Freddie Mac are the exception. They can sometimes go up to 85 percent.

Creative Financing

Apple's Steve Jobs was often referred to as a visionary. Not only did he popularly revolutionize phones and computing, he also impacted our movies, music, and shopping experiences. Those who knew him claimed he had a "reality distortion field." He constantly perceived things as they could be rather than as they were. He refused to believe in limitations because, to Jobs, dedication and creativity could overcome any obstacle. He relentlessly pursued new ideas, often without any precedent.

Take, for instance, a famous episode from the earlier days of Apple computers when Jobs and his team were introducing a new computer called the "Lisa." He tasked his designers with creating a new type of mouse. Jobs wanted a mouse that could move freely in any direction, something we take for granted now but which was a new idea back then. An engineer on his team dared to tell Jobs it was impossible and not commercially viable. Jobs fired that employee immediately, and the next designer on the team said, "I can build that mouse."

The majority of lending institutions will tell you there is only one way to finance your deal, but I want to expand your perspective. Just like Jobs, you can distort their "reality" and uncover some truly creative ways to find the money you need. One's ability to be creative is a predictor of success for financing properties. They say that necessity is the mother of invention. It seems I come across a brand-new financing method every week, usually through an investor who wanted to challenge the traditional way of securing financing.

Creative financing is the strategy that allows an investor to own a property without a huge cash payment up front. It's even possible that by using these strategies you can secure an investment without any down payment at all. But these solutions are not magic wands that turn bad deals into moneymakers. You still have to find the right property at the right price before you decide on which, if any, creative financing option to use.

As I cover these options, I'll give my opinion about when it makes sense to use them. Remember that every creative financing option applies differently to different investors and risk tolerances. Pass these options through your own filter as you consider if they're right for you.

Seller Financing

What if you were looking at a home to buy and instead of getting the money from a lender, you got the seller to finance the purchase? This is exactly how seller financing works. You create a contract that allows you to finance the deal with money provided by the seller of the home. Essentially, the seller provides the mortgage that a bank would normally offer.

If a seller has an active mortgage with a remaining balance still owed to the bank, then they would need approval from their bank before offering seller financing to the new buyer. This can be a time-consuming and complicated process, which is why things generally go a lot smoother (for both buyers and sellers) when the seller owns the property free and clear without a mortgage.

One of the principal advantages of seller financing is that you avoid the hassle and paperwork inherent in dealing with a large lender. Closing fees can be expensive, and a seller-financed option lets you save thousands of dollars by doing the deal directly through the seller. Motivated sellers eager to unload the property are often open to seller financing. Many may not even require a down payment. No down payment means more cash on hand, which comes in handy when you need to renovate, update, or bring a property into compliance as you seek to land the perfect tenants.

Taking on the debt of a seller-financed deal does not get reported to credit agencies. This will not affect your ability to get traditional loans in the future.

In normal market conditions, finding a seller willing to finance your purchase of their property can be extremely difficult. In a typical transaction, buyers with the right credit, income, and employment background can obtain a traditional mortgage to finance their purchase. Most sellers would rather deal with a buyer with a bank loan in place than a buyer looking for seller financing—why take the risk? But in situations with few (if any) potential buyers, with properties in disrepair, or with tight credit options in a major recession, the only way for some sellers to get the price they want is to offer seller financing on a portion of the sales price—essentially offering a loan to the buyer. Figure 18 illustrates the mechanics of such a loan.

fig. 18

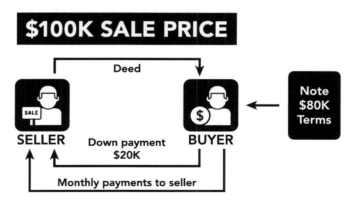

A normal down payment, 20 percent in figure 18, is common in these types of deals. They also typically involve a period of monthly loan payments, similar to that of a normal mortgage but often culminating in a large balloon payment at the end of the term.

Sellers interested in this type of deal, however, may have a clause in their current mortgage that prevents it. This is known as a "due on sale" clause and requires that the seller pay off their own mortgage in full when transferring the property to a new buyer. Unless the seller has the cash to do this, it will impede their ability to offer a seller-financed loan to a new buyer. Seller financing also happens to be expensive, at least in comparison with prevailing mortgage interest rates. Generally, sellers ask for higher interest rates to compensate for the risk they accept.

If you want to find a seller-financed property, look for the following conditions:

» A buyer's market
» Motivated sellers eager to make a deal
» Sellers who own their property with no outstanding debts . . . OR
» Sellers with small outstanding principals with loan payoff costs that are less than the down payment you will make

Hard Money Loans

It's possible that even with a solid investment plan, conventional lending institutions won't consider your proposal. A poor credit score or a spotty employment history can harm your chances with cautious banks.

Self-employed people can face steeper obstacles with banks and credit unions because they don't have the perceived stability of an employer.

In these cases, you can pursue private lenders, also known as **hard money lenders**. I know many of my students secure hard money loans through friends and family to land their first deal, but I would not advise this. Owing money to family changes the dynamics at the family dinner table. Holidays can get awkward when you have $10,000 of Uncle Jordan's money tied up in a rental home.

In the world of residential real estate, most lenders will close their coffers after awarding you an initial loan. If unexpected renovation costs blow your budget and you ask your lender for a new supplemental loan to "bridge the gap," don't expect any love. Not only that, you'll be looked at skeptically when you come to that lender for your next project. "There's the guy who couldn't get his estimates right." On the other hand, hard money lenders are apt to be more flexible should you need additional funds to cover project overruns.

Hard money lenders use the property you own as collateral, which is why they are also known as asset-based lenders. In making their lending decisions, they allot more weight to the value of your property than they allot to low credit scores or past lending history. If you can present a strong case for investment and back it up with projected rental returns, that will heighten the chance of a yes from a hard money lender. In return for sidestepping the more traditional institutions, you will be asked to pay higher costs. But if you're coming to the game with a low credit score, those costs may be worth it if it means securing financing.

Subject-To Deals

When a homeowner is in financial distress, they may be open to accepting a "subject-to" deal. In these deals, the buyer simply takes over the loan repayments from the seller. The mortgage and the deed to the property remain in the seller's name, and, as the investor, the buyer is responsible for making payments to the seller, not to the lender. Sellers are typically open to these types of deals when they have impending foreclosures, a looming financial hardship (a lost job or a big medical bill), or are unable to make necessary repairs to a home.

These deals can work in your favor because they don't require you to qualify for a loan, meaning that as long as you and the seller agree to the terms, you can begin finding tenants for the property and collecting rents right away. If the seller has missed payments or faces repossession, they can improve their credit score with the payments you are making on their behalf. However, you need to be careful if the seller wants to transfer the property into your name, because most loans come with the "due on sale" clause that demands immediate full repayment of the outstanding debt principal in a change of ownership to the title. Thoroughly screen your potential partner, because the types of sellers who accept subject-to deals are also more likely to file for bankruptcy due to other debts in their name. If the seller declares bankruptcy, the lender can foreclose on the property. Also, it's your responsibility to check for any past balances owed on utilities, unpaid repair bills, or any other possible liens on the property.

Be sure to use a reputable intermediary, such as a lawyer or title company, to maintain a transparent payment plan that's timely and trustworthy for both parties. Subject-to deals are regulated differently from state to state, so be sure to check with your local laws to remain compliant.

Chapter Recap

» The way you finance your deal can vary from property to property and is not restricted simply by the amount of money you have.

» Debt, or leverage, can be advantageous in real estate, but too much debt can harm your returns.

» When securing a loan from a lender, you must present your investment as you would a business, demonstrating the potential for returns, cash flow, and limited risk.

» Beyond traditional lenders, you can seek out creative financing solutions, often without putting up any money of your own.

| 3 |
Understanding Real Estate Cycles

Chapter Overview
» Identifying the Four Phases of a Real Estate Cycle
» Creating a Financial Plan Based on Future Projections
» Future-Proofing Your Investment from Unexpected Downturns

The whole future lies in uncertainty. Live immediately.

– SENECA

I'm going to give you a quotation, and I want you to guess when it was written. Here it is:

"The last major [economic] downturn was around 1990, which would put the next major recession around the year 2008."

Well, what do you think? 2005? 2007? These words were penned by Fred Foldvary, a brilliant yet maligned economics professor who included them in an editorial way back in 1998. In that same article Foldvary predicted the upcoming tech bubble collapse in 2000. In the world of finance, a lot of people make a lot of predictions. Sometimes they get it right and often they don't. I can't tell you whether Mr. Foldvary just got lucky or whether we were witnessing a genius at work. What I *can* tell you is that there are some basic premises and models that, though far from a crystal ball, can prove insightful.

In 1879, economist Henry George introduced the idea that all economies go through cycles, predictable in their progress but not always predictable in their timing. The real estate economy is no different. Barring unforeseen events, the cycle is constant and has been observed for nearly two hundred years in the developed world. When one phase of the cycle ends, another phase begins. What's astounding is the cycle's regularity. Real estate seems to peak in value every eighteen years, barring the occurrence of global catastrophes.

GRAPHIC

fig. 19

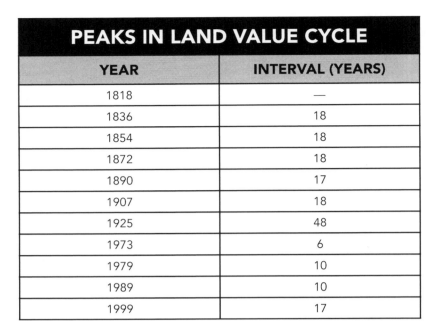

PEAKS IN LAND VALUE CYCLE	
YEAR	**INTERVAL (YEARS)**
1818	—
1836	18
1854	18
1872	18
1890	17
1907	18
1925	48
1973	6
1979	10
1989	10
1999	17

source: Fred E. Foldvary, "The Depression of 2008"

Barring major global upsets, the real estate cycle is almost like clockwork in its regularity.

The Four Phases of a Real Estate Cycle

QUOTE

This, too, shall pass.

– MEDIEVAL PERSIAN PROVERB

The ability to identify the current phase in the real estate cycle can help to predict what is to come. But as I'll cover later in this chapter, there are "black swan" events, a term coined by author and hedge-fund manager Nassim Nicholas Taleb. These are events that no one could predict; they're beyond the scope of expectations. According to Taleb, people tend to underestimate the frequency of these events on the whole, when each of them, considered individually, seems very unlikely. At the time of writing, we are in the midst of such an event, with the entire world shut down and self-isolating at home due to a pandemic no one could have foretold.

The typical flow of the real estate cycle proceeds from recovery to expansion to hypersupply to recession. While the entire cycle averages eighteen years in length, the length of each individual phase varies from around three to five years. Unless an unforeseen event disrupts the pattern, the four phases discussed here can be used to reliably point us toward the future. It's important to note that here we're only addressing the real estate cycle and not making comments on the general economic cycle, which can appear to run in a similar fashion.

Pandemic Journal Entry: As I am writing this, the market is experiencing an unprecedented event that has effectively shortened the current market cycle; what was gearing up to be the early stages of a hypersupply phase with growing new construction suddenly looks like the beginning of a long recession fueled by massive unemployment and economic disruption. Under normal conditions, the market would probably have peaked in the mid-2020s before heading into another recession to mark the beginning of the next market cycle. Massive market disruption can stretch or compress market cycles—World War II led to a nearly fifty-year period between real estate peaks, from 1925 to 1973, while the Fed's raising of interest rates to historic highs led to a premature peak of the next market cycle. The extraordinary impact of the global pandemic will in all likelihood produce an early peak in the current real estate cycle, even though prices have so far stayed relatively resilient and in some cases have gone up in spite of the pandemic. In light of the tens of millions of jobs lost, many permanently, this widespread job and income insecurity will have profound economic reverberations in the years to come. It's therefore difficult to forecast any significant growth in the next few years.

There are two primary factors relevant to the real estate industry, namely, occupancy levels and construction projects. Just looking at these two factors alone gives you enough data to identify the current phase of a market cycle. In the following graph, you can see the various phases: recovery, expansion, hypersupply, and recession.

Though the pattern is universal, the global economy is not universally in sync. Some nations, states, and regions seemingly lead the way, and others lag behind. For instance, rural California might be in the recovery phase while the urban coastal areas of the state might already be experiencing expansion. It may take the lagging areas as long as a year to catch up.

In light of the information presented in figure 20, one might feel as if it's easy to implement a "buy low, sell high" strategy. When prices are low, as in the recession or recovery phases, then it's time to buy; you know that prices will climb as you enter the expansion phase. On the other hand, if your current market has been in the expansion phase for the last two to three years, it could be a sign that prices are about to fall and you're entering the hypersupply phase.

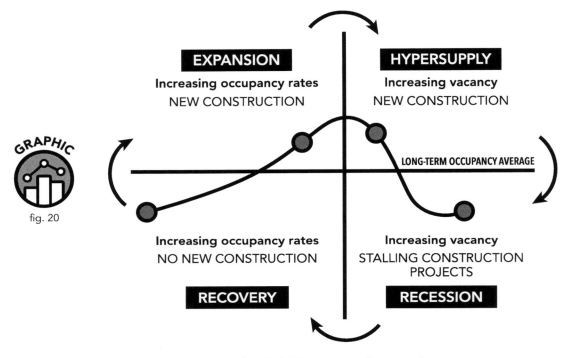

A typical eighteen-year real estate cycle

The Recovery Phase

When you can see the bottomed-out real estate prices behind you, the real estate cycle will have entered the recovery phase. Another sign is when the Federal Reserve steps in and lowers interest rates. This will prompt businesses to build and consumers to buy. Employment rates begin climbing as people go back to work. The demand for new housing increases as people now have both the money to spend and the need to find a place to live near the site of their new job.

We know from the law of supply and demand that we learned about in Economics 101 that an increase in demand will increase the price of the properties on the market. More competition pushes rent prices upward as well, while the economy steadily improves. The housing market, much like the stock market, is based on consumer confidence. As confidence in the economy grows, people increasingly compete for the available inventory of properties.

As a rental property investor, you are paying attention to those increased occupancy rates, a sign that the economy is moving in the right direction. And on the flip side of the same coin, as occupancy rates rise, vacancies drop. You can see this, for example, in the state of California. The first hint of a drop in vacancy levels happened in mid-2009, and by mid-2011 vacancy levels were steadily falling as the economy was in a full recovery phase (figure 21).

fig. 21

VACANCY RATES FOR CALIFORNIA

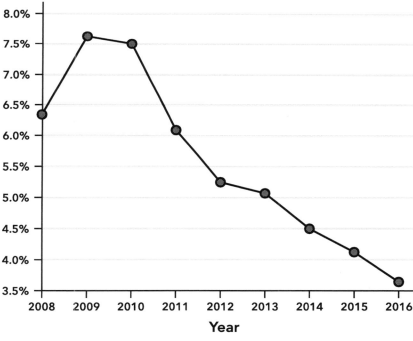

source: Federal Reserve Economic Data

Falling vacancy rates in California

Rental property investors should move quickly to buy properties when the time is right. If you can catch the recovery phase early on, you can buy properties that people want to offload from a recession-era deal, often at a fraction of the value. While you cannot yet charge optimal rental prices, you are in a position to slowly increase the rent, using the rising occupancy rates (more competition for rentals) to your advantage.

With the number of available homes on the market dropping and interest rates going lower, construction companies will green-light more permits for new projects to capitalize on the demand for new housing. But all this rapid growth leads inevitably to the next phase.

The Expansion Phase

Officially, an expansion phase occurs when occupancy levels across the entire market exceed the long-term average, but prices and demand are still climbing. Simply put, the demand for homes has exceeded the average. As an illustration, let's imagine that typical occupancy levels for rental properties in Seattle are 95 percent. During a recession, occupancy fell to 90 percent as people struggled to afford their rents and mortgages. But as the recovery began, those numbers started rising. Rapidly, rental occupancy rates increased to 97.5 percent, well above the 95 percent average for the area. As soon as those occupancy rates rose above the average, Seattle entered an expansion phase.

For the rental property owner, expansion is an ideal time to be in the market. Finding a new property will be difficult, as competition is fierce. What won't be difficult is collecting more rent on the properties you own. To illustrate, look at the dramatic rent increases that occurred during an expansion phase in Los Angeles soon after the recovery of the 2008 housing collapse. During the recovery phase, rent prices stayed relatively stable, but as we shifted into the expansion phase, when occupancy rates climbed, the rent prices (figure 22) climbed with them.

fig. 22

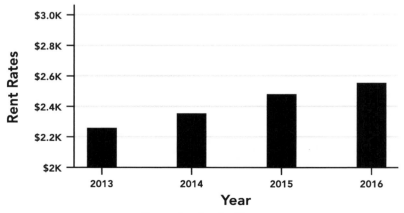

AVERAGE LA COUNTY RENTAL PRICES INCREASING DURING EXPANSION PHASE

Source: Los Angeles Almanac

Growth cannot continue forever. In the recovery phase, businesses rush to get new permits and begin construction while interest rates are low and demand is high. When the expansion phase kicks in, all those new projects are in full swing. More and more new properties enter the market in response to the increased (and still increasing) demand. But there comes a point when the rising availability of the properties on the market begins to shift the whole housing economy into a new phase of the real estate cycle.

The Hypersupply Phase

Rental property owners will watch the expansion phase closely, studying rent prices as they rise along with occupancy levels. Builders are watching the same phenomenon, looking for the opportunity to profit from building new properties. In the expansion phase, you will see projects popping up all over the place, because new construction looks financially attractive. But as completed projects begin to advertise more vacancies, you will see a transition into the next phase: hypersupply.

As more properties become available and occupancy levels drop again, the number of vacancies on the market will begin to climb steeply. There is a point where the number of rental properties exceeds the number of people searching for a place to live. This is like the housing market saying, "OK, we're good! We don't need more properties! We have enough!" Unfortunately, because feedback between vacancy and new construction is delayed, there is no stopping the number of new homes on the way. With more property choices for renters, property owners are forced to lower rent prices in order to attract tenants.

When charted on a graph, it is easy to spot the transition from the expansion phase into the hypersupply phase. The relationship between vacancy and housing starts (also known as new construction) helps to clarify this point (figure 23). Leading up to 2006, housing starts were trailed closely by vacancy rates. As more and more housing units were built, it led to a glut of properties, a hypersupply. By 2006, with no more properties needed to satisfy demand, and as builders began to severely reduce the number of new projects, housing starts took a steep dive, causing vacancy to peak. This gave the market time to absorb the excess supply, ultimately reducing the vacancy rate again.

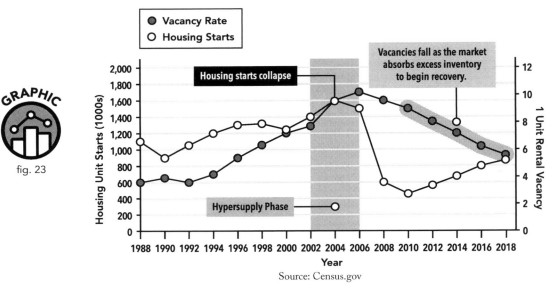

Source: Census.gov

Vacancy rates for single-unit properties in the US

In figure 23, it's easy to see the beginning of the end for the housing market. At a certain point, beginning around 2002, the supply of new housing began climbing in near-parallel alignment with the increase in vacancy rates. In other words, demand was perpetually unable to catch up to supply. A steep rise in vacancies with levels well above historical rates is a sign for property owners to pay special attention and exercise extra caution when buying. While new construction may seem attractive to purchase, the hypersupplied market is saturated. Dwindling demand cannot support the sheer volume of properties available and, in turn, rent prices will stagnate or even start to fall. This is a sure sign that the economy is about to experience a recession.

The Recession Phase

The old joke is that a recession is when your neighbor loses his job; a depression is when you lose your job. By early 2008, unemployment levels had begun to rise. There was a slow but gradual climb from the typical, stable 4.5 percent rate, peaking at 10 percent unemployment by October 2009. As expendable income levels fell, so did *consumption* as people sought to spend less and save more money. The gross domestic product (GDP) gap, which measures actual national output compared to potential output, increased to 6 percent, representing nearly one trillion dollars in lost production as the whole US economy slowed to a halt. Economists love using these data for interpreting a recession, but real estate investors are concerned with something different.

When there's a glut of properties on the market and occupancy rates are low, owners and builders have no choice but to accept lower prices for their assets. Keep in mind that many new properties are built late into the expansion and hypersupply phases. They arrive on the market too many and too late, and with little demand for them.

Once occupancy levels fall back below the national average, real estate has officially gone into a recession phase. And this phase comes on fast. Economic factors like raised interest rates and rising unemployment levels accompany the onset of recession. In the world of rental property owners, however, the key element of recession is a general lack of interest in buying and occupying properties. This is for good reason: people are hesitant to spend money, showing little to no confidence in the current state of the economy.

A recession generally lasts around three to five years before the market recovers. In figure 24, you can observe the drop in housing prices, a sure sign of a recessive market. In Seattle, peak housing prices occurred in July 2007. By the end of that year, housing prices were falling, and the Great Recession had officially begun. That downward trend lasted until February 2012, almost a full five years after the initial drop.

GRAPHIC

fig. 24

SEATTLE HOME PRICES
(RELATIVE TO JANUARY 2000)

Source: Federal Reserve Economic Data

The housing price collapse in Seattle during recession

Savvy investors can weather this storm and even make money on it. A recession, especially toward the end of the phase, is a great time to make a purchase from homeowners eager to sell. We will elaborate in chapter

8, but this is a good time to peruse the foreclosures on the market to locate excellent properties at incredibly low prices. Rent prices will not increase at this time; you may even have to concede to lowering rents to keep tenants in the property.

And as surely as a recession begins, it will eventually end. The Federal Reserve will lower interest rates, just as it has always done. The market will slowly gain confidence, just as it always has. And the real estate cycle will continue, just as it has predictably done in the past.

Planning Your Entrance into the Market

If you have even only heard of ice hockey, then you likely know the name Wayne Gretzky. His nickname, The Great One, is well-earned and deserved. Skating almost as early as he walked, Gretzky grew up playing hockey from a very early age. His keen sense of the sport, as well as a preternatural talent, helped propel him to become, arguably, the best hockey player who ever played the game. Many of his records, some set more than thirty years ago, remain unbroken.

Compared to other players, Wayne was never competitively fast or large. He was diminutive and young; in fact, the National Hockey League had to grant a special allowance for him to start playing professionally at just seventeen years of age—the official age minimum was twenty. But above all else, Gretzky was known as a smart player. Part of his skill was that he was always ready to strike, with an instinct to be in the right position at the right time. When he was just a small boy, his family would gather around the TV every Saturday night to watch hockey games. Wayne would take a marker and a piece of cardboard cut into the oval shape of a hockey rink. Throughout the game, he would trace the path of the puck on the cardboard. Maybe this habit helped him develop his sense of always skating where the puck was about to be, and not where it was.

It is tempting to make property investment decisions based on the market conditions of the past twelve to eighteen months. A successful investor, however, considers what the market will look like in the future. During the housing boom in the mid-2000s, people watched investors make their millions with real estate, at least on paper. It seemed almost too easy to buy properties and create an entire profitable portfolio from day one. But when investors tried to use past data to extrapolate future prices, they fell short. They were skating where the puck was—not where it was going to be. And then the bottom fell out and all those who had made assumptions based on past performance were suddenly left with millions of dollars' worth of properties that were upside down in their mortgages—meaning the investors owed more than the assets were worth.

Another tempting idea is to believe you can foresee the future. While the nature of real estate is that it operates in a cycle, there is nothing scientific about it. It is not a repeatable experiment that produces predictable results. For example, who could have predicted there would be a global disease that, in addition to killing more than a million people worldwide, caused millions to lose their jobs, leaving them unable to pay their rent? Historically, we call these black swan events. This is the equivalent of "expecting the unexpected." Typically, the best way to future-proof your investments from these kinds of events is to invest in strong markets that have strong historical results. Speculative markets, in which you hope for strong growth in the future, can collapse under the weight of these unforeseen events.

One of my clients rents out luxury high-rise apartments in Seattle, a historically strong market. I spoke to him during the COVID-19 lockdown to see how he was faring. He informed me that the rent payments he received had dropped from being 94 percent on time to being 89 percent on time. It was hardly a blip on his radar in the midst of a pandemic that could have cost him thousands, all thanks to investing in a strong rental market supported by reliable tenants with high-salaried jobs.

Underwriting Your Assumptions

Understanding the current data and the current phase of the real estate cycle helps you make decisions about where the market will be in the future. In the lending world, they use the term **underwriting** to describe the way lenders assess the viability of people seeking a loan. The term comes from a time when lenders would write their name on the contract underneath the borrower's name, legitimizing their belief in the borrower's ability to repay the debt. In return for the risk of lending the capital, they received a reward in the form of the interest owed on the loan.

Think of yourself as an underwriter, looking at your potential investments as a lender looks at a borrower. In other words, are you willing to undertake the risk of making the purchase in return for the reward of making profits from your investment?

Official underwriters make assumptions about people asking for loans. They assume they have good credit, that they will continue to have good credit in the future, and that they have the ability to repay the loan according to the agreed-upon terms of the contract. Researched and proven assumptions help underwriters lessen the risk and maximize their return. It is no different in property investing. You make assumptions about the property, namely, that it will appreciate in value and provide a stable source of rental income for years to come. The better you are at making those assumptions, the less risk you have in making that investment.

In the real estate cycle, your assumptions should be based on future phases of the cycle, not on past performance. Imagine two investors, Alex and Ben, both looking to buy rental properties that are similar price and potential. The only difference between the two is that Alex discovers his property in 2006, and Ben discovers his in 2010.

"Alex from '06" sees many of his friends owning property and decides to get in on the action. After all, the numbers his friends are reporting about their investments sound too good to be true. He looks at past performance and decides to pull the trigger on a home that has just come up for sale. Alex from '06 makes his underwriting assumptions based on the past, and he pays higher than market value for the property because he expects he will easily pay off the loan with his correspondingly high rental income. But Alex from '06 is at the tail end of the hypersupply phase. Rents look high, but the vacancy rates have been climbing as well—a result of the excess supply hitting the market. Alex soon finds out that because of this excess in supply, rental prices have stalled and even begun to decrease. In the end, this market underperforms by far compared to his initial expectations. Alex assumed that his high rental rates would continue to rise. Nope. Alex from '06 essentially overpaid to ride in a hot air balloon right before it popped.

In comparison, "Ben from 2010" is looking at a similar property. But prices are still falling from the recession, and it makes him overly pessimistic. Ben from 2010 looks back a couple of years, noting the falling housing market, and conservatively assumes that rent will be flat for a long time. Poor Ben from 2010. He doesn't understand that once the existing oversupply is absorbed, rents will likely trend upward again. As a result, he undervalues his investment opportunities by underestimating their potential returns. He settles on a lesser property in a market with lower potential, and the tragedy of it is that he's done so at a time when a slightly more expensive property in a market with higher potential would have been well worth the price premium. If Ben were more optimistic and realistic about the future, he'd have seen the opportunity that was there for the taking. Ben from 2010 settled for the "thrills" of the kiddie roller coaster when he could have been having the time of his life on Space Mountain.

The main problem with both Alex's and Ben's rental property purchases is that they were based on false assumptions, costing each investor profits that they could have made had they taken the time to understand the future of their markets. Your decision to purchase a property must take into account the purchase price as well as the reasonable expectation of future rental income.

When to Buy In

It is generally accepted that your house will, eventually, appreciate in value, barring any major disrepair or calamity. The housing market has seen a steady 4.18 percent increase in value over the last fifty years. In fact, only one year, 2010, saw housing values fall below previous levels. Growth is slower in some years and in some markets, but growth is consistent (figure 25).

Source: US Bureau of Labor Statistics

Year-over-year price increases for US housing

Knowing what you now know about real estate cycles, you can buy properties at lower than market value and capitalize on the expected future growth in the next phase of the cycle. For example, if you buy a property in the recession/recovery phase, you can reasonably expect to see aggressive growth in the value of your home and the rent you charge. Knowing that you are in the recession/recovery phase can help you make better offers, going in with the assumption that the current sales price likely sits below the property's accepted market value. You could underwrite the lower rents you will get in the near term with the anticipated appreciation of the asset's value in the future.

All investment strategies are a version of buying low and selling high.

Alternatively, if you recognize a booming expansion/hypersupply phase, that could be a sign to be suspicious of the current sales price. Not to say you should never buy a home in a phase like this, but you will need to proceed with prudence and careful planning. Because the risk to your future home's value is high, you need to take extra caution when negotiating the final sale figures.

At the time of this writing, our country is experiencing an unprecedented amount of quantitative easing with trillions of dollars being injected into the economy. Economic analysts are predicting that this will lead to rising inflation rates over the next decade. Historically, the Federal Reserve has used 2 percent as its annual inflation target ceiling, not allowing inflation to rise any higher. Now, that same 2 percent target is an *average*, not a fixed maximum, meaning the Fed's mandate will permit rates of inflation above the target, especially following years of below-2-percent inflation. For rental property investors, this will present an attractive buying opportunity post-fallout from the pandemic that will be on par with, if not greater than, the period after the Great Recession of 2008.

I also believe that this period of uncertainty can be an incentive to invest your money in inflation-hedging investments, such as rental property. Inflation can be difficult to guard against, with a limited number of options to protect your money. Rental investments can withstand the volatile nature of an adjusting economy and offer solid ground in a turbulent financial whirlpool. Moreover, even after everything settles down, rental properties will remain one of your best investment options.

What Rents Could/Should Be

In a way, a rental price is a textbook example of the law of supply and demand at play. All things being equal, when tenants have the freedom to choose from a multitude of properties, any property charging higher rent is likely to be passed over. Excessive supply in the market decreases the demand for the product. Conversely, when the supply of available homes is low, the demand for that product goes up, in turn pushing rent prices upward until the balance is reached (figure 26).

fig. 26

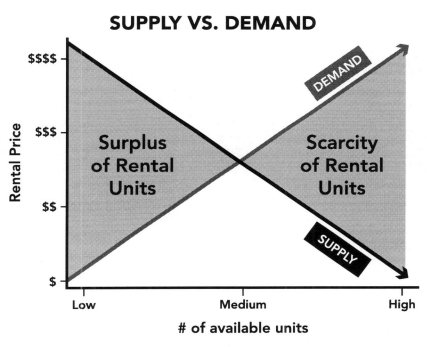

How supply and demand laws affect rental prices

Going forward, let's look at some assumptions we can make about how much you can charge for rent. If, for example, the market cycle is currently in an expansion phase and you know you can charge high rents, the price you would have to pay for a property would be affected. You could pay a higher purchase price because you are optimistically assuming that rents will increase in the future. It might not make financial sense at the time of purchase, but your underwriting assumption plans for a better future. It's tempting to remain conservative about the rent prices you set, but by doing so, you could miss out on incredible opportunities because it could lead to undervaluing rental properties. Being risk-averse and aiming too low might cost you money in the long run.

Chapter Recap

» Real estate falls in a predictable and routine cycle of four distinct phases: recovery, expansion, hypersupply, and recession.

» Only two factors apply to rental property investors in the context of the phases: the occupancy/vacancy levels and the construction volume in the market.

» Rental property investors don't use the real estate cycle to time the market. Instead, they use their knowledge to evaluate the likely future returns on their investment.

» When considering a rental property, imagine yourself as a lender underwriting an investment. Evaluate the likely future risks and returns rather than basing your decisions on past performance.

| 4 |
Building Resilient Cash Flow

The key to financial freedom is a person's ability to convert earned income into passive income.

– ROBERT KIYOSAKI

Building your cash flow, at least in principle, is simple. You buy a property. You put tenants in that property who pay you every month. If they pay you more than it costs to own that property, then you keep the profits and build a passive cash flow. Repeat to your heart's content. But while the concept is simple, it is not always easy to implement. For one thing, how do you know which property to buy? How do you know if it will generate the cash flow you need to make another investment in the future? And when you buy it, how do you set it up so that the money keeps coming in for a long time? These common questions are part of what we'll cover in this chapter.

Part of the challenge in creating a book like this is that people live in various markets around the country. For the same amount of money, you can buy big in some markets and barely scrape by in others. One million dollars sounds like a lot of money, but have a look at some examples of properties you can buy in different markets. Figure 27 shows some recent examples I found for sale while scouring through several communities. With a million dollars, you could buy a gated, sprawling piece of land with a 7,000-square-foot mansion in El Paso, Texas. You could buy a large, two-bedroom condo overlooking Lake Michigan in Chicago, or you could buy a tiny one-bedroom Manhattan apartment.

GRAPHIC

fig. 27

	LISTING PRICE	PROPERTY SIZE (SQ. FT.)	PRICE PER SQ. FT.
San Francisco, CA	$1,195,000	1,069 (condo)	$1,118
El Paso, TX	$1,000,000	7,251 (house)	$138
Chicago, IL	$1,000,000	1,611 (condo)	$621
Austin, TX	$1,000,000	1,990 (house)	$503
Manhattan, NY	$1,000,000	744 (apartment)	$1,292
Jacksonville, FL	$1,000,000	5,482 (house)	$182

MY TAKE

I've heard that you should aim to clear $250 a month per $100,000 in property value, after all your expenses have been paid. In my experience, however, that is too low in some markets and too high in others.

With so much variation in the relationship between price and size, it can be difficult to set a hard-and-fast rule that dictates how much rent you should plan on collecting.

DIGITAL ASSETS

You can find several rental calculators for different property types in your Digital Asset Vault. Visit **www.clydebankmedia.com/rental-assets**.

A common response to the question of how much rent should you should collect is the "one percent rule." This rule simply states that you should target your investing at properties for which you will be able to collect 1 percent of the total property value in monthly rent. For example, if the property is valued at $200,000, the one percent rule dictates that your target rent is $2,000 a month or more for a solid investment return. While it's adequate as a starting point, that rule doesn't apply to every market equally. For instance, I find that in coastal cities with very high property values you can't come close to achieving this benchmark. In figure 28, you can see the average ratio of cities like San Francisco and San Jose barely reaching 0.25 percent. The 1 percent benchmark is not impossible in these types of markets, but using this guideline creates an unreachable standard. On the flip side, the one percent rule is easier to achieve in other markets like Memphis or Jackson. The rule is a starting point, not an ironclad guide. Because there are so many local factors that come into play, set your gauge at a 1 percent ratio and use the comparable rent prices to see how close you can get.

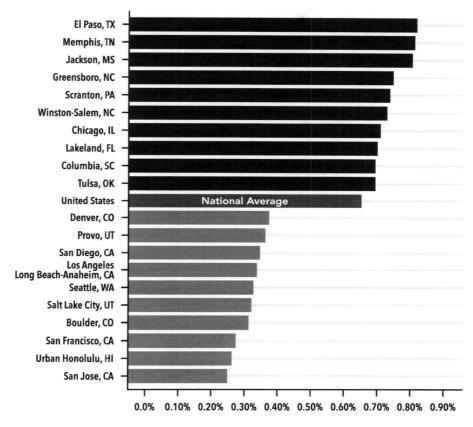

THE 10
BEST AND WORST MARKETS
FOR PURSUING THE 1% RULE

GRAPHIC

fig. 28

Source: Zillow Research Data 2020

DIGITAL ASSETS

The chart in figure 28 shows the highest and lowest rent-to-property-value ratios in the country. You can find a complete analysis of more than one hundred markets in the Market Analysis Tool found in your Digital Asset Vault at **www.clydebankmedia.com/rental-assets**.

As you begin sorting through properties, you'll need a method of weighing the rent you should collect against the price you pay for the property. In this chapter, I will introduce a few of the metrics that rental property owners use to evaluate the efficiency of their investments.

I will also show you how to compare two properties and create a simple measurement that shows what each property can earn. This allows you to make a valid comparison between two very different options, kind of like converting an apples-to-oranges comparison back to apples-to-apples.

Using Comparables to Maximize Profits

Eventually, and hopefully soon, you will identify a property that has the potential to be a great investment. It's possible that it will be a "plug and play" property, where you simply take ownership and start charging rents. Or maybe you'll have to make some repairs before you can post the "For Rent" sign. To find the right rental figures, you'll have to compare your property against others like it in the area. These are your *comparables*, or comps, as they are more commonly known. Comps let you see what purchase prices and rental prices look like in a given area.

Comps are used to discern competitive rental prices. If you don't know what the comps are, you could end up asking too much and scaring away prospective tenants. Or you might ask too little and lock yourself into a contract at a price below market value. Comps also help you determine if the purchase price of your home is too high or if it is priced below market value. If it is priced lower than what other homes sell for, comps can help you see the underlying causes for the disparity. Let's dig deeper into how to evaluate comps and discover the perfect price for your property.

Comparable Market Sales

Patrick is looking at rental property in Aurora, a thriving suburban city just outside of Denver. He finds what looks like a great home for sale, built in the last five years, with four bedrooms, a modern kitchen layout, and a fenced, landscaped backyard. The advertised price is $390,000. But is that a good price? Is it too high?

When looking at a potential market, it helps to see what homes are selling for right now, as well as what they sold for recently. Narrow down your search to properties that have been sold in the last thirty days. I would not recommend looking at sales prices any further back than ninety days, because market conditions can change quickly.

One of the best ways to pull together aggregated data for these comparable analyses is to use a site like Zillow. In the appendix I've included several other site options for overseas readers, but I like Zillow for use in the United States because it allows you to use filters to narrow down your search terms. Your goal with a comparable market sales analysis is to get a solid sense of what price homes are listed at and what they have sold for in the area. Once you know this, you can accurately tell whether a property's purchase price is accurate, inflated, or ready to move quickly.

A home's selling price is not an objective thing. I can't pull out my Kelley Blue Book to assign a value to a home based on a few key features. There is a subjective nature to a purchase price that requires some due diligence to uncover. In our example above, Patrick was eyeing a property in Aurora that was listed at $390,000 in good condition. At first glance, that might seem fair, but when Patrick pulls up the data for houses that have sold in the last month, he uncovers a different story. One telling statistic is the *months of inventory*, a metric used by real estate agents to determine how long it would take to sell all homes on the market at the current rate. With thousands of homes listed right now, Aurora has eleven and a half months of inventory on the market, which is a very high number for this statistic. This means that if no new homes were listed, and all the homes now for sale sold at the current rate, it would take nearly a year to clear the board of available properties. This statistic could mean that there are too many homes listed right now or that people aren't buying very quickly.

To continue to refine our take on the market we need to look at some more data points and metrics.

When looking at recent sales, Patrick discovers that homes in the neighborhood have sold at 93 percent of the original asking price after 124 days on the market. That tells him that people in Aurora aren't in a rush to buy, at least not at the prices advertised. Moreover, there are at least four other properties in a five-block radius of Patrick's choice with similar characteristics, each priced slightly lower than his. Although Patrick's dream home looks good, it seems that the $390,000 price is too high, at least in the current market. That does not mean Patrick needs to give up on the property; it simply gives him some wiggle room to negotiate a better price if he decides to pull the trigger and make an offer.

Comparable Market Rents

In your comps analysis, you should also compare the price that homes are currently renting for. Just as we did with purchase prices, you can use a site aggregator like Zillow to draw rental data, using filters to create an apples-to-apples comparison to find similar properties. In some ways, comparing rental prices is slightly more challenging than comparing purchase prices. Where it starts to get difficult is in ranking and pricing the various amenities of a property. While one amenity may be necessary in Aurora, like central heating, it may not make sense in other markets like Jacksonville or Fort Worth. Hence, renters will likely pay more in Aurora if the property includes central heating, whereas in Jacksonville they may not care one way or the other.

It may be difficult to assess a fair rental price, but good sites allow you to see what other homes are offering as amenities to attract their tenants. Do they provide backyards for pets? Are they offering good parking for young urban professionals? Do they have three or four bedrooms for larger families? When you are looking at comparable market rents, you want to know these three factors: the rental price, the amenities offered, and any incentives included. To remain competitive in the market, you need to maintain a consistent offering of all three factors. It's no use having the cheapest rent in a neighborhood full of families if you don't offer a landscaped backyard for the children to play in. Likewise, what will tenants think of your home if you offer all the best amenities but have a rental price that's 50 percent higher than anything else in that community?

I've created a Rental Comparison Worksheet to help you identify and quantify the amenities offered for the size and scope of the current rentals on the market. You can get your copy in the Digital Asset Vault at **www.clydebankmedia.com/rental-assets**.

Let's borrow some of Patrick's thunder and track Aurora's rental market. We have created a simple spreadsheet listing some of the features of current rentals in Aurora. We have narrowed our search to single-family homes, because Patrick would prefer to lease his property to a family. Aurora experiences much colder winters than I do in California, but they do get warm summers. Therefore, I have included heating and cooling options as amenities for each property.

fig. 29

PROPERTY	BATHS	SQ. FT.	RENT	YR. BUILT	KITCHEN (1-5)	HEAT? A/C?	YARD (1-5)
3 br	2.5	1,700	$1,995	1979	1	Y/N	1
3 br	3	1,678	$2,195	2010	3	Y/Y	5
3 br	2	1,740	$2,095	2008	2	Y/N	3
3 br	2.5	2,600	$2,250	2001	2	Y/Y	4
3 br	2	1,939	$1,950	1979	2	Y/N	1

As you can see in figure 29, Aurora has a good selection of both older and newer homes, and they are all different. We have set up a ranking system for the backyard to judge cleanliness and size, as well as a ranking for the style and age of the kitchens in each property. These numbers are subjective, of course, but in this example, the higher the number, the better the tenant appeal.

Look at the first property, for instance. We can see that it is an aged home, over forty years old, with an unkempt backyard that families would not appreciate. The kitchen is desperate for a modern overhaul, as much of the décor is untouched from its original build.

To use this data, we have to assign a price point for each amenity listed for these homes. In other words, how much more per month would a tenant be willing to pay for a good yard or a fourth bedroom? To keep it simple, we'll look only at the three-bedroom homes and we'll narrow our field to just three basic amenities.

fig. 30

PROPERTY	RENT	SQ. FT.	YARD (1-5)	KITCHEN (1-5)
A (1979)	$1,995	1,700	1	1
B (2010)	$2,195	1,678	5	3
C (2008)	$2,095	1,740	3	2

Property B is clearly a nice home with a good yard and an attractive kitchen, both amenities that families in this area seem to value. The rent is $200 more per month than a home with a poor yard and kitchen (Property A). Property C's amenities are only slightly better than Property A's, and it advertises at a rental price halfway between the other two options. They all have very similar square footage, so only the amenities account for the different rental prices.

To calculate the price of each amenity, we need to start with a base rental rate, which is what the home would rent for in this market without all the additional amenities. Let's start by assigning values to each amenity, inasmuch as we can estimate them. In our example, we can estimate that an excellent backyard and kitchen each seem to add an extra $100 per month in value. If they are just so-so, they add $50 per month. We can also assume that newer homes push the price upward, so let's figure a further $100 per month for the appeal of a newer home. We now remove those figures from the asking price to arrive at the base rental rate for each property.

» **Property A**
$1,995 - $0 (offers no amenities, so no adjustments needed) = $1,995

» **Property B**
$2,195 - $300 ($100 + $100 + $100) = $1,895

» **Property C**
$2,095 - $200 ($50 + $50 + $100) = $1,895

Finally, take the average of all the properties to arrive at what you can expect to earn from a basic rental property in this specific market.

» ($1,995 + $1,895 + $1,895)/3 = **$1,928**

In this very simplified version of your comparable analysis, a three-bedroom home in Aurora has a base rental rate of around $1,930 per month. You can use this number to calculate the rents you can expect to earn once you include all the amenities of the property you want to buy.

Base rental rate: $1,930
+ Modest backyard: $50
+ Modern kitchen: $100
+ Less than 10 years old: $100
+ Study/den/office: $75
+ Air conditioning: $20
+ Garden shed: $20
+ Five minutes to stores: $35
+ Across from park: $25
+ Attached two-car garage: $40
= **$2,395/month**

Patrick has the capacity to charge $2,395 per month for his property, with all that it includes. He could also use this method to account for how much he could charge if he modernized and upgraded amenities to increase the potential for higher rent. For instance, if Patrick spent $500 to hire a local landscaping company to clean up the backyard, he could charge an additional $50 a month in rent, paying off his landscaping bill within the first year.

Measuring Investment Gains

Although I presented several strategies for investing, always with the aim of moving on to the next property—an approach that I believe is the key to building wealth—most rental property owners will choose to buy a stable investment property and hold on to it for as long as it produces positive investment gains. But to achieve consistent gains for years, you need to know what to expect before you even make an offer. While planning their careers, most people make rational, informed decisions about the path they plan to take before they invest years and tens of thousands of dollars in their education. You have to know how much a doctor gets paid before you decide to take on a six-figure tuition bill over eight years of intense education. Think of this process in the same way. You want to have a steady rental income that lasts as long as you operate your property. The analysis process is your way of predicting how high your "salary" will be so you know if it's worth it to commit to a given property.

To project your investment gains, you must understand how they're generated. As we mentioned in chapter 1, cash flow from rental properties can take several different forms. The most obvious form is that of the rent check you collect every month. It's tangible and easy to count. Next, you have the appreciated value in the home, either from an improving market or from renovations to the home. Appreciated value, however, does not technically become cash flow until you sell your property and take profit. Another form of cash flow comes from your debt reduction, as you pay down the loan and build equity in your investment. In the simple net worth calculation of assets minus liabilities, you increase your net worth when you increase your assets *as well as* decrease your liabilities. In other words, paying down debt generates wealth.

Where it starts to get complicated is in how you measure and compare the potential gains from different properties you could invest in. Let me illustrate. Let's say you are looking at two properties, both in similar markets. Option A is in a good neighborhood with strong historical rental rates and higher property prices but slower expected appreciation. The second, Option B, sits on the outskirts of town with lower property prices, but city planning is forecasting explosive growth sometime in the next ten years as they improve transportation and infrastructure in that area. One investment is solid and stable, and the other involves some speculation but has potential for greater returns. You do some basic math on a napkin while you sip coffee at the local Starbucks. Here's what you've mapped out:

> **Option A**
> Purchase: $300,000
> Rent: $2,000/month
> Estimated property value after ten years: $350,000 (assuming only 1.6 percent annual appreciation)

> Option B
> Purchase: $150,000
> Rent: $1,100/month
> Estimated property value after ten years: $350,000 (assuming 8.8 percent annual appreciation!)

Don't jump ahead and pull out your calculator—there is a lot more to weigh before you make a decision. Option A is stable, so you shouldn't have any problem getting tenants right away. Homes in Option A's market are older but established, and they attract families who want to find a good long-term agreement with their landlord. On the other hand, the age of the home cuts into the appreciation, because you will need to pay for repairs and maintenance along the way. Option B is in a brand-new community, but there are risks there as well. If the city doesn't come through on its infrastructure plans, that community won't be as attractive anymore, and the appreciation you hope for will not exist. Rent will be lower because of the lack of amenities in the area.

If you look just at total returns over ten years, Option B is ahead, with a cash flow income of $332,000 ($132,000 from ten years of rent + $200,000 profit from final sale) compared to Option A's $290,000 ($240,000 from ten years of rent + $50,000 profit from final sale). But the method of getting that cash involves more risk with Option B, which assumes a very high annual rate of increase in appreciation of the property values in that market. Option A gets the bulk of its total return through higher rent payments, while Option B must wait ten years for the final sale to make the bulk its profits. Which is the better investment? The answer, it seems, is not intuitive. One involves greater confidence in the rental assumption, the other in the appreciation assumption. One provides more consistent cash flow, and the other greater potential returns at exit. Each has different kinds and degrees of risk.

That is why investors use special metrics to make it easier to compare these options. Once you account for the capital you invest in each property, the risks involved, how fast the money comes back, and your profits after all expenses are paid, it is easy to see which of these two options would be the attractive choice for the savvy rental property investor. Let's cover the basic metrics you will need, as well as some advanced ones that you will use once you branch out into more adventurous investments.

Rental Yield

The majority of people reading this book will be interested in a strategy that helps them find a good property, buy it at a good price, and collect stable, sizable rent checks for years to come. These are the income builders, those that see the value of rental properties to increase or replace their own incomes as they work to achieve financial freedom.

MY TAKE

If you are new to rental property investing, this is your best bet. Take the time to understand how a rental property operates with a solid buy-and-hold strategy. And once you have experience in this field, you can expand your portfolio to include properties with more inherent risk and return potential.

To understand your own potential income, you have to calculate the net rental yield. This is the calculation of the rent you will collect against the money you spend to invest in the property.

Imagine there are two properties you are considering for your very first rental home. To make it consistent, let's bring back those options you thought about in the Starbucks: options A and B. Option A makes $2,000 rent per month and Option B makes just $1,100 per month. Option A looks like the better investment because it brings in almost twice as much money, right? That is only half the equation, however, because you need to account for how much money you invest to have the right to collect those rents.

In a typical rental investment, you put money in at the beginning (your investment) and you collect money on a regular basis throughout the life of your investment (your rent, less expenses) (figure 31). The yield measurement takes both figures into account so that you can create accurate comparisons of several options.

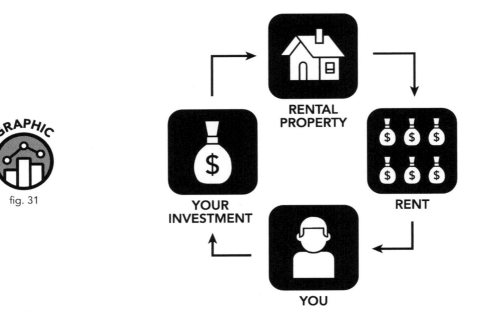

To increase your yield, or the amount of money you make per dollar you invest, you can either increase your rent, decrease your expenses, or invest less money (figure 32). All three options allow you to maximize your rental yield, even if the amount on the rent check is smaller. You can also use this yield formula to compare your investment against other types of investments, such as stocks.

GRAPHIC

fig. 32

This calculation takes the yearly profit you earn divided by the cash you put in.

Now, let's apply this to the two options we looked at earlier. In Option A, you have to pay $60,000 as a down payment plus a further $12,000 in closing costs, agent fees, and some repairs, putting your total investment at $72,000. Option B allows you to invest just $33,000 with your down payment and closing costs.

>> **Option A**
Rent: $2,000 per month, or $24,000 per year
Total investment: $72,000
Yield (yearly rent / investment): 33.3 percent

>> **Option B**
Rent: $1,100 per month, or $13,200 per year
Total investment: $33,000
Yield (yearly rent / investment): 40 percent

Once we do the calculations, it becomes clear that Option B earns more per dollar of investment than Option A. As an added benefit, you only have to invest half as much money, risking less to make a better yield.

Advanced Investing Metrics

Rental yield is quite a simple way to measure your rental income. First, it assumes you are looking at properties from similar markets and with similar risk profiles. Once you branch out into different markets, say, properties that require more renovations, you will need an advanced understanding of how to compare them. The rental yield also assumes that the investor intends to make most of the money from the monthly rental income, not factoring in a final sales price as part of the returns. As I mentioned earlier, there are more methods of making money on your rental than merely collecting the tenants' checks. While these metrics may not apply to your first investment, you will certainly find them useful as you progress on your journey.

I am touching only briefly on these metrics to expose you to some advanced options and ideas. I cover these measurements extensively in my previous book, *Real Estate Investing QuickStart Guide*.

The best way to measure your investment is to consider how quickly you get paid, how large the payoff, and how likely it is to happen—or, in investor terms, the efficiency, magnitude, and risk of a deal.

Internal Rate of Return

The principle behind the concept of ***internal rate of return*** (IRR) is that money today is worth more than money tomorrow. IRR is the measurement that quantifies that statement. The reason this measurement matters so much is that your rental property will earn different amounts at different times throughout the life of your investment. You collect monthly rent. But maybe for one year, you use the rent checks to fund a massive renovation, offsetting your rental cash income. And then after fifteen years, maybe you think it's time to move on to a new property. So you sell the old property and cash in on the large amount of equity you've built up in it.

When you factor all these figures into the IRR, you create a simple percentage that you can use to compare two different rental investments. Imagine that you had eight investing options that you wanted to compare. You invest $200 in each option, and after ten years, each investment returns $1,000. But the timing of those returns is very different. This is where we use the IRR to create an equal comparison of multiple options. Which option is best? The IRR tells you which investing options earn you more money the quickest.

GRAPHIC

fig. 33

Investment	IRR	DAY 1 1/1/20	YEAR 1 1/1/21	YEAR 2 1/1/22	YEAR 3 1/1/23	YEAR 4 1/1/24	YEAR 5 1/1/25	YEAR 6 1/1/26	YEAR 7 1/1/27	YEAR 8 1/1/28	YEAR 9 1/1/29	YEAR 10 1/1/30	Total Cash Flow
#1	49%	-200	100	100	100	100	100	100	100	100	100	100	1,000
#2	51%	-200	100	100	100	200	0	100	100	100	200	0	1,000
#3	54%	-200	100	100	200	100	0	100	100	200	100	0	1,000
#4	59%	-200	100	200	100	100	0	100	200	100	100	0	1,000
#5	69%	-200	200	100	100	100	0	200	100	100	100	0	1,000
#6	27%	-200	0	0	0	0	500	0	0	0	0	500	1,000
#7	28%	-200	0	0	0	0	500	0	0	0	500	0	1,000
#8	31%	-200	0	0	0	500	0	0	0	0	0	500	1,000

The IRR of each of the different $200 investments

NOTE

The numbers in figure 33 are purposely oversimplified to help you understand the concept. While the numbers used don't correspond to real-world investment scenarios, the patterns do. For example, you might go without collecting rent for months at a time, and some investments do indeed bring in returns only after years of patience and hard work. This data is presented to help you understand that the timing of investment returns, not just their amounts, is important to consider.

In figure 33, investment number 5 returns your money in the most efficient way. Number 6 is not efficient at all. I like this metric because it factors in both the yearly income and the end returns from a successful sale, allowing me to simplify a complicated cash flow schedule in a way that makes it easy to compare and contrast.

Cash Multiple

The *cash multiple* is a simple way to measure how much money is returning to you—the magnitude of your return on investment. The idea is that you can measure how much money you will get back from every dollar you invest. If you spend $100 and get $200 back, that is a 2x cash multiple. If you spend $100 and get $300 back, that is a 3x multiple. Simple, right?

The problem with this metric, at least on its own, is that it doesn't account for the timing, like the IRR would. For example, I could sell you a property that I advertise as a guaranteed 2x multiple. It is only after you make the investment that you discover you do not get that return for another twenty-five years. When you consider that inflation will eat into your profits, that 2x multiple doesn't sound so good anymore.

Net Present Value

By calculating IRR, you know the timing of your returns. By calculating the cash multiple, you know the size of your returns. Both measurements together give you a decent picture of how well separate investments will do. As an investor, you should always be looking to balance all the factors to make the best informed decision. This is where the *net present value* (NPV) comes into its own. NPV allows us to assess risk and think about future dollars in present-day terms. The more risky an investment is, the greater the rate of discount applied to your projected future cash flows. Because of inflation, money due to you in the future is already inherently less valuable than money obtained today. And any risk of said money not materializing at all in the future, or materializing to a lesser extent than projected, further diminishes its present-day worth. In a moment I'll walk you through the mechanics of the NPV calculation. But for now, I want you to take a step back and consider why it's important that we use multiple evaluation metrics when assessing critical investment decisions, particularly when comparing one potential investment against another.

If you have two investments and you only have the IRR and the cash multiple as your data points, it's like you are looking at a two-dimensional representation of the investments. You are missing the third component of any investment—the risk profile. NPV provides you with a means to quantify risk (to the best extent possible). By considering NPV alongside your IRR and cash multiple metrics, you obtain what I call a "full-dimensional" picture of the investment under consideration.

The net present value is based on a risk percentage called the **discount rate**. This is essentially the opportunity cost you incur by not placing your investment moneys in a safe alternative, like a T-bond or mutual fund, summed with a quantification of the unique risks presented by the particular investment opportunity under evaluation. It's a mouthful. Let's break it down. Let's say you could safely make 5 percent returns if you put your money in a diversified mutual fund full of bonds. That would put your base risk rate at 5 percent. Next, you raise your rate further to account for the risks involved with your investment. For example, if you have construction risks with a renovation, then you might add a further 3 percent to your base rate. Along with your base rate (5 percent), you add up the additional construction risk to come up with a final discount rate of 8 percent.

NOTE

These figures, obviously, are subjective to each investor. The risk I would incur for renovating a property might be significantly higher than that of Chip and Joanna Gaines on HGTV's *Fixer Upper*. More experience drops the risk rate as you become more familiar with the process.

The NPV is the amount of money you would get if all your theoretical future returns were paid as a lump sum today. To calculate this theoretical value accurately, we must discount the money from the future. If you stuck $100 under your mattress and left it for a year, it would have less buying power when you pulled it out, due to inflation. If you left that same $100 bill under your mattress for ten years, it wouldn't be able to buy nearly as much. This same concept is used when valuing your prospective investment returns using NPV. If you have a property paying you the same rent for the next ten years, then the rent you collect in year ten will have less value than the rent collected in year one. And it's not only about inflation; it's also about uncertainty. As we project our expected future incomes, the further we go out into the future, the less certain we can be of those incomes actually materializing. The present-day value of all these nearer-term and longer-term anticipated returns is what the NPV measures.

I'll give you an example of a fictitious investment of $200. Option A returns $172.90 each year for ten years, giving you a total of $1,729 after ten years of your holding the property. Option B uses that same $200 investment but pays nothing until the tenth year, when you get a payout of $100,000.

GRAPHIC

fig. 34

Investment	IRR	DAY 1 1/1/20	YEAR 1 1/1/21	YEAR 2 1/1/22	YEAR 3 1/1/23	YEAR 4 1/1/24	YEAR 5 1/1/25
A	86.2%	-200	172.7	172.7	172.7	172.7	172.7
B	86.2%	-200	0	0	0	0	0

Investment	IRR	YEAR 6 1/1/26	YEAR 7 1/1/27	YEAR 8 1/1/28	YEAR 9 1/1/29	YEAR 10 1/1/30	TOTAL CASH FLOW
A	86.2%	172.7	172.7	172.7	172.7	172.7	$1,727
B	86.2%	0	0	0	0	100,000	$100,000

Notice that the IRR is identical, which, if considered alone, would give the false impression that these investment opportunities are identical. They are clearly quite different.

Intuitively, we know Option B is better, but in real-life scenarios it's rarely that easy. Over the same period with the same initial investment, Option B achieves 57.8 times the total cash flow of Option A, but the IRR was unable to convey even this drastic difference on its own. This is precisely why savvy investors will rely on not one but several measures.

This is how the NPV can quantify what we sense is true but haven't measured yet. In each option (figure 34), we're going to account for the risk involved (which, for simplicity's sake, we'll assume is the same), and we will use a discount rate of 8 percent for each investment. Remember that the NPV represents the total amount of money you would have if all future returns, through the duration of the investment period, were paid today discounted at a chosen rate that matches the assessed risk level in the investment. Money tomorrow is always worth less than money today due to discounting. But don't be deceived. That is not to say that future money has no worth whatsoever—on the contrary (figure 35):

GRAPHIC

fig. 35

Investment	IRR	Cash Multiple	NPV
A	86.1%	8.6	$889
B	86.1%	500.0	$42,703

Even with an identical IRR, the NPVs and cash multiples of Investment B show that we have a clear winner.

In Option A, you invest $200 and get an immediate return of $889. But in Option B, you invest $200 and get a return of $42,703 today. The choice is clear in this example. In the real world, you can use the IRR, cash multiple, and NPV together to form a 3D "full-dimensional" model that will help you choose between several investment properties. The value of this model is that it gives you, the rental property investor, a tangible number that makes it a lot easier to determine that Property A is better than Properties B, C, and D.

As an exclusive bonus for my readers, I've created a downloadable template that allows you to chart and determine each of these metrics when evaluating prospective rental properties. Take the BOE (Back of the Envelope) Rental Property Calculator and plug in your own numbers to analyze your investment options. Download it by visiting **www.clydebankmedia.com/rental-assets.**

Chapter Recap

» To build a strong rental cash flow, planning and analysis must be done before making an offer on a home.

» Since purchase prices and rents are subjective, using comparable properties in the area allows you to assess potential returns and spot good deals.

» As rental owners build their income, they need to analyze their yield, which accounts for the cash flow coming in compared to the amount they invested to earn the right to collect that cash flow.

» To compare different investment options, you need to use metrics that tell you how much you'll make, how quickly you'll make it, and the risk tolerance needed to make it.

| 5 |
Exits and Exchanges

Chapter Overview
» Planning If and When It Makes Sense to Sell
» Handling Tenants and Contracts When Selling
» Understanding the Tax Advantages of a 1031 Exchange

A poem is never finished—only abandoned.
— W. H. AUDEN, PARAPHRASING PAUL VALÉRY

The Permian Basin in West Texas is a hot place to be—in more than one sense of the word. This oil-rich area of the country has been extremely prosperous and has seen an influx of jobs. As a result, there has been increased interest in the properties and communities of the area. Towns based entirely on the oil economy have been booming, and real estate prices have seen the effect. As an interesting side note, small mountain villages in nearby New Mexico are also benefiting from this boom, as residents of the oil towns seek to find winter homes to escape the relentless sun.

In the town of Odessa, with a population of less than 100,000, the oil economy has been kind, especially to those who already owned property there. Ten years ago, a typical house cost $105,000, but today the same property is worth nearly double that amount (figure 36). The real estate in Odessa has been featured nationwide as one of the fastest-moving and most prosperous investing hotbeds in the US, although you would find similar results in Dallas, Amarillo, Kermit, and Midland. The rise began fifteen years ago, and it is typical of what we find in towns where oil is the primary industry.

Although people tell tales of incredible wealth coming from these investments, the writing is on the wall for these towns. The oil price recently traded below zero for the first time ever. The OPEC price war in Russia and Saudi Arabia has caused instability in the American oil town economies. As a result, people who live in places like Odessa are losing their high incomes and can't afford to buy property anymore. Lost jobs mean no more financing as banks struggle to say yes to homeowners who need it. Unfortunately, the future of these oil towns is uncertain, and uncertainty is never an investor's friend.

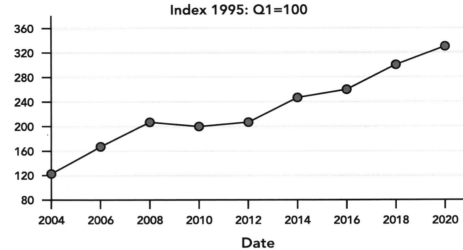

fig. 36

HOUSE PRICES IN ODESSA, TX
Index 1995: Q1=100

source: Federal Reserve Economic Data

The housing price index for property in Odessa, Texas

What I've described is a situation of lost faith in the economy's ability to support the real estate market. Oil towns are volatile and jumpy, responding quickly to market conditions and plummeting rapidly along with the price of a barrel of oil. It's during times like these that you need to have an escape plan, a life preserver strapped to your back for when the leaks begin to spout. Otherwise, you're going down with the ship.

It seems early to talk about exit scenarios, at least at this point in the book. But I want to emphasize that your exit scenario is crucial. When you understand how and when you'll exit, you'll make better decisions when you buy. You'll also have a ready-made plan that helps you avoid the pitfalls that threaten to undo years of hard work in a rental property. I see three main exit scenarios that could occur during the life of your investment.

» **"It's not me, it's you."** Similar to the situation I described in West Texas, there may come a time when you no longer believe in the sanctity of the market you once thought was so great. I find examples of this in every economy, especially when rental property owners try to capitalize on a rapidly rising growth rate within a niche sector.

» **"Economy class? Nah, I'm flying first class."** The most likely reason you will want to get out of a deal is so that you can grab on to a better deal. With experience acquired during your first investment, you will understand how to do it better the next time. When that "next time" rolls around in the form of a more stable, better-producing rental property, you can—and should—have a plan in place to sell your current property so that you can upsize to a better deal. Later on in the chapter, I'll introduce you to a tax-saving scheme designed specifically for this purpose.

» **"Till death do us part."** A legitimate plan for rental property investors is not to leave their property at all. You have a stable income, you have a market that works well, you have great tenants; why disrupt a good thing? Unless you need the capital from the first property to trade up to a better deal, it's a perfectly realistic plan to hold on to a property for decades.

Unless you are planning on scenario number three, let's cover some of the aspects of getting the best sales price and how to use your exit scenario to your advantage.

Selling Your Rental Property

Whether it's simply time to cash out or you'd like to take your money and move on to bigger properties, selling a home takes skill. Get it right, and you'll put more money in your pocket. Get it wrong, and your property could stagnate on the market, costing you all those rental returns you diligently collected over the years.

Part market research, part psychology, and part timing, the sale of a rental property can be likened to an art form that you can work at to improve. Forget all the variables that are beyond your control and focus instead on what you can control. By the time you are ready to sell, you should have built up a significant amount of equity in the home, have a deep understanding of the market, established good relationships with your tenants, and have measurable data to support your claim that your property will provide value to the next owner.

Silicon Valley companies have learned to rush to market with whatever product they have to offer. Often, people complain that the products are buggy, flawed, or not yet complete. That is intentional. In fact, engineers working in Silicon Valley joke that failure is a feature. These companies intentionally launch products that have not been fully fixed, calling them the "minimum viable product," just one notch above unfinished. And then they sit back and watch. As users report what works and what doesn't, these engineers take that information to iterate to a better product, launching version 2.0 with all the lessons they learned from their first attempt. This purposeful method of failure and feedback allows engineers to find out what doesn't work and what users actually want, and to tailor the product for better performance in the future. While this strategy may be frustrating for the early adopters, it's a clever way to save money. The risk is too great for companies spending millions of dollars developing products. If a fully fleshed out product fails on day one, it could capsize the entire company. But using this method, the research and development costs are deferred until the company absolutely understands what the market wants and how its product can perform better on the next iteration.

As a real estate investor, use your exit period to analyze your own feedback. The "postmortem" part of the rental investment is one of the best times to understand what went right and what went wrong. Using some of the metrics discussed in the previous chapter, you can calculate your IRR and NPV on past performance. We talked about how we might use these metrics prior to making a purchase. We used plenty of assumptions and estimates. We tried to predict what the future would look like. Reality is always more complicated. Oil prices suddenly crash and communities buckle. People lose their jobs and move on. Alternatively, perhaps the city where you invested built new roads and upgraded the infrastructure, an unanticipated boon to your real estate holdings. In any case, once you've spent time in the arena as a property owner, you don't need to do quite as much estimating and projecting. You will have the immeasurably valuable ability to use real data to evaluate your progress. You can check your actual performance against your predictions. And you can use those lessons to inform you as move on to your next rental property with a rock-solid plan to do better.

Listing Your Property

It's been said that a property has to sell three times before your buyer signs on the dotted line. It first must be sold when a potential buyer views the listing. Then it gets sold on the drive-by of the home and neighborhood. Finally, it's sold when the home is shown. That means you should put as much effort into the listing of the home as you would when showing a potential buyer through the property. The listing is the first point of contact for your buyer and the first impression your property will make that will influence how the rest of the deal progresses.

Unless you have experience in the real estate industry, this is not the time to DIY your listing. Save that responsibility for the experts and list with an agent who has experience in your community and understands the market at a deeper level than you do. An agent will have a network of contacts who would love to see your property. You might spend more in fees to work with an agent than you would if you listed the property on your own, but because you save precious time, the trade-off is worth it.

One of the best ways to nudge the purchase price in your favor is to plan your sale around the seasonality of the market. No two time periods are equal, at least in the real estate market. Sales predictably rise and fall based on the time of year. In some locations, like college towns, real estate sales revolve around the school year and the influx and outflow of students to the area. In other locations, the weather affects the sales market, often by as much as three or four times in volume. The key is to understand what seasonal factors affect your market and plan accordingly.

In figure 37, you can see the clear sales seasonality in Denver. Low season coincides with February, typically one of the coldest times of the year in Denver. But as spring and summer come along, sales volume can spike, even double. If you know that a seasonal spike is just around the corner, it would be worthwhile to practice some patience and wait the few months until your property can sell for a higher amount. We see similar patterns throughout different markets in the US, each with its own variables affecting the volume.

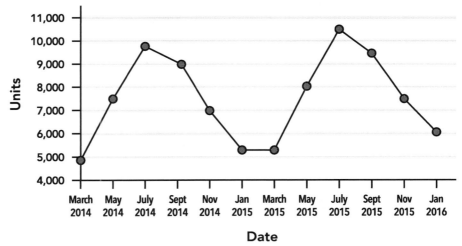

fig. 37

DENVER MONTHLY SALES

Source: Federal Reserve Economic Data

The peaks and troughs of sales volume in Denver

Often, these patterns are dictated by the weather. Therefore, you wouldn't use the seasonal sales data from San Francisco for your property in Milwaukee. Check local patterns online or with a local real estate agent before deciding on the best course of action.

Pricing Your Property

One of the reasons I advocate using a listing agent to sell your home is that it removes you from the equation. Subjectivity is not your friend when you price your home, because it can be hard to remove your personal biases from the final figure. This is a common occurrence with for-sale-by-owner (FSBO) sellers. Often an owner will set the price based partially on the market value, but significantly more on what they feel the home should be worth. This can be a dangerous stance to take when the home's excessive valuation repels potential buyers. It ultimately causes the property to remain on the market longer than it should. And when a home has been "for sale" for too long, buyers tend to have a negative perception of its value.

Have you ever noticed a house that repeatedly shows up in the listings, often with a "Price Reduced" banner to help draw more eyeballs to the listing? And what do we all tend to think when we see that? "I wonder what's wrong with that place that they keep dropping the price." It's a downward spiral that's hard to escape. You drop the price to attract buyers, but you scare buyers away because a dropped price also signals a lack of interest. And so you drop the price further in an effort to attract buyers. And so on and so on . . .

REMEMBER

The market value of a property and the listing price are independent of each other. It is possible to sell a home at, below, or above its value, depending on the market conditions.

Listing agents use comparable properties, much like you did in chapter 2, to help determine a fair market value for a home. I like to use comps to discover what other properties are advertising and then list my own home with distinguishing amenities that set it apart from the others in the same market. In a suburban community, for instance, I'll advertise a property with a spacious, landscaped backyard to emphasize the family-friendly aspects of the home; the goal is to drive up interest, and therefore the price.

There's a psychological aspect of setting a price that I find riveting. A couple of the tactics I use (conceding a win and setting an anchor price) were learned directly from professional FBI negotiators. In his book *Never Split the Difference*, Chris Voss relates his experience as a hostage negotiator and how the principles carry over to everyday life. One of the tactics he uses for financial dealings is setting an "anchor price" (in his own mind) for the sales price, but allowing some wiggle room so that the other party ends up feeling like they've had a win. This method can be used by either a buyer or a seller. When buying, Voss consistently uses a set formula. He starts with a particular price in mind that he would be willing to pay, but does not disclose it. Instead, he offers 65 percent of this target price, knowing that it's not likely to be accepted, but it establishes an anchor point in the mind of the other party. He then "concedes" and increases his bid to 85, 95, and finally 100 percent of the price he originally wanted to pay. It is an incredibly tactful and clever way to negotiate.

In real estate, I use something like this when setting a price with my listing agent. Let's say I want to sell the home for $250,000. I like to set the price higher, just to anchor a value in the minds of those who look at my property, but not so high that I risk scaring off potential buyers. If the market can support it, I'll list it at, say, $263,000, all the while planning on conceding the price during negotiation by as much as $13,000. It feels like a win to the buyer, and I have achieved the price I originally wanted.

Handling Tenants in the Handover

Beyond all the figures and dollars that get thrown around during the sale of a home, there is a human element to it all. If you have tenants in the home you're planning to sell, you'll need to help ease the transition from one landlord to the next. You can do this by taking some steps before you ever put the "For Sale" sign on the front lawn.

First, it's entirely possible for your tenants to become your buyer, taking over ownership of the property they have obviously loved so much. In that case, you could employ the seller financing option we discussed in chapter 2, becoming the bank and financing the deal yourself for a potentially higher sales price, lower tax bills, and the ability to keep up the *passive income* stream you've built.

Existing tenants can be both an asset and a liability during the sale of your home. New landlords like the idea of not having to spend time filling a vacancy in their new property. The stable income from an existing tenant can draw buyers who value the time saved in locating reputable renters.

On the other hand, the tenant you signed is an unknown variable to the new landlord. To prevent this from becoming an issue, provide the buyer with a rental history for the house, or for each unit of the house or apartment complex (for example, "unit A has had uninterrupted rent payments since the beginning of the lease eighteen months ago"). Show deposit receipts as appropriate. You might also inform the buyer that the current tenant(s) has passed your background checks.

As privacy laws are becoming more well defined, it's best not to share personally identifiable information about your tenants without their consent. All of the disclosures mentioned previously can be provided to a prospective buyer while keeping personally identifying information anonymous.

Tenants who have built up a solid relationship with you also face uncertainty with a new landlord. Lease agreements they signed with you need to be renegotiated with the new owner. They worry about increasing rents and the responsiveness of the new owner concerning repairs and other issues. Any existing lease agreements remain in place during the takeover, so before selling the home, discuss the possibility of signing a new lease agreement that extends the term; this will potentially ease the fears of tenants, at the same time creating a more stable value proposition for your buyer.

Also, keep tenants in the loop about your plans, even from the very beginning of their lease term. If you plan on selling in three years, inform your tenant. An unexpected or last-minute notice that you're selling the property strains the relationship and could harm the deal if the tenant decides to leave as you progress through the sale.

The 1031 Exchange

We have what it takes to take what you have.
– SUGGESTED IRS MOTTO

An inescapable reality of any exit strategy is that you will have to pay taxes on the sale of your home. If you make profits on the sale, you will incur capital gains taxes on those profits. It's like a punishment for doing well on your property investment. But, luckily, there is a way to kick that tax bill down the road. The 1031 exchange program was designed to offer a mitigation of that expensive tax bill while at the same time providing an option to trade up to bigger and better properties using the equity you have in the investment.

Essentially, the 1031 exchange, named after Section 1031 of the tax code, allows you to defer taxes when you use the gains to invest in a "like-kind" investment. This simply means that all the profits you make from the sale can be kept tax-free as long as you buy another investment that is similar to the one you sold. You can't keep your gains and speculate on the stock market. But you can invest in another rental property. Rental investors love the 1031 exchange because it opens up the possibility of using their gains as leverage toward a bigger or better property. It's like a cheat code that lets you upsize quickly to bigger profits. The IRS allows this for any investment, not just real estate. It's in the agency's favor as well, as the IRS gets to collect a bigger tax bill if you operate and profit from a larger property in the future. In order to use this advantage, you must abide by the rules of the 1031 exchange:

» **Equal or greater value swap:** The next property you invest in must be of equal or greater value than the property you sold. The point of the exchange is to upgrade, not to keep profits in your pocket. But it doesn't have to be just one property. Let's say you sell a $400,000 home and you use the 1031 exchange to translate that into two $250,000 homes in another market. Because the combined value is greater than the property you sold, it fulfills the requirement.

» **Like-kind investment:** This is an easy requirement for real estate investors because as long as it's real estate, you can make a swap to an entirely different type of property and it will still be considered a like-kind investment. Many investors use this exchange to trade up from a townhouse to a single-family home, or from an apartment to a duplex.

» **45-day identification deadline:** You must identify the property or properties you intend to buy within forty-five days of the sale of your original property. That is an incredibly quick timeline, so it makes sense to have something in mind before you sell the property. The good news is that you don't have to limit yourself to just one property. You can identify up to three potential options in case the first one should fall through. Also, this does not mean you have to make the offer just yet; you simply need to identify the prospective property so the IRS can grant you the 1031 provision.

» **180-day closing:** Although you will have provided the IRS with written intention to buy the property you identify, you have six months to officially close the deal. Use this time to negotiate prices and finalize all your due diligence before you sign on the dotted line.

MY TAKE

The 1031 exchange is an IRS vehicle, which by some hidden official statute means it is far more complicated than I have depicted. Consult with a tax specialist when considering the 1031 exchange option so you can use it to its full advantage without falling astray of the taxman.

Chapter Recap

» The best time to plan your exit strategy is before you ever enter the market.

» You have three exit scenarios, which include losing faith in the market, trading up to larger properties, and never exiting at all.

» Selling a property can be risky. If you're not careful, you can end up undoing all the effort you've put in and all the profits you've made from monthly rental returns.

» Pricing your property is part psychological and part analytical, best done in coordination with a professional real estate agent who knows the market.

» The 1031 exchange, when done correctly, allows you to use 100 percent of your profits toward a better property with higher earning potential.

PLANNING TO WIN WITH THE RIGHT PROPERTY

| 6 |
Rental Property Types

The question of what you want to own is actually the question of how you want to live your life.

— MARIE KONDO

Not all properties are created equal. In the first part of the book, we discussed how to plan for and charge the right price for your rental property. But the right price only serves you well if it's applied to the right property. The following story is a bit apocryphal, but it applies. Michelangelo was once asked how he came to sculpt the masterpiece *David*. He claimed that it was very simple. He merely looked at the block of marble and chipped away anything that wasn't David. Your process of finding the right property is identical. You look at the market and simply reject all the options that aren't perfect for you. Practice saying no to the countless "good" options that come your way, and you'll be ready to say yes when the "great" option presents itself.

I have a friend who despised eating at Subway. He claimed that no matter what he tried, he always found the food unsatisfactory. If you're familiar with Subway, it's hard to hate what you eat there because *you* select everything that goes into *your* sandwich. One day my friend realized why he was left disappointed every time he ate there. It was a problem of choice.

You see, my friend liked all the individual ingredients he could add to his subs. He liked the pickles and cucumbers, the mayonnaise and hot sauce, the onions and olives, the cheeses, and all the other options. Naturally, he figured, since he liked all the ingredients, he should really love the sub if he packed everything into it. And so, no matter what type of sub he got—pizza, meatball, turkey, tuna, chicken—he'd include every filling. And it always tasted terrible. Once he understood that his sandwich would taste a lot better if he simply selected a few key ingredients that work well together, he became a Subway superfan.

There's nothing wrong with pickles, mayonnaise, and barbecue sauce on their own, but together they can make for a bad sub. My friend's story is not that dissimilar to the problem of rental property choices. It's easy to get overwhelmed with the options available. Real estate is a very broad term that encompasses many different types of assets. In each category, you'll find assets that sound both appealing and profitable. But you don't need to choose them all. In fact, you'll make a more profitable return if you simply select the one or two properties that work for you, based on your available capital, risk tolerance, and market.

Although real estate properties can be either residential or commercial, almost all rental property investments are residential, in the sense that the sole purpose of the property is to provide a home, whether for a family, a business, or an industry. For a thorough explanation of commercial properties, grab my *Real Estate Investing QuickStart Guide*.

Single-Family Homes

fig. 38

Single-family homes, often shortened to SFHs, are the most common property type in the United States. These homes share no walls with other properties, sit individually on a lot, and may or may not have a garage included on the land. Over the last eighty years, 60 percent of all US housing units built have been single-family homes. Even though demographics and preferences have changed over time, the ratio of single-family homes to other types of property has barely shifted.

For that reason, the ***Case-Shiller Index***, a home price index commonly used by investors, is based on the sales records of the single-family home. Every month, 60,000 new single-family homes are added to the current 70 million SFH units around the country. Suffice it to say that rental property investors will never suffer from a lack of choices. These assets are almost entirely suburban, with some exceptions in inner-city communities. This makes the single-family home an ideal choice for families as opposed to single occupants or students, who prefer living closer to city centers. As an investor, you will face competition from homeowners for the single-family homes on the market.

Because of the consistent demand in every market and the ease of financing, the single-family home is the best investment for a beginner rental property investor.

There are significant advantages to buying a single-family home. It is an asset that is built to last for decades. You can expect to earn high rents, but that rental return is often offset by higher debt service costs, at least compared to those of apartments, condos, and townhouses. With many financing options aimed at single-family homeowners, it's extremely easy to purchase this type of asset.

But along with the good comes the bad. One of the challenges associated with SFH investments is that these properties tend to be costly, both in purchase price and maintenance costs. Because SFHs include both the structure and the land, there is simply more of the asset for you to maintain.

Within the SFH asset type are countless variations:

» **Bedrooms**: Consider who buys and lives in a single-bedroom home: the single tenant or the young couple. These tenants generally see one-bedroom SFHs as starter properties. And then what happens? People meet people. Families grow. And that cute little single-family home is suddenly too small for their needs. On the other hand, large family homes with four to five bedrooms mean that your tenants likely have children. Kids will put extra wear and tear on your property. Thus, until you become accustomed to being a landlord, you may do better with smaller families as tenants. I suggest limiting your rental home to one with two or three bedrooms to reduce the likelihood of excess wear and tear.

» **Garages**: Whether attached or detached, the garage is a crucial amenity. We all like to accumulate stuff, and your tenants are no exception. Even if your garage isn't used to shelter vehicles, it's an ideal storage spot that, in the eyes of your tenant, adds value to the property.

» **Yards**: To attract the type of tenants you want, find a property with front and back yards that will appeal to that type. For example, if you are looking for a family to rent your SFH, ensure the property has a functional, fenced-off yard for children to play in. Even if the yard is just a small, well-kept garden, the allure of a nicely maintained outdoor area adds value to your property in your tenants' eyes.

» **Size**: Every year, people build larger homes. In the last forty years, the average new home size has increased by one thousand square feet. Most people prefer SFHs with more space, but there is such a thing as too much space. Older couples, especially empty nesters, generally prefer to downsize. Larger homes are more expensive to heat and cool, and it takes more time to clean and maintain them. The size of the property you choose needs to reflect the type of tenant you want to attract.

GRAPHIC

fig. 39

REAL ESTATE SCORECARD **Single Family Homes (SFH)**	
Advantages	**Disadvantages**
• Strong long-term fundamentals • Tax advantages • Easier to get started • Attracts quality tenants • Easiest to sell • Cheaper financing	• Limited profit potential per property • Concentrated tenant/property/market risk • 100% vacancy possible • Fewer financing options • Repairs and maintenance

Cost	Cash Flow	Appreciation	Investment Return	Fundamentals
4	5	8	7	9
All scores 1–10 (1 = worst, 10 = best)				

Townhouses

fig. 40

Slightly different from the single-family home is the townhouse, a property type defined by there being at least four units in a single building. The unit shares walls, often on both sides, and includes a small parcel of land. As a cost-saving measure, townhouses are often built with identical floorplans in each unit, sometimes mirrored in neighboring units. Townhouses were originally a British solution for people moving from rural communities into towns, hence the name "town house."

Cities like Brooklyn and San Francisco have row houses, which look similar to townhouses but have a different ownership model. Each row house, although sharing common walls, is a wholly owned individual property with no fees or communal amenities.

Townhouses are part of a community, meaning that the owner is often liable to pay *homeowners association* (HOA) fees. These fees, used for communal benefits, often cover minor landscaping jobs such as grass cutting or snow removal. Many landlords enjoy operating townhouses, knowing that much of the burden for maintenance is shared with a communal association. They are normally free to make changes to the unit, so long as they adhere to the guidelines established by the HOA. Unit upkeep falls to the owner, giving them free rein to renovate and repair as they see fit. Townhouses tend to incur steeper repair costs because, unlike condos and apartments, they include exterior walls and land.

Compared to other residential property types, the townhouse is a relatively sparse asset, representing less than 5 percent of the total housing units in the United States. They can be found in both suburban and urban areas, anywhere that space is at a premium. Consider investing in townhouses in family-friendly communities, the main target for this type of investment property. With low purchase prices, townhouses can be a lucrative first investment. But you have to factor HOA fees and repairs into your rental yield projections. Though rents can be good, this property type tends to appreciate rather slowly and may even lose value over time. Note that you can manage only your individual unit; you have no control over how diligent the neighbors are about doing their fair share of maintenance. An unkempt neighboring property reflects poorly on the whole building.

fig. 41

REAL ESTATE SCORECARD **Townhouses**				
Advantages		**Disadvantages**		
• Affordable • Good locations • Less repairs and maintenance • Easier to manage • Tend to be newer • Higher rental yields • More tenant amenities		• HOA fees • Costlier than condominiums • Tougher to finance • Lower appreciation potential • Subject to community restrictions		
Cost	**Cash Flow**	**Appreciation**	**Investment Return**	**Fundamentals**
7	6	4	6	8
All scores 1–10 (1 = worst, 10 = best)				

Condominiums

A condominium is a single unit within a larger building of units. As an investor, you buy and control the single unit, leasing it out to tenants for rental income. Condo units share walls and often ceilings and floors with other units. Within the four walls of the unit, all repairs and maintenance are up to the owner. Other costs, such as lawn maintenance, parking, snow removal, trash collection, and upkeep of common areas (lobbies, elevators, hallways, etc.) are taken care of by the condo association. The cost for this maintenance is included in the condo association fees paid by every owner.

Land is not included with condominium properties, but common amenities like laundry rooms and gyms often are. Condos tend to be built in urban centers, making them popular with single people and professionals. They are advertised with a dollar-per-square-foot amount, mainly intended to attract buyers who want to live in the unit. One of the advantages of this property type is that once you find a suitable condo building, you can also choose the right unit within that building. The purchase price is cheaper than that of single-family homes, but be careful: the appreciation of your condo's value depends on the condo association's effectiveness at maintaining the building. Your unit can have the latest in modern amenities, but things like an outdated décor or lack of lawn care can cause depreciation.

NOTE

If you're considering this type of asset, ask to see the minutes of previous association meetings. You can discover any major repairs, complaints, and issues that previous tenants and owners have raised in the past, as well as how swiftly the association dealt with the issues.

The volatile nature of condo prices gives you the opportunity to use the "buy low, sell high" tactic during market swings. You can generate rental income and make substantial returns on the appreciation, but only if you buy at the right time. Consider condos for steady rental income streams but not as long-term profit plays dependent on value appreciation gains.

fig. 43

REAL ESTATE SCORECARD
Condominiums

Advantages	Disadvantages
• Affordable • Good locations • Least repairs and maintenance • Easier to manage • Tend to be newer • Extensive tenant amenities	• HOA fees • Harder to sell • Tougher to finance • Lower appreciation potential • Subject to community restrictions • Most sensitive to market cycles

Cost	Cash Flow	Appreciation	Investment Return	Fundamentals
8	7	3	6	6

All scores 1–10 (1 = worst, 10 = best)

Apartments

fig. 44

At first glance, it appears that condos and apartments share many of the same traits. For the average homeowner, that might be true. But an investor approaches apartments very differently than condo units. Most apartment complexes are considered commercial units, bought as an entire building and then rented out en masse. This strategy puts rental apartment investing outside the financial scope of the average first-time investor. Even so, it's still worth knowing the potential benefits and drawbacks of operating an apartment building as an investment.

Apartments are often built in inner-city neighborhoods, catering to tenants who value proximity over space. They can be cost-effective solutions for tenants who find single-family housing out of their price range. If purchased correctly, an apartment complex is a rental investment that has the potential to earn consistent returns in the long run. In many urban neighborhoods, tenants live in the same apartment for years. But the general rule is that apartment units have higher turnover rates than single-family homes, and they also have higher vacancy rates. When you analyze the income and expenses associated with the investment, you have to factor in the costs of those potential vacancies. If you can afford them, apartment complexes can be a handsome addition to your investment portfolio.

MY TAKE

I cover the ins and outs of investing in apartment complexes in my *Real Estate Investing QuickStart Guide*. Grab your copy to go deeper into the topic of analyzing and investing in multifamily properties.

GRAPHIC

fig. 45

REAL ESTATE SCORECARD **Multifamily (apartments)**	
Advantages	**Disadvantages**
<ul><li>More financing options</li><li>Additional income sources</li><li>Tax advantages</li><li>Strong long-term fundamentals</li><li>Lowest price per unit</li><li>Economies of scale</li></ul>	<ul><li>Costs more</li><li>More sophisticated competition</li><li>More regulations than SFH rentals</li><li>More complex than SFH rentals</li><li>Concentrated risk in single property</li><li>More expenses overall</li></ul>

Cost	Cash Flow	Appreciation	Investment Return	Fundamentals
3	9	6	5	10
All scores 1–10 (1 = worst, 10 = best)				

Mobile Home Parks

fig. 46

Mobile homes are prefabricated structures that are built off-site and moved into place. Other common terms for this asset are trailers and manufactured homes, though they refer to the same type of property. When we discuss investing in mobile home parks for rental property, we take a slight detour from our previous examples. Rental investment in mobile home parks is not at all about the buildings, but rather the land on which they sit.

Mobile home structures are a terrible investment. The home, due to its prefabricated design, depreciates rapidly. Resale figures show little to no appreciation at all. According to the IRS, a mobile home structure is not even considered real estate but rather personal property, having more in common with a vehicle than a home. The land on which it sits, however, *is* considered real estate property, which for our purposes makes for a much more attractive option. This is why investors in this asset class are technically only buying the lots and not the actual buildings in a mobile home park. The residents own and maintain the depreciating buildings while the investor collects rent on the nondepreciating land.

Lonnie Scruggs, one of the more popular real estate investors from the '70s, '80s, and '90s, was a pioneer in mobile home investing strategies. You could even argue that Scruggs was one of the original real estate "gurus," his name almost synonymous with mobile home investments. His deals, also known as "Lonnie deals," usually involved buying a used mobile home for cash, turning it around with renovations, and using seller financing to lease it to the new homeowner.

Although outside the scope of rental property investing, "Lonnie deals" can be profitable ventures if you know what you're doing. As an example of a Lonnie deal, one investor bought a mobile home for $250, cleaned it up, and then sold it to a buyer for a $1,500 down payment and a monthly installment plan of $250 per month for forty-two months on a seller-financed contract.

Mobile home structures are risky investments, but the land they sit on is a much better deal. After purchasing the lot, you charge rent and utility hookups to the mobile home tenant. One of my students, whom you'll meet in a moment, has been heavily involved in these types of deals, having executed $30 million in mobile home park acquisitions in the last three years. Even within the last ten years, mobile home investor millionaires have become increasingly common. As other types of investments have become crowded with investors and overvalued, mobile home parks have gained serious interest from investors. Mobile home lots are simple to operate, with almost no ongoing maintenance costs. In return for a cheap purchase price and low maintenance, you can make a very solid yield on your investment.

MY TAKE

I'm very bullish on mobile home parks in the medium and long-term forecasts. It's my opinion that across the board in real estate, we're going to see an influx of people trading down, reducing their rental expenses in response to fewer jobs and decreasing wages. According to one study, leading economists predict that up to 40 percent of job losses from the COVID-19 shock will be permanent, leaving tens of thousands with income and job insecurity. In some markets where the rental alternatives are few and far between, mobile home parks allow renters to save on rent and costs of living.

GRAPHIC

fig. 47

REAL ESTATE SCORECARD **Mobile Home Parks**				
Advantages			**Disadvantages**	
• Resilience during strong economic downturns • Generally lower cost per unit • Easier maintenance • Strong support from demographic trends			• Potential risks with sewage management • Still have stigma although improved in recent years • Typically located outside of city centers	
Cost	**Cash Flow**	**Appreciation**	**Investment Return**	**Fundamentals**
8	9	5	8	10
All scores 1–10 (1 = worst, 10 = best)				

DETOUR

FROM THE FIELD: Allow me to introduce you to a close friend of mine, Dan Ryu, who is utterly killing it with investments in mobile home parks:

I'm about to board a twin engine Cessna for the first time and land two hours away on an asphalt strip in the middle of a grassy field (aka the "airport"). The pilot provides me with no comfort when he asks me how much I weigh before I board the plane. Uh, seriously? That matters?

Despite all appearances, my new venture does not involve "muling" white powder across the border, though I wouldn't blame you for thinking that—I mean, why else would I be landing in a grassy field?

The reality of my adventure is not at all criminal, but it is an adventure nonetheless. The plane I'm about to board will take me to the site of an off-market deal—a mom-and-pop seller who's developed a mobile home park from the ground up and is looking to sell and retire.

If you were to buy in to the stereotypes of how "trailer parks" are portrayed in TV shows, movies, or even in passing references, then the last thing you'd be thinking is "how can I invest in one of those?" The perception created by click-bait news stories and entertainment media is one of crime-infested, low-income, run-down assets filled with problems and problematic tenants. But I invite you to take a moment to dig beneath the surface, where you'll find a reality that offers attractive risk-adjusted returns, stable cash flows, and an asset that has become the darling of the private equity world, with big name investors like Sam Zell and Warren Buffett prominently involved.

When you invest in mobile home parks, you're buying the land and infrastructure. The tenants own their own mobile homes. They pay you "lot rent" (also known as "space rent") but since they own their own home, they're responsible for the repair and upkeep of it. When the toilet breaks, or the unit needs new siding or a new roof, or the HVAC or refrigerator needs replacement, the responsibility falls on the homeowner, not on you. Expenses, as a proportion of rents, are much lower with mobile homes than with other property types. Mobile home investors enjoy expense ratios of about 30-40 percent, depending on whether water and sewer utilities are rebilled to tenants.

Another key advantage of investing in mobile home parks is the relative lack of competition. One thing I notice when I visit an area undergoing lots of growth is all the cranes! You hear the loud construction noises of high-rises being built and more units being created to deal with housing shortages as people pour into the area. But what you seldom, if ever, see is more mobile home parks being built. According to Charles Becker, PhD, an economics professor at Duke University, municipalities are reluctant to allow construction of mobile home parks because data show that they consume more in public resources than they provide in taxes. Not only are mobile home parks not developed, they often are scrapped to make room for another type of development. Add in the general stigma of the trailer park and what do you get? You get an asset class that's scarce, with low supply.

To paraphrase mobile home park investor Sam Zell, it comes down to supply and demand; while the demand for affordable housing continues to grow, the supply of mobile homes on the market remains low for the reasons just mentioned. The end result is that there is never any shortage of prospective tenants.

If you decide to explore this asset class, you won't need to hopscotch across the country in commuter planes looking for deals. You can begin your journey by checking out deals online and getting to know the brokers involved in this space.

As head of acquisitions for a private equity group, Dan Ryu oversaw the purchase, diligence, and transition of over $30 million in mobile home parks. For more information on Dan Ryu, visit www.athenamhc.com or connect with him on LinkedIn at: linkedin.com/in/danryu.

Short-Term Rentals / Vacation Homes

In a traditional rental property investment deal, you buy a property, install a tenant, and collect rent for the lifetime of that deal. This is also called a long-term rental investment. **Short-term rentals** (and vacation homes) change just one variable in that format: the tenant. Instead of just one tenant, the short-term rental provides an ongoing string of "tenants" or guests that pay rent. A short-term property is a fully furnished property, allowing your guests to stay as little as one night and still have everything they need on location. A short-term rental property is defined by guests agreeing to stay for a particular period of time for a specific purpose. In most markets, a short term is defined as anything less than twenty-eight to thirty days, but that definition is subject to change.

fig. 48

The short-term rental market and the vacation home market overlap in many ways, so for the sake of brevity I'll refer to them both as short-term rentals, or STRs. There are several platforms that operate short-term rentals, Airbnb being one of the more popular options. Although you can get your feet wet in the short-term rental market by listing an extra bedroom in your own home, you can use these platforms for entire properties as an additional rental investment deal.

If you're interested in becoming a host and want to operate your short-term rental listing effectively, check out my blog, www.learnbnb.com, for free resources on short-term rental hosting best practices.

Key Distinctions of Short-Term Rentals

Although you could technically operate a short-term rental with any of the aforementioned asset types, it's the way you operate them that differs. According to a recent study, the average Airbnb host earns just $924 per month. Only 10 percent of all Airbnb hosts make more than $2,000 per month with their listings. Short-term rentals sound lucrative and easy, but you must be aware of how they differ from long-term rentals in order to make this asset profitable.

To begin with, understand that most Airbnb operators are in the hospitality business. When you operate an STR as a host, you are essentially running a private hotel. You cater to the whims and wishes of your guests, tending to and restocking the property during the turnover period. Cleaning, repairs, and emergency issues all fall to the host and must be resolved quickly to keep the property functional. STRs listed on platforms like Airbnb are at the mercy of the rating system. If your property doesn't have a five-star review from guests, your occupancy rate suffers.

Traditional rental property owners are not in the hospitality business; they are in the rental property business. To turn your property into a functional STR while maintaining a healthy distance from your guests, you need to have systems in place. Professional management companies and several third-party apps can handle the hospitality side of the investment, keeping you as the investor rather than the on-call concierge. But these conveniences cost money, eating into your profits. Your daily rates and occupancy levels must compensate for those costs.

Another key difference between short- and long-term rentals is the markets where properties are located. Traditional long-term rental properties operate in every market because people, for one reason or another, want to live there. STRs only function well in certain markets. Vacation homes are exceptionally prone to seasonal fluctuation, as they are often lake cabins, beach town homes, or ski chalets. It's an investment that can only operate at capacity during the summer (or winter) months. Excessive vacancy due to poor weather conditions (or lack of tourism) is a real risk to an STR investor. You can still profit as an investor in non-tourist areas, but only if your properties serve a different specific function outside of tourism. Rentals close to hospitals, schools, and in urban environments can have consistently high occupancy rates when guests are not tourists. These guests have an alternative purpose, such as attending a job interview or visiting patients in long-term care.

One of the ways to succeed when you invest in STRs is to maximize your profitability. In a traditional rental, you set the rent price and that rent is locked in place for a year or longer. With STRs, you have much more flexibility. If you need to fill vacancies immediately, you can lower the rate or create discounts for extended stays. And once demand is high, say for a sporting event or a college graduation, you can increase your rates as much as you like.

One investor I know operates four STR properties in Austin, Texas. But because he wants to operate them as an investor and not as a hospitality owner, he uses a computer program to set his rates according to the demand in the area. His program automatically detects events that prompt more visitors, such as parents flying in for the University of Texas awards night, and adjusts his rate accordingly. For big events like South by Southwest, he can charge up to three times his normal rate and still achieve 90 percent occupancy.

One of the disadvantages of a short-term rental property is that unless you are in a tourism-heavy market, you may be subject to ever-changing laws. In cities where the hotel industry has a lot of clout, these hospitality businesses may put pressure on city hall to enact strict guidelines about operating short-term rental properties. We've seen this happen in cities like Las Vegas, Amsterdam, New York City, and here in SoCal. Santa Monica has some of the strictest short-term rental laws in the world. Currently, hosts are required to collect 14 percent occupancy tax from guests, physically live on the property while guests are staying there, and register for a business license. Many markets set limits on the number of days in a year that you can list a property. If you can only have guests stay for 60, 120, or 180 days, that leaves your property unoccupied for most of the year. These laws, prone to change at a moment's notice, can turn a once-profitable short-term rental property into a dead weight on your portfolio overnight.

GRAPHIC

fig. 49

REAL ESTATE SCORECARD **Short-Term Rentals**				
Advantages			**Disadvantages**	
• Generally higher rental revenue/s.f. than traditional rentals, especially in core tourist markets			• Increased regulation will likely limit upside in many cities. • Requires more active operations	
Cost	Cash Flow	Appreciation	Investment Return	Fundamentals
4	8	9	9	8
All scores 1–10 (1 = worst, 10 = best)				

MY TAKE

In the immediate fallout of the pandemic, travel around the world came to a near standstill. Necessarily, that meant that STR owners felt the pinch more acutely than any other investor, with no guests to fill their vacancies. Across the country, revenue dropped by 80 percent. Owners were forced to give up their properties due to a lack of demand. But on the flip side, those who held on to their STRs found themselves in a less competitive environment. As people begin traveling more, these stalwarts will have their fill of customers. The income streams of STR properties will be spotty in the near term, but as things go back to normal and the economy recovers, there will be opportunity for massive long-term gains. My advice is to endure the storm now so you can win the calm later.

DETOUR

FROM THE FIELD: Allow me to introduce you to James Svetec. James is one of the finest short-term rental investors I know. He's the owner and founder of bnbmastery.com and he coauthored (with yours truly) *Airbnb For Dummies*. Take it away, James:

As we emerge from an unforgettable 2020, it's a severe understatement to declare that the global COVID-19 pandemic had a big impact on the entire short-term rental industry. With travel restrictions instituted globally, short-term rentals saw travel-related demand drop significantly in most markets. In some major cities, demand dropped by as much as 90 percent in the early months of the pandemic.

Yet, with the arrival of promising vaccines and widespread distribution underway, there is finally reason to be optimistic as we look ahead. What will the future look like? Where will the opportunities and risks lie going forward for short-term rental investors? In order to answer this question, we must first look at how the industry has already adapted to the pandemic.

I maintain that there's been a permanent alteration to travel demand.

With many fewer flight routes in service and countries requiring long quarantine windows for arriving travelers, people are traveling locally and discovering previously ignored destinations that are within driving distance, places with plenty of nature and space. Such regional excursions and "stay-cations" provide an alternative from the thick crowds of the cities and typical tourist destinations. Moreover, with remote working becoming the norm, these regional tourists can live away from home and work remotely for weeks or months at a time.

On the investment side, buying rental properties in the new "Zoom towns"—the gateway communities within two hours of major metropolitan areas—could yield solid short-term rental revenue in the near term and sizable price appreciation in the long run. From Bend, Oregon, to Kelowna, British Columbia, from Martha's Vineyard to Bozeman, Montana, and everywhere in between, small communities located away from the city centers and near national parks, lakes, and mountains are finding themselves inundated with long-term vacationers or residents in search of a permanent relocation.

There's been a significant drop in inventory (i.e., competition). With bookings all but dried up in previous Airbnb hot spots, many hosts who took out extra financing to acquire short-term rental properties have been forced to leave the market and sell their properties—their rental revenues became insufficient to cover their mortgage payments. According to AllTheRooms.com, a leading short-term rental analytics data provider, some cities saw as much as a 35 percent drop in available listings from October 2019 to October 2020.

Another idea for clever investors is to buy rental properties in previous Airbnb hot spots and rent them out as traditional rentals for the near term while looking to revert them back to short-term rentals when demand begins to recover. In the best Airbnb markets, the short-term rental revenue potential can outpace traditional rental revenue by 4x.

When travel habits return to normal and demand is reasserted in traditional spaces, we can expect a massive influx of new short-term rental hosts.

This recovery of travel norms will be aided by successful mass distribution of COVID-19 vaccines and the ensuing abatement of fear in the general public. We may even see the norms exceeded, with travel spiking higher as eager travelers make up for canceled vacations.

Bottom line: although it may take well into 2022 for short-term rentals to fully recover from the global pandemic, this period of massive disruption also presents opportunity for those with a discerning eye.

James Svetec is the coauthor of *Airbnb For Dummies.* Through his coaching and training programs, James has worked with hundreds of short-term rental entrepreneurs from all around the world, helping them to build successful businesses and become masters of Airbnb.

Chapter Recap

» Any choice of property can be fodder for a good rental investment, but you should select properties that fall within your risk tolerance, available capital, and chosen market.

» Single-family homes are the most commonly operated asset, but the cost can be prohibitively high for first-time investors.

» Apartments, condos, and townhouses come with a smaller purchase price tag and require less ongoing management, but appreciation is much slower.

» Mobile home parks are a profitable field for rental investments, as long as you invest in the raw land and not the mobile home structures.

» Short-term rentals and vacation homes can be operated with any property type but are highly dependent on market conditions and local laws to be successfully profitable.

| 7 |
Market Analysis

The real voyage of discovery consists not in seeking new landscapes, but in having new eyes.

– MARCEL PROUST

There is a joke I've heard that I'm told is quite well known in India: One morning, a fisherman was sitting at the end of a long dock catching crabs when a young boy walked down to see what he was doing. Upon meeting the man, he saw that he had three crab pots at his feet. The first pot had a lid, and he asked the fisherman what was inside.

"Those are Mumbai crabs. They are strong and are always trying to escape, which is why I need the lid."

The second pot also had a lid, but it was weighed down with rocks, and the boy could see the crabs trying desperately to get out. He asked the fisherman about the second pot.

"Oh, those are Delhi crabs. They are also strong and fight hard to get out, so I need to use extra weight to hold down the lid."

The boy noticed the third pot, which was full to the brim with crabs but had no lid to keep them from escaping. He asked the fisherman about this pot.

The fisherman smiled. "Oh, those! I don't need to worry about a lid. Those are Bengali crabs. If any crab tries to escape, the other crabs simply pull it back down again."

There is a lot you can do to a property to improve its value. You can renovate it, paint it, fix it, or enlarge it, changing it as much as you want. But you can't change its neighborhood. Just like the crabs hopelessly struggling to escape the Bengali pot, an investor can pour out a ton of money and effort to improve the value of a rental home, but the condition and amenities of the neighborhood can drag the value back down again. Because of this, you cannot evaluate a property on its own. Properties must be evaluated within the context of their locations. Receiving $2,000 a month for rent may sound good in and of itself, but how does that compare to other properties in the neighborhood? In Waco, getting $2,000 a month might be a lofty goal, but in San Francisco it could be pitifully low. The right property in the right market—that's our goal.

Market analysis allows you to begin evaluating everything from a high level, comparing a particular region to others and then narrowing down to neighborhood analysis and finally to individual properties (figure 50). If you want to cut down your own Christmas tree, you don't go to the rain forest. You need to identify the right forest before you go looking for a specific tree. In real estate, you need to scout groups of properties initially from a bird's-eye vantage point before you zoom in to look more closely at individual properties.

MARKET ANALYSIS

fig. 50

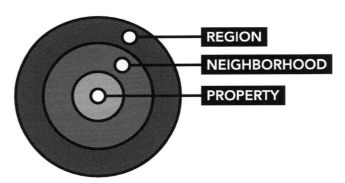

The narrowing field of vision of market analysis

Finding the right market also depends on the niche of your desired type of tenant. Suburban communities are perfect for families, but those same communities can be a nightmare for early-career builders. Single twentysomethings working in corporate jobs don't need single-family homes in good school districts with large parks close by. They prefer communities with good transportation options and proximity to downtown areas.

Above all, there is one mantra to keep in mind throughout the process of market analysis. It's the same mantra we use when evaluating individual properties. It's so crucial that I made it the wallpaper background on my computer (you should do the same). It is "Learn to say no to the good, so that you can say yes to the best."

When I was in school, we did this experiment to create our own water filtration systems. We first lined a funnel with a coffee filter, then with a layer of activated charcoal. Then we layered sand and gravel over that. Finally, we put the funnel over a glass. When we poured dirty, cloudy water through our filtration system, the water that dripped into the glass was clear and drinkable. The sand and gravel removed large particles. The charcoal removed microbes, and the coffee filter removed any remaining small particles. What was left was pure drinking water. This market analysis process has the same effect. We want to "filter" all our potential markets, removing the "good" markets so that what remains is a great market with excellent rental potential.

Comparing Different Markets

I admit that looking at properties is still exciting for me. Although I have gone through this process hundreds of times, I still enjoy looking at pictures and taking walk-throughs (virtual or in person) of potential rental properties. It's fun, but it can be a waste of time if you have not done your due diligence beforehand and identified your target market. Before we graduate to looking for the right rental property, we need to locate the best source for the property. We need to step back and expand our view to look at an entire market. And by market, I am not simply referring to a city. Generally, we can make assumptions that Los Angeles property is more expensive than property in Mobile, Alabama. But we can also assume that there are poorly performing properties in LA, just as there are profitable properties in Mobile. Although we can begin by comparing the markets of entire cities, we eventually need to look at properties at the level of a neighborhood, comparing them to other neighborhoods in the same city.

You can find the Market Analysis Tool as a free resource in your Digital Asset Vault. Find it at **www.clydebankmedia.com/rental-assets**.

I know of many investors who want to be able to touch the investment they make. They like the feeling of being close enough to manage their investments personally and visit their properties often. Although I understand the preference of those rental property investors, I feel they risk doing themselves a disservice by ignoring the potential rental returns that might be available if they considered markets beyond their own backyards.

Have you ever been in a plane when it's landing? It's interesting to watch the ground get closer and closer as you come in to touch down. But have you ever looked out the window while the plane is descending through clouds? You see nothing until the clouds clear, and then you suddenly notice that you're only two hundred feet from the ground. Now, imagine these two separate landings—one in the clear view of day and the other through a cloud—except this time imagine that you are sitting in a seat without any window, and you can't see out. You would have no idea, in either case, whether the landing was being made in sunny, clear conditions or through a bank of fog. So long as you reached the ground, it would always feel like a perfect landing.

I like to compare rental property investing to the pilot landing his plane. Some investors want to see and touch their investments; they are like the pilots who would prefer to land in clear conditions. They'd rather use their own eyes, see the ground coming, and tailor their landing in response to their immediate sensory input. But when visibility is poor, the pilot must choose to rely on his instruments to guide him. Although he cannot physically see the ground, his altimeter and speed gauges relay enough information for him to safely land the plane. This is what it's like to operate a rental property in a different market, from afar. You can still achieve a profitable return, even when your rental property is all the way across the country. You simply have to trust and know how to use certain tools to help you make it work.

Rents and Property Values

If we want to eliminate markets quickly, we need to look at the trends of property values as well as rent values over time. We have at our disposal two essential evaluation metrics: the Case-Shiller and Median Rental indices.

Our goal throughout this analysis is to say no more often than we say yes.

fig. 51

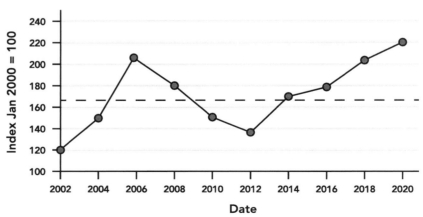

CHANGE IN HOME PRICES OVER TIME

The Case-Shiller 20-city composite index

The Case-Shiller Index is based on the sales prices of single-family homes across the country. Using this index, we can see how a market is performing right now as well as how it compares to other markets over time. Figure 51 shows a twenty-city composite of this index. From its lowest point after the 2008 global financial crisis until today, home prices have recovered past the peak values achieved in 2006 nationally. But looking at each market individually, we will see differences that give us a baseline from which to make comparisons.

Now, let's say that you live in the western United States and you'd like to consider some markets around you. You decide to look at the Los Angeles, Las Vegas, and Denver markets. Although the general shape of the curves (figure 52) is similar to that of the national curve, the differences between these markets are drastic.

fig. 52

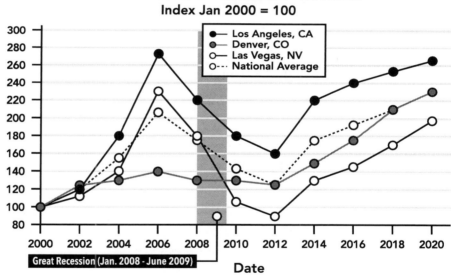

Source: Federal Reserve Economic Data

The Case-Shiller indices for Las Vegas, Los Angeles, and Denver

Las Vegas home prices haven't increased much over time. After the crash of the 2008 recession, home values bottomed out in 2012, below 2006 peak levels, and although the market has recovered significantly, current home prices are still more than 10 percent below the peak levels. The curve for Los Angeles also dipped post-2008, but the dip was far less severe and the recovery has been faster and stronger; home values in early 2021 were well past their 2006 peak levels. The Denver curve tells an entirely different story. Unlike most other markets, Denver home prices did not see a big spike in the mid 2000s and subsequently saw a very modest dip in the 2008 recession. Yet, like other cities, home prices have steadily climbed and are nearly twice their 2006 peak values. By comparing each city's Case-Shiller charts to the national average and to each other, we can get a better understanding of the local market recovery as well as how it fared in the previous downturn.

What does the data tell you? Perhaps that the housing market demand in Los Angeles is more robust and resilient than the housing market in Las Vegas. That the Las Vegas housing market is far more susceptible to market downturns. And what about Denver? Has there been some major demographic shift in the local area? Since the mid-2000s, Denver has seen an influx of technology companies establishing headquarters and regional campuses there, creating a "Silicon Rockies" that has attracted thousands of high-paying tech jobs. As you can see, these charts alone won't tell you the whole story about the local markets, but they are a great starting point.

Choose the right market and you can make more money from appreciating property values. But that is only a side benefit of rental property investing. Monthly rent is what makes or breaks a rental investment. As such, you want to know how good rental returns are in a given market. For that, we can use a simple median rental price index showing the average monthly rent prices in an entire market. If we overlay all three cities onto a median rental graph (figure 53), we can see the trends at work.

fig. 53

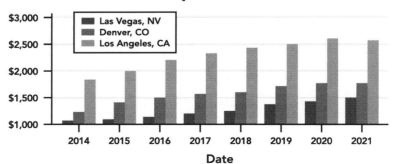

Source: Zillow

Median rent prices in Los Angeles, Las Vegas, and Denver for the last seven years

GRAPHIC

fig. 54

YEAR-OVER-YEAR CHANGE IN RENTS

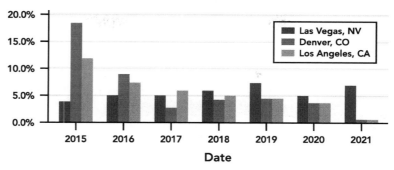

Source: Zillow

YOY change in median rent prices since 2015

Although rents in all three cities increased consistently during the period from 2014 to 2021, the rents in Denver saw a much greater increase from 2014 to 2015. Both Los Angeles and Denver had good rental increases from 2014 through 2017 but more modest increases from 2018 to early 2020. Then, since 2020, we see Denver and Los Angeles rents remaining essentially flat while Las Vegas has a steep rise; this is attributed to the fact that many ultra-large cities have seen an exodus of residents to smaller nearby cities (like Las Vegas). It is too early to tell if a rental spike like what we're seeing in Las Vegas will be permanent or is only a temporary increase.

NOTE

Ideally, you want to see the growth in rental prices exceed the appreciation in property value; in other words, that property values in the market have not risen relative to the increase in rents. This means you'll get more rent for every dollar you spend on purchasing the property—more bang for your buck—while still benefiting from the appreciation potential.

Even though home prices in Las Vegas may not be subject to such dynamic upward (and downward) price swings as those observed in other markets, like Los Angeles, the growth in Las Vegas rental prices makes this market highly attractive.

Neighborhood Trends

Once you have narrowed your search to promising markets, you can analyze the neighborhoods within them. We're not yet looking at individual properties, but we're getting closer. We want to analyze what makes a certain neighborhood stand out, what gives it that unique selling point that distinguishes it from others.

NOTE

Many of the trends depicted in figures 52, 53, and 54 can be evaluated using online sources, but if you're investing close to where you live, then you should supplement these metrics with a "boots on the ground" approach. Take drives through your prospective neighborhoods at different times of day, talk to locals, and spend time in the neighborhood for a deeper appreciation of its amenities and charms.

Here are some key characteristics that define a desirable neighborhood.

» **Amenities**: Does the neighborhood offer community parks? Walking trails? Proximity to major shopping? Most tenants don't want to live somewhere that is thirty minutes from the closest grocery store.

» **New construction**: If there is a lot of new construction in the area, or plans for major infrastructure developments, that's a good sign. It means that municipal officials have identified that neighborhood for growth and targeted it as a profitable location.

» **Job market**: A desirable neighborhood often has a strong job market associated with it. I was doing an analysis (for my blog) of the best-performing markets around the country for rental investments. In terms of rental yield, the number one market in the country was Brownsville, Texas. Why was this small border town consistently outperforming other markets? Part of the reason is that in 2014, SpaceX announced that Brownsville would become their next commercial launching site. With that announcement came new construction, better technology jobs, extra infrastructure, and an increased demand for housing. The regional job market can make (or break, as with the oil towns in Texas) the rental economy of a neighborhood.

» **Schools**: Good school districts can define good neighborhoods. A reputable school district, at least compared to lesser ones in the area, can also push home values upward. But keep in mind that the school district is not relevant to all tenants.

There are websites that aggregate data from multiple sources to help you compare the desirability of neighborhoods, one against the other. For instance, Walkscore.com has listed and ranked every community in the US, Canada, and Australia. You can see the walkability of a neighborhood (its pedestrian friendliness and distance to nearby places) as well as the transportation score (how well public transport serves the neighborhood). To give you a comparison, Brooklyn Heights in New York City has a Walk Score of 97 and a Transit Score of 100, and Beaverton (a community outside of Portland, Oregon) has a Walk Score of 50 and a Transit Score of 37. These numbers may not be absolute, but they can offer an overall sense of a place from afar.

MY TAKE

I've had success with rentals in communities that have uncannily expedient commutes to major commercial centers and job locations, where my tenants may live in less popular areas but enjoy faster commutes. These communities might once have been run-down, but tenants are attracted to lower costs and higher convenience, and, as the community improves, I can charge higher and higher rents and expect my property values to appreciate.

Environmental Trends

I don't hear much talk about this in other real estate circles, but I believe you should be mindful of environmental concerns when evaluating the long-term trends of a neighborhood. In the last eighty years, Louisiana has lost more than two thousand square miles to rising waters. Every ninety minutes, it loses the equivalent of a football field's worth of land. The National Oceanic and Atmospheric Administration recently retired the names of thirty-one geographic locations in a small area of Louisiana because those places don't exist anymore. Flooding in the Mississippi River Delta has caused many of these places to disappear, and I don't think that will be an uncommon phenomenon in the future. In flood-prone areas, insurance companies have also noticed this trend, jacking up flood premiums to as much as three or four times what they were just ten years ago. I'm not saying it's certain, but it's a very plausible scenario that global warming will devastate entire regions and create new coastal regions that could become the new tourism destinations.

I won't get too dramatic about the health of our world, but natural disasters are occurring more frequently, and that can have a significant impact on the market of your choice. Over the last forty years, the frequency of tornadoes has increased across many areas of the Great Plains. Rising temperatures have caused cities like Las Vegas and Phoenix to experience record temperatures and extended drought seasons. It seems that wildfires are the norm rather than the exception here in Southern California. And all those natural events will impact rental prices in the future. Very few people will be willing to pay high rent in a neighborhood with summers in the 120s. How can you find tenants for some neighborhoods when they are constantly dealing with hurricane-force winds? With so much uncertainty ahead, I advise putting a premium on markets with greater potential to offer long-term stability.

Rates and Taxes

When notorious gangster Al Capone was finally brought down from his perch as the king of crime, it wasn't guns, extortion, or murder that undid it all. It was tax evasion. Even if the money Capone earned was illegal, it still had to be declared to the Internal Revenue Service as income. His years as crime boss, overseeing countless crimes and orchestrating many deaths, were all undone thanks to the tax law.

You have to take taxes and rates seriously, because they can have a major impact on your rental investment. From state to state, you can find markets that treat your property-related earnings differently, at least in terms of taxable income. The two major taxes you'll pay on your rental investment income are capital gains taxes when you sell the property, and property taxes that you owe the state.

In chapter 5, we discussed how you can use the 1031 exchange to defer your capital gains tax bill.

Property tax rates vary from state to state, and some states are more friendly to landlords than others. You can also find states with low tax rates but high average home values. In other words, considering the tax rate alone isn't enough; you'll still be stuck with a huge tax bill if the property is expensive, as you can see in figure 55. Even if you invest in a state with a low tax rate (see Hawaii), you could still be stuck with a hefty tax bill.

	EFFECTIVE PROPERTY TAX RATE	MEDIAN HOME VALUE	ANNUAL TAX BILL
Hawaii	0.29%	$620,400	$1,799
Alabama	0.40%	$130,500	$522
Louisiana	0.51%	$147,200	$751
West Virginia	0.53%	$97,600	$517
Wyoming	0.55%	$226,300	$1,245
South Carolina	0.56%	$165,100	$925

Source: Investopedia

The six lowest property tax rates by state

Although Hawaii has the lowest tax rate in the country, the average home value is very high, giving you an average annual tax bill of close to $2,000. On the other hand, Alabama's median house price makes it very tax advantageous to buy and operate rental properties in the state.

CAUTION

Irrespective of tax implications, it is important to note that higher home values do not necessarily translate into higher rental income checks in your pocket. It's important not to conflate buying a property in an expensive area with the idea that you will realize greater profit margins. While the actual dollars you could charge for rent in an expensive market like SoCal might be three or four times what you would collect from a property in Alabama, the average yield in SoCal is far less than that in Alabama. It's about how much rent you get to collect and keep for every dollar you put into purchasing the property. Moreover, it might sound like a winning idea to put yourself in a position to charge $3,000 per month for a San Francisco rental property, but you have to account for how much it costs you up-front to have the right to collect that rent. It may not be as glamorous as it appears.

Choosing Your Niche

I want to challenge you to analyze markets through two different lenses. The first lens is what we've been applying throughout the course of this book—the lens of the rental property investor. Through this lens, you're analyzing your rental investment potential, calculating advantages in the market, trying to capitalize on value and rental returns. The second lens—the lens of the tenant—might feel foreign when you first look through it, but it's important that you do so. You want to see the neighborhood as your tenants will see it. You want to understand what they value, how they assess where they want to live, and what factors into their decision to rent a property.

In the sales world, the importance of "defining" the client or customer is often prioritized. To help clarify how to design and market a product, those who work in the field will spend time fleshing out their ideal client. They give those clients fictitious names, create backstories, and identify their wants and needs. Using demographics like age, gender, family status, education, career, values, and income level, you can imagine your likely or ideal tenants and strive to envision their search for a home through their eyes. Doing so will make it easier for you to identify the properties that are irresistible to them. Let's have some fun and look through the lenses of three different tenants: Emil, Jessica, and Tyson.

No neighborhood is entirely homogenous. Even in a community dominated by families, there might still be properties that would appeal to a tenant outside of that "family" mold. Although you should always try to secure investment properties tailored to your target market, such as a single-family home in a neighborhood of families, sometimes you have to work with what you have. For instance, if you can find only small one-bedroom condos in a neighborhood of houses, then work hard to create a property that would appeal to singles and young couples, despite their not being the neighborhood's core demographic element.

Families

Emil is a forty-three-year-old husband and the father of two growing boys. He and his wife rent a small two-bedroom house in Scottsdale, Arizona. Emil's boys, ages eight and twelve, love playing baseball and riding bikes. Emil works at a high school closer to Phoenix and was recently promoted to vice principal. He works long hours during the school year, but he loves to spend time with his family when he can; they often hike up in the mountains together on nice evenings and weekends. Emil's family owns one car, as his wife works part-time at home, managing the books of a local theater. They make a combined $85,000 a year.

Emil loves his family, and it's growing. It was simpler when the boys were smaller and they were content to share a room. However, Emil's oldest boy is about to become a teenager and has been pestering his parents for his own bedroom. That seems fair. And Emil's wife just convinced him that a dog is exactly what the boys need, but their landlord doesn't allow pets. Emil needs to upgrade to a home that can accommodate his rambunctious boys as well as provide some room for the new family arrival. With his recent promotion, he's confident they can upgrade to a larger property within their means without looking too far out of the city.

Q: What does a family man like Emil care about when looking for his next home?

Emil's main concerns center around how the new home will serve his family. Here are some of the features that he's looking for:

» **Extra bedrooms:** Emil wants to find a house that has a bedroom for each boy. Three bedrooms would be fine, but a fourth bedroom could be used as a home office for his wife. At any rate, a two-bedroom home just doesn't cut it anymore.

» **Fenced yard:** It's a rarity, but Emil needs to find a landlord who offers pet-friendly terms, and a fenced yard is a must. Not only will it give his family somewhere to barbecue and play, but the new pet will need room to run around.

Pets and kids can be deal-breakers for many landlords. I have chosen not to rent out properties to tenants with pets or kids, but that is my decision to mitigate the extra risk of damage to the property.

» **Storage:** Families tend to accumulate a lot of things. Storage is a necessity for Emil, for sporting equipment, for clothes, for toys, for all the miscellaneous stuff that families tend to acquire over the years. Closets and a garage would help Emil immensely with his storage needs.

» **Multiple bathrooms:** Gone are the days when the single-bathroom home is enough. Any property that offers two or two and a half bathrooms is high on Emil's list of considerations.

» **Good school district:** Emil doesn't want to move again after this, so he's thinking long term. And because of that, he wants to locate a property in a good elementary and high school district. It's still a few years away, but high school is coming fast for his oldest boy.

» **Low crime rate**: It's a nonnegotiable fact that their new neighborhood has to be safe. Emil can peruse the crime rate statistics often provided by municipalities for their communities, which will help him narrow down his search to safer neighborhoods.

» **Separate living areas**: It gets cramped quickly in Emil's current home. The kids need a space of their own to watch TV, play video games, or have friends over. A second living area would solve that problem, not to mention giving Emil and his wife some peace and quiet.

Emil's family is unique, but his desires for a rental property are common to many families. Families are typically stable tenants looking for single-family homes or townhouses. The type of property you manage dictates the type of family you will attract. Some neighborhoods tend to attract more families, both as homeowners and as renters. City census reports can be useful in finding these neighborhoods. These reports break down the occupants of a community into number of people per dwelling, average age of the community, and the ratio of age groups within that community.

Students

Jessica is a twenty-four-year-old full-time student with a bachelor's degree in biomedical engineering from Ohio State. She recently got accepted into her first-choice university for her postgraduate degree at New York University (NYU). She is ecstatic because she gets to work alongside some incredibly brilliant scientists and researchers, using the most up-to-date technology in the industry to create advanced prosthetics. Jessica wants to develop robotic limbs that incorporate artificial intelligence for better mobility, and NYU's program is at the forefront of that field of research. This is a dream come true, but she knows that it will take a lot of hard work. Although she lived on campus in Columbus, she needs her own space if she's going to succeed in this highly competitive field. Money is tight, but with the help of some scholarships and a part-time hostess job, Jessica hopes to find a small one-bedroom apartment in Brooklyn or Williamsburg.

Between NYU's intensive program and her job, Jessica won't be home much, but she needs a quiet place where she can study. She grew up in a small Ohio town and is unfamiliar with city life. This is Jessica's first time in New York City, so she wants a place that has everything she needs close by.

Q: What does a student like Jessica care about when searching for her next home?

Because Jessica is studying full time, her budget is very tight. But she is unwilling to compromise on getting her own apartment. Sharing with others, even in an expensive city like Brooklyn, would distract her from her goals. The program lasts two years, and Jessica's goal is to find an apartment that can be hers and only hers for the entirety of her time in New York City. She doesn't want disruptions to her schedule or her privacy, or to be put in a position where she needs to change residences in the middle of her program.

» **Proximity:** Jessica wants to live close to school, but the middle of Brooklyn can be expensive for a single occupant. If walking distance to NYU is impossible, then she needs to find somewhere close to the subway so she can get to the lab quickly.

» **Furnishings:** Jessica has a few things, but other than her bed, she has no large furniture. The ideal rental would already be furnished, or at least semi-furnished.

» **Amenities:** Jessica won't have a car, so she uses Walk Score (walkscore.com) to calculate the walkability of different neighborhoods. To Jessica and many students like her, the home is just a place to sleep and study. Her living room will be the city itself, so she needs amenities close at hand like grocery stores, laundry facilities, cafes, and good shopping.

» **Price:** No matter what Jessica finds, the cost of rent is her main consideration. She was lucky to secure a couple of scholarships, but she still doesn't have a lot of flexibility with her desired price point. If she can apply and get approved for an apartment in her price range, then she's willing to be lenient on many of her other requirements.

Jessica is an outlier as a student, living by herself in a big city. It's much more common to find students looking for shared accommodations to cut down on costs. Although student tenants can present more risk as first-time renters, the demand for student accommodation is consistent. The trade-off is that vacancy rates can be higher due to students leaving during the summer and the more frequent turnover of student tenants.

However, year after year, you know when students will be looking for new housing and when to begin advertising for new occupants. Look for communities around major universities or in college towns.

Professionals

Tyson is a thirty-four-year-old working as a junior executive at JP Morgan Mortgage in Chicago. Tyson has been steadily climbing the corporate ladder ever since he was hired as a client processor straight out of the Wharton School. His current role is enviable, especially considering his age, but Tyson seems to have stalled out. He wants to achieve more in his career, but maybe JP Morgan isn't the right place to do that. As a rising star within the company, he has attracted headhunters. Some of the offers sound appealing, putting him on the fast track to a senior executive role within five years. One headhunter has offered Tyson such a position with an insurance company based in Atlanta. Tyson has to admit that it would be nice to escape the blustery winters of Chicago in favor of warmer weather down south. He currently earns a salary of $135,000, but the new position is offering $150,000 plus some very attractive signing benefits, such as a luxury company car.

Tyson's present apartment sits along prestigious Lake Shore Drive with an unimpeded view of Lake Michigan. If Tyson can find similar accommodations in Atlanta, then he will seriously consider the offer, as it might be the career boost he needs. Plus, with the salary bump he has been offered, he can afford to look at renting some luxury townhouses with additional space and amenities. A townhouse would be nice because parking will be a necessity for his new BMW 5 Series sedan.

Q: What does a working professional like Tyson value when looking to rent a new home?

Tyson's a single guy who values living in comfort and luxury, because, well, he can afford it. After years of hard work and long hours at the office, this new offer could be the break that pays dividends for all his efforts. Tyson wants a townhouse that shows off his status and caters to his specific whims.

» **Proximity:** The suburbs are for families. Tyson wants to find a townhouse close to the office, and that often means an inner-city townhouse or one close to the central business district. Tyson also wants his home to be central to the action, meaning that great dining and entertainment are just a few blocks away.

» **Modernity:** Tyson's not looking for a property with history. He wouldn't mind paying higher condo or townhouse fees if he could have the latest and greatest amenities. Central heating and cooling, sound systems, laundry services, and high-quality appliances are all on Tyson's "must have" list.

» **Views:** You don't pay thousands in rent every month to stare at a brick wall. Tyson would love a property with a striking city view of some kind.

» **Privacy:** If Tyson is going to upgrade his home, he wants it to be in an exclusive neighborhood, private and secure. It has to have covered parking and security access and must be in an upscale neighborhood where he can network with and entertain fellow professionals.

» **Size:** Property prices in Chicago meant that although his apartment was nice and he was paying top dollar for it, it was pretty small. Tyson wants a townhouse or condo that gives him more space to enjoy. He also doesn't want to feel like he's living on top of his neighbors, listening to their every conversation.

A professional's career-minded focus makes him a tenant with unique goals and desires. On the professional's checklist, you'll find proximity and amenities as high-priority items. Although these types of properties generally cost more than comparable suburban housing, the rental yield for the investment can be strong. I have colleagues who focus their portfolio entirely on apartments and condos for high-income professionals, and they have weathered many economic downturns because of it.

Chapter Recap

» The goal of analyzing markets is to begin with a broad perspective, narrowing your scope from a region to a neighborhood and finally to individual properties.

» In every stage of the market analysis process you must learn to say no to the several good options so that you can say yes to the best. In real estate analysis, "good" is the enemy of "great."

» Markets have their own unique characteristics and must be evaluated alongside one another before you decide where to invest.

» Once a market is selected, the individual neighborhoods within the market must also be compared, analyzed, and, when possible, explored.

» The right property must be paired with the right tenant. Learn to see properties through your ideal tenant's eyes to understand what they value in a home.

| 8 |
Where to Find Property Deals

Chapter Overview
- » Property Sources for Every Investor
- » The Advantages of Using Real Estate Agents
- » Finding Properties through Public Records
- » Creative Ways to Source Potential Deals

Wealth is not about having a lot of money—it's about having a lot of options.
— CHRIS ROCK

With fifteen years of experience in working with $500 million worth of completed real estate deals, I go to the same sources when looking for my next great rental property investment as I did when I was just getting started. Those sources include local real estate agents, online listings, classifieds, and reaching out through my network of investors. The great thing about the sources I use is that you can use them too. Sure, over the years I've developed a personal network of friends and associates who often help me locate the best properties, and such a resource can only be built through time and experience. But many of the powerful tools I rely on are tools that you and anyone else can use, starting today!

If you continue down this path toward becoming a successful rental property investor, as I hope you will, you will want to work on continuously building your network. Get in the habit of broadcasting your intentions. Let people know you're looking to buy a rental property, and it will likely open a world of options. You have no idea when you will be in conversation with someone with access to a deal you never knew existed.

Real Estate Agents

I touched on this in the introduction, but when I was first introduced to rental property investing, it was as the analyst for a group of investors I worked with. We called ourselves "the Weekend Fund" because we all had full-time careers that prevented us from meeting during the week. With our pooled money, we wanted to find property that made solid rental income. Among the members of the Weekend Fund, I had the most relevant experience in real estate, which is why the group looked to me to take the lead role in defining our investment process. Although many Weekend Fund members brought deals to the table for the group to consider, I brought the most by far. I didn't work any harder, I just knew where to go. I relied almost exclusively on real estate agents to help me source properties for consideration. I would sift through their leads, looking for properties to suit the Weekend Fund's investment objectives.

I focused on sourcing deals from agents in part for the agent's preexisting networks of clients and properties, but we also found their broader knowledge of local regions and neighborhoods to be useful. We were investing in markets in Nevada and Arizona, and it would have been impossible for us to visit these potential properties in person. The real estate agents filled in the gaps for us. A lot of people seem to underestimate the humble real estate agent, in my opinion. It's true that the incentive of an agent—to make a quick sale—isn't always in line with your own incentive to find the best property, and therefore you might tend to distrust an agent's recommendations. I have not found that to be an issue. I view real estate agents as "boots on the ground" help that can direct me to relevant neighborhoods and properties I would have otherwise overlooked. Their local expertise gives them an edge in understanding the market in a way that outsiders never could.

MY TAKE

The best real estate agents are those who have personally invested in rental properties. Their experience means they intuitively know which properties will return good rental yields, a metric that not all agents will appreciate.

If you present yourself as a serious investor with an intention to fill your portfolio with rental properties, agents will bend over backward to help you, because you are a potentially solid source of income for them if they do their job well. The best way to work with agents is to give them a template of the types of properties you want to consider. Narrow down the search to the number of bedrooms, the age of the property, the price, and the neighborhoods, and let them populate your inbox with options. Even as I write this, I have dozens of unread emails from agents who keep me in the loop with properties they want me to consider. And because I have so many options, I can quickly throw out the "good" ones in favor of that "great" property that becomes my next excellent rental investment.

Multiple Listing Services

One of the reasons you want to work with a real estate agent is that she has access to a local database of listings that you do not have. At least in North America, this database is a known as a *multiple listing service*, or MLS. Real estate agents across the continent populate these listings with the properties they are currently selling. The listings provide up-to-date information on thousands of properties that are on the market for sale right now (figure 56). The MLS databases are ostensibly only accessible to licensed real estate agents, but most agents host their local MLS on their website for free. Although part of the reason I personally obtained my real estate license was to have unfettered access to MLS sites around the country, you don't need to take such drastic measures. The easier approach is to simply make friends with a few real estate agents who have MLS access and can help you find what you're looking for.

I obtained my real estate license so that I could collect finder's fees for any deals I helped to arrange (you can collect a finder's fee only if you're licensed).

There are now many MLS data aggregators (some free, like Redfin and Zillow, and some paid, like Privy) that compile the information from MLS databases for easy public access. Using these aggregator sites, anybody, regardless of whether they have a real estate license, can comb through the property options in most markets. But be advised that data contained within the free resources may be incomplete and spotty in some markets. The paid resources provide a more complete and rich data set tailored to the investor audience.

The advantages of using an MLS are many. The MLS provides accurate, reliable information on any property that is publicly listed for sale. You can see at a glance the options in a given market and get pictures, relevant data, and asking prices. You can set alerts, using a number of filters, that actively contact you with new properties that meet your search criteria. The advantage to sellers of such a public listing is that it leads to increased competition for those same properties. For the seller, the MLS is ideal because they want as many eyes on their property as possible.

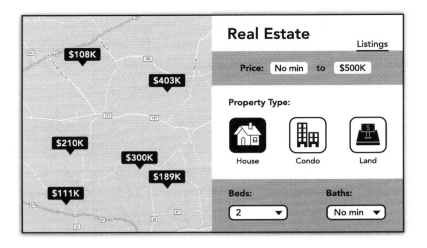

Real Estate

Listings

Price: No min to $500K

Property Type:

House   Condo   Land

Beds: Baths:

2   ▼   No min   ▼

An example layout of a real estate aggregator site. These sites, like Redfin.com or Zillow.com, draw from locally hosted MLS sites, allowing users to filter through the available properties in a market.

Pocket Listings

Another reason to have a good real estate agent on your side is to get access to exclusive listings known as pocket listings or "off-MLS" listings, which don't appear on public forums, usually for anonymity or privacy reasons. Because much of the owner's information in a sale is trackable online, some markets rely heavily on pocket listings to sell high-value, high-profile properties. Los Angeles and Washington, DC, are gold mines of pocket listing deals, as famous faces hide behind them when buying or selling properties.

EXAMPLE

Sotheby's International Realty, which works exclusively in the Hollywood Hills, estimates it generates 70 percent of its business through pocket listings. They rely so heavily on the unofficial listings of movie stars, musicians, and athletes that they have created their own exclusive real estate agent platform for pocket listings. It's a database for listings that don't want to be advertised on a database. Hmmm . . .

Pocket listings may give you exclusive access to hidden deals, but they can be hiding important information. When a property is publicly listed, you know the date it was listed. When a property sits unsold on the market for a long time, buyers become leery about whether the purchase price may be too high. To avoid that, sometimes sellers like to keep their property unofficially listed to hide how long it has been available. Pocket listings can also be dubious because the real estate agent often ends up representing the buyer and the seller. If your real estate agent is receiving commissions from both sides of the sale, they have no incentive to protect your interests. Though it's not illegal, this could go against the Realtor Code of Ethics, a one-hundred-year-old code of practice designed to protect you from dodgy real estate agents.

Classified Listings

It may seem dated, but you can still trust classified ads, both in print and online, as a reputable source of properties for sale. Real estate agents and brokerages still list properties in the newspaper. You'll often find these properties on an MLS site as well, but they are highlighted in newspaper classifieds for a different reason. Agents love to use the newspaper, not just as a way to advertise properties, but to advertise themselves. The most common purpose for using newspaper classifieds is to bring attention to the real estate firms. Most firms and real estate brokerages tend to specialize in a particular type of property; by studying the classifieds, you can get a sense of the types of properties they represent. You can also look in the classifieds for highlighted price reductions or recently listed homes. If real estate brokerages are willing to pay money to list it in a newspaper, there is a reason they want more eyes on the property.

As an alternative to print media, online classifieds are becoming a popular way to list property. Using sites like Craigslist or Oodle, which aggregate listings from many sites like Facebook and eBay, you can find online listings from owners that want to sell directly to buyers. These for-sale-by-owner (FSBO) ads circumvent the traditional real estate agent and can save you thousands in closing costs because you deal directly with the seller.

Many of the listings on online classified sites are for homes that wouldn't sell as a traditional brokerage listing, such as uninhabitable properties with severe structural issues. Buying these properties without the protection of a reputable real estate agent could be more trouble than you bargained for.

You don't have to wait for a good property to pop up in the classifieds. There is a way to use classified ads proactively. You can post ads offering to buy homes, or even target struggling landlords, offering to take over their problem properties if they're willing to cut you a nice deal. I know from personal experience that many people quickly get in over their heads as landlords and want a way out. You can find these distressed landlords with your own ads and offer to take their "ready-made rentals" off their hands.

REOs/Foreclosures

Real estate owned (REO) and foreclosed properties are essentially the same thing. The only difference is that a foreclosure is a property *in the process* of being reclaimed by the lender, and an REO property has already been reclaimed. In either case, you're dealing with the bank or lending institution that has repossessed the home due to a defaulted loan on the property. The lender has now become the seller.

Buying foreclosed or REO properties can be daunting for the first-time investor, but it doesn't need to be. Once you become accustomed to how the foreclosure process works, you can find incredible deals on properties that other risk-averse investors skip past.

For the most part, lending institutions work hard to avoid the whole process of foreclosure. The lender has several steps designed to provide an "out" to the borrower before they take action to repossess the property. In some states, the lender must receive court approval to undergo the repossession process, and the borrower can challenge the foreclosure. Banks want to sell REO properties quickly and at a discount, which they often do in an "as is" condition.

NOTE

Lenders get their own inspections done when they take possession, so ask for the inspection report when considering an REO property.

So, how do you find these REO properties? It depends. State to state, there are different regulations about how lenders advertise their REO assets on the books.

> » **Lender listings:** Some lenders have their own private assets listed for online browsing. This is usually the case for portfolio lenders that have not sold their mortgages to Fannie Mae or Freddie Mac (see chapter 2). On these private sites, you can search through the assets the lender wants to sell as soon as possible.

> » **Government websites:** The Department of Housing and Urban Development (HUD) has a large selection of REO listings held by different lenders. Using the HUD web page, you can see, for example, the assets held by the IRS that have been repossessed for tax liens. These listings are available to the public via the HUD website, hud.gov.

> » **Fannie Mae and Freddie Mac:** Combined, these government-sponsored enterprises have guaranteed almost half of all mortgages

in the US. You can search their websites, fanniemae.com and freddiemac.com, for the REO properties on their books.

» **Public MLS sites:** Websites like zillow.com contain filters that help you find foreclosed properties. Rather than going through public records in each market, these websites make it easy to find all relevant foreclosures and REOs in your area (figure 57).

fig. 57

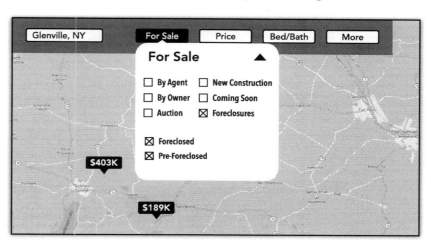

» **Real estate agents:** Because lenders work with real estate agents to sell their properties, you can find REO properties through your local agent. They have access to multiple lender listings within your market.

Getting Creative

By the late 1970s, Kuwait was becoming rich. It was discovered that this tiny Arabian country was sitting on top of an untapped oil reservoir, what amounted to 10 percent of the total global reserves. With a rise in global demand for oil, everyday Kuwaitis were suddenly flush with cash. Such widespread wealth was an unprecedented situation, given that the country's history was such that money belonged in the hands of the ruling elite. At the time, the only stock market in the region was known as the Boursa. It was strictly controlled by the sheik, and only a handful of Kuwaiti companies were publicly traded on this market. Even the investors allowed to participate on the Boursa were tightly controlled, and trading was restricted to the old-world money families. In response, the country's nouveau riche created a new stock market in 1982 known as the Souk al-Manakh.

This unofficial stock market was housed in a parking garage and quickly became the most exciting, enticing way to spend all this newfound cash. Non-Kuwaiti companies that would never have qualified to be listed under the Boursa were welcomed into the Souk al-Manakh, and many of them flourished. The newly rich turned to this underground market as a form of entertainment, making millions within hours. Investors were so revved up about making money hand-over-fist in the Souk-al-Manakh that many of them wrote post-dated checks for more than they could afford in order to secure bigger investment positions.

Trading went wild. The relationship between a company's performance and its stock price became unintelligible. Investors continued to trade billions in post-dated checks. In one extreme example, a young passport clerk was able to trade $14 billion in stocks, all based on post-dated checks that he could never have covered. But, as all bubbles do, the Souk trading frenzy popped suddenly and with great force. Some $240 billion had been floating in the Souk al-Manakh when the crash happened, making it the third-largest stock market in the world behind the US's New York Stock Exchange and Japan's Tokyo Stock Exchange. Although the Kuwaiti government offered some assistance, it refused to bail out the largest investors involved in these trades. And the fallout left the country economically stagnant for a decade.

I tell you this story to show you how the Kuwaiti people got creative with their cash. With the Boursa, they faced steep barriers to the traditional way of investing, so they created a new stock market that forged a new path around the obstacles. It was just a matter of thinking differently, albeit in the wrong direction. When thinking about where to find your next potential rental property, I want you to have the same mindset. I want you to look for opportunities where they didn't exist before. When you look for properties where no one else is looking, you'll find properties that no one else is finding. And I implore you to be unlike the reckless and greedy investors in the Souk al-Manakh; temper your creativity and opportunism with thoughtfulness, sound judgment, and discretion. Here are some ideas to get you thinking outside the box:

Driving for Dollars

I have an associate who operates short-term rental properties. Although he started with renting out his spare room on Airbnb, he now operates dozens of STR properties. In his early days, he would spend his evenings and weekends looking for new potential properties for his ever-growing portfolio. When asked what he was doing, he would always respond, "I'm driving for dollars."

The term, which at first I thought he had coined, refers to the practice of driving around a community looking for properties that aren't listed. Some of these homes will not even be currently for sale, but there will be obvious signs that the owners might be receptive to an enthusiastic buyer such as yourself. Maybe there is an unkempt yard, the house is in great need of repairs, or there are other clear indications that the owner doesn't value the house as much as the neighbors value theirs.

This type of process can be tedious at best, so narrow your search to nicer neighborhoods where homes in disrepair stick out like a sore thumb.

Once you've noted the addresses of these properties, you can look up the owners' information in public records or by using a reverse address search online. You can then contact the owners to test their receptiveness to selling their property. If you find a willing owner, you can buy these distressed homes at a discount and, after some renovation, rent them out for a hefty profit. The neighbors will love you for it, and you'll be building a good reputation along the way. Big wins all around!

Public Eviction Records

Much like you did when looking through the REO property listings, you can access eviction notices in your area through public records. Eviction is a long-drawn-out process that can take months to complete. Of course, the simplest solution is to properly screen one's tenants, and we'll discuss that in chapter 10. Every once in a while, however, a bad tenant can completely wear out a landlord. It may be possible to convince those distressed landlords that it would be worthwhile to sell their rental property to you. But be sure that your offer to buy the property happens *after* the eviction process and not during it!

Each county has different regulations and procedures for processing eviction records, but it's all accessible to the public. In most states, you have to go to your county's administration office, which should have a list of current evictions for you to view in person. If not, someone there can certainly direct you to the right location.

Viewing eviction records often requires a face-to-face visit, which is not feasible if you're purchasing or managing properties in markets that are far away from where you live. If you're intent on finding eviction records in markets where you can't physically visit the county records office, it may be possible to find a local real estate agent who can create a list for you.

Wholesalers

Wholesaling is often touted as a solution for people who have no money to invest in real estate properties. Essentially, a wholesaler is a middleman who makes a deal between a motivated seller and a buyer. The wholesaler often spends long hours trying to locate troubled sellers, such as those underwater on their property or stuck with massive repairs they can't afford. Wholesalers create a deal wherein the seller agrees to sell the property at a certain price. The wholesaler then sells that contract to a buyer for a small profit. For example, if a wholesaler were able to find a seller willing to write up a contract to sell a property for $90,000, then the wholesaler could sell that contract for $95,000, netting $5,000 for mediating a deal between the two parties.

The appeal of wholesaling is that it simply takes work, a lot of time, and a little luck to pair up two parties. You aren't required to invest any money, just the "sweat equity" of finding the deal in the first place. As a rental property investor, a wholesaler can be your friend. Through a process called "bird dogging," wholesalers work for you to find these sellers, bringing you deals once they've located a property that shows promise. What do the wholesalers get out of it? They gain experience from spending time with you, learning the trade of rental property investing. They also get a cut of the deal in return for the work of locating the property. You get to save the time it would take to find these properties. With a successful wholesaler on your side, you get ready-made deals handed to you, all set to dissect and analyze, without the hassle of searching for them.

A successful partnership with a wholesaler would require that you spend time training the person so they would understand the kind of properties you need.

Chapter Recap

» Once you've identified the right market, you can narrow your search to find the right property within that market.

» Many of the sources used by licensed real estate agents and highly experienced investors are accessible to the public. You can use these same sources to find the best property for yourself.

» When you're looking at long-distance markets around the country, real estate agents can be an invaluable source of local knowledge.

» REO properties, where the lender is acting as the seller, can be an excellent source of profitable deals.

» If you are willing to put in the effort, you can find motivated sellers for properties not currently listed for sale.

PLANNING TO WIN WITH THE RIGHT PEOPLE

| 9 |
Building Your Team

The fastest way to change yourself is to hang out with people who are already the way you want to be.

— REID HOFFMAN

I once heard someone say that if you're going to do something for the rest of your life, you might as well learn to do it well. Since I'm going to be eating food for the foreseeable future, I took some time to learn how to cook. I have practiced my knife skills. I have become familiar with spices and seasonings. I have been diligent about getting better with some cooking techniques like basting, shallow frying, and sous vide. I am no chef, but I have improved the quality of the food I make. One of the best lessons I ever learned was the concept of mise en place. Literally translated from the French, it means "set up." Mise en place means that before you begin cooking, you have everything in place and ready to go. You have your vegetables and herbs cut, your spices portioned out, and your implements on hand. Because I'm not searching for the spatula or scrambling to measure out a teaspoon of salt, I can freely focus on the cooking. I've done the prep work which has set me up for a successful meal.

In the first section of the book, we talked about the mise en place of price. You do your hard work at the beginning of your investment journey, making your money when you buy. By doing the prep work, you set yourself up for a profitable return on your investment property. In the second section of the book, we talked about the mise en place of the property. By analyzing where to buy the right property and determining who the property is for, you can reject the good options in favor of the best. But, if I can be so bold as to run a little further with this kitchen analogy: no restaurant chef cooks on his own. In any commercial kitchen, there is a whole team of people diligently working together to produce world-class meals. While one chef cooks the meat to perfection, another chef is simmering the perfect sauce, while yet another is preparing the sides. The kitchen team works synchronously to produce the meal on your plate.

A successful rental property is not a solo venture. Don't get me wrong, you alone are responsible for your investments, and you alone reap the profits. But a successful rental property investment depends on several different people along the way. For instance, you might depend on a professional **_property manager_** to find suitable tenants for you and supervise the daily operations of your rental properties. Or you might learn about better investment opportunities by spending time with experienced investors who have been there, done that.

The Advantages of a Network

I have a friend named Josh who runs an ESL (English as a second language) class on the weekends. His students are usually immigrants. The class is open to anybody who wishes to join, although it's aimed at beginning English speakers. It is not uncommon for whole families of immigrants to attend the class together. The goal is to create an informal and safe setting in which to practice reading and speaking English. Josh's students hail from a multitude of different countries, have been in the USA anywhere from three weeks to five years, and hold varying levels of English-speaking proficiency. Across the board, however, it's fair to say that their English is quite limited.

The class always starts the same way. Josh asks if anybody has practiced English during the week. Maybe it was at a store. Maybe on the job site with coworkers. Most of the class sheepishly admits they spoke very little English during the week. The common issue with many immigrants is that it's much more comfortable for them to speak their native tongue. They shop in ethnic grocery stores that serve them in their language. They never speak English at home with their families. They tend to get jobs with people who speak the same language as they do. For many, this ESL class is the only two hours of the whole week when they'll speak English.

One week, a new family comes to the class. Josh greets them and discovers that they recently emigrated from El Salvador and have been living in the US for six months. Josh notices that their English is much more advanced than that of many others in the class, including students who have been in the country for years. He remarks on their language skills and asks if they've attended other ESL classes before this one.

"No," says the father. "When we moved here, we chose a neighborhood with no other Latinos at all. We sent our kids to an English school. We work in jobs where we only speak English. It was hard for us at first, but we had no choice but to learn to speak the language."

What's the reason for the skill disparity between the regular attendees of Josh's class and this El Salvadorian family? The difference is solely based on whom they surround themselves with. While the other immigrants in the ESL class chose to remain in their own cultural bubbles, this family made a conscious choice about who they would (and wouldn't) spend time with. Just six months later, at least in respect to their language skills, that decision has made all the difference.

This story is not fiction. It is real-world proof that the people around you affect your decisions and abilities. Make wise choices about your investing network of associates and colleagues, and you'll have stronger results with your property investments.

MY TAKE

I would argue that, in addition to analysis skills, the people you surround yourself with have the most impact on your rental property investment outcomes. Without the like-minded aspiring investors of the Weekend Fund, I would not have pursued property investing as purposefully as I did, nor would I have attained the same great results. My real estate analysis skills only became relevant once I was part of a network of investors that pushed me to use them.

Here are just a few of the benefits you'll reap from having a solid network in place:

» **Wisdom:** You're not out to reinvent the wheel. There are people out there who have been successfully operating rental properties for years. You can, and should, replicate their success by learning from them. Maybe you have problem tenants and wonder if it's the right time to evict them. Maybe you're sizing up two similar properties and having trouble making the final decision about which one to buy. Or maybe you just want to know the best way to approach a tenant about a rent increase. There are investors out there who have navigated these types of situations dozens of times and can offer precious advice.

» **Motivation:** Rental property investing is hard work. There is no doubt you will experience bad days when you feel like throwing in the towel. I find that partners, both personal and professional, can motivate you to press on. Find role models who have achieved the dream of passive income, built a sizable retirement portfolio, or operate rental properties across the country. If one investor can do it, so can you.

» **Opportunities:** In chapter 8, we talked about the sources for your next deal. None are as important as the network of people around you. My network of colleagues and investors has provided a constant flow of rental opportunities for years. I depend on my personal and professional circles to help me locate my next great rental property.

» **Connections:** You cannot simply open Google and type "best lawyer / real estate agent / mortgage broker" and expect to find a suitable partner for your investment journey. More often than not, my Rolodex of partners has expanded because someone I know connected me with someone they know. "Oh, you should meet my contractor. He does incredible work." In this way, I make connections with people I would otherwise never meet. These people also come with recommendations from people I trust, which is a simple way for me to vet the best partners for my ever-growing team.

» **Perspective:** I can only view an investment through my lens, my perspective. Sometimes it pays to have someone else look at a property while applying their own distinctive vision. A contractor might view a property for its potential appreciated value after renovations. A real estate agent could point out the appeal of a certain neighborhood (or lack thereof). I depend on the perspective of a group of people to help inform me about my best course of action.

It's your duty to develop a "dream team" who will work with you to produce the best possible rental property investment.

Beware of the temptation to simply focus on finding the "star players" in each professional field. The term "dream team" became popular during the 1992 Olympics and referred to the USA men's basketball team, which was made up of a veritable who's who of basketball greats. Michael Jordan. Magic Johnson. Larry Bird. Patrick Ewing. Karl Malone. These legends of the game came together and won gold for America, and as a result, they came to be known as the most dominant team ever assembled. But when the USA tried to replicate that success at the 2004 Olympics, they fell flat. The names on that team were just as big. LeBron James. Dwyane Wade. Allen Iverson. But the team barely managed to secure bronze against an arguably weaker Lithuanian squad. What was the difference? In 1992, the dream team was an actual team, all striving as one for the same goal. But in 2004, many critics argued that the players were merely a group of skilled individuals, not a real team. Without that singular goal, they lost focus and failed to take the podium.

As we continue in this chapter, you'll see the value of teamwork and shared goals within your network of partners.

Professional Partners

You don't build a business. You build people and then people build the business.
— ZIG ZIGLAR

On your team there will be two types of people: those you pay to work with you and those you do not. Those you pay are also known as your professional partners. You rely on professionals at every step of the rental investment journey. You depend on mortgage brokers to help you finance your property. You require lawyers to draw up legal paperwork for a sale. And because you depend so heavily on this subgroup of people, you need to invest time and energy in selecting them with care. Be selective about your choice of partners. Train your professional partners to understand your goals by clearly communicating the strategy you have to build your rental investment portfolio.

There was a time, believe it or not, when George Clooney had difficulty landing acting roles. Audition after audition, he struggled to capture the attention of casting agents and directors. But after some intense self-scrutiny, Clooney uncovered the root of his problem: his intentions. Clooney walked into these casting offices hoping that the decision-makers would like him. He came across as needy and self-serving. But once he altered his perspective, he started getting callbacks. What did he do differently? He realized that casting agents and producers are hoping to find the right man for the job. Clooney simply presented himself not as a hopeful candidate but as the solution to their casting problem. He would deliver the role they wanted and make it easier for them to do their jobs. And because of that mentality shift, he's become the A-list celebrity we know today.

What distinguishes you from all the other clients your future professional partners have? Lawyers, mortgage brokers, real estate agents—the best practitioners in their field might already have enough work to keep them busy. Much like Clooney's solution for getting recognition, you should present yourself as a powerful asset to these professionals. They would be foolish not to want to adjust their busy schedules to meet with you and work with you. Rental property investors are terrific moneymakers for the partners who work with them. While the average homeowner might buy one property every five years, a successful rental property owner could buy several. If you're successful, they are successful. For example, I have a multitude of real estate agents filling up my inbox with potential deals because they recognize me as a source of constant income. They want me to find the best properties because when I do, I want to work with them again and again. Treat these professionals as if you were the answer to their desire for sustainable, reliable work—because you are!

Real Estate Agents

In chapter 8, we talked about the value of real estate agents as a source for finding your ideal property. But here I want to stress the impact of having a good real estate agent as a part of your *network*. In his book *The Tipping Point*, Malcolm Gladwell highlights three types of people with particular social skills that create viral sensations, like overnight fashion trends or the popularity of a product. One of those three types is the Connector, someone who is adept at making friends and introductions. Either through curiosity, confidence, or just good social skills, Connectors have ties to people beyond their social, economic, professional, and cultural circles. In other words, you can recognize a Connector by how often they say, "I've got somebody I think you should meet."

Although not all real estate agents are Connectors as Gladwell would describe them, a high proportion of Connectors are naturally drawn to the profession. Because being a real estate agent is a relational job, social people naturally thrive in that environment. A great real estate agent helps you get connected with everyone else in their network. They can introduce you to quality contractors, reputable accountants, experienced lawyers, and even other successful investors. The best real estate agent isn't always the person with the most ads on bus stop benches or listings in the local paper. Search out the real estate agents with quality connections to many different industries that can help you build your team of professionals.

Contractors

Although it may not be with your first or even your second rental property, you will eventually find an investment that requires some rehab work. This is where you'll need a reputable contractor on your contact list.

The profession is so rife with unscrupulous contractors that Spike TV created a reality show on the subject. *Catch a Contractor*, hosted by Adam Carolla, worked with unlucky homeowners who were stuck with unfinished renovations. The TV show's crew would track down the disreputable contractor who left these homeowners high and dry and in debt for tens of thousands of dollars. The hosts would confront the contractors about their work and questionable business practices. And if the contractor was unable or unwilling to return to finish the job, then the TV crew would complete the renovations for the homeowner. The show's concept was so popular that its first episode became the most highly viewed premiere of an original program in Spike TV's history.

I encourage you to spend time developing a good relationship with a contractor you can trust. Once they have an appreciation for the kind of work you require and the quality you expect, it can make your job a lot easier.

More and more, I am discovering that the opinion of a contractor holds a lot of weight when I am analyzing properties. My contractor's expertise with renovations helps me decide which deals would go smoothly and which properties would be too risky to take on. I can send him before-and-after photos of a recently completed renovation project in the area and get a reliable estimate of how much it would cost for me to do something similar. With the help of my contractor's eye, I can accurately determine the potential value of a property.

Lawyers

How many lawyer jokes are there? Three. The rest are just true stories. All jokes aside, lawyers are a valuable asset on your rental property investment team. One of the reasons to recruit a trusted legal team is that you're going to be contacting them again and again. For every tenant agreement, for every sale, for every alteration to a contract, you will be contacting your lawyer.

I cannot stress enough how important it is to find a good legal team. An expeditious lawyer can help you secure good deals. Every now and then, you will come across a property on the market that is so attractive it draws in investors like sharks responding to the smell of blood. If your legal team can quickly draw up a contract to buy the property, your bid holds more weight for the seller by virtue of its promptness. With the help of your legal team, your quick action can circumvent a potential feeding frenzy in the form of a bidding war.

On more than one occasion, I've found divorce lawyers to be an excellent source for properties about to come on the market. In an impending divorce, the separating couple often looks to sell the major assets that are co-owned. A divorce lawyer is often the first outside party to be aware of the potential sale. With an investor like you as a contact, divorce lawyers can advise their clients that the home will sell quickly if they give your number a call.

Brokers

Within the broker category, there are mortgage brokers and insurance brokers. In both cases, the broker acts as a middleman between you and companies offering products. You may be asking, why not just walk into the bank yourself and ask for a loan? Well, you could try that approach, but the advantage of working with brokers is that they have access to products from a multitude of sources. There are hundreds of mortgage options out there. Furthermore, some lenders work exclusively with brokers, which means that unless you work with a broker, you may not have access to all the available financing options on the market. If you find a broker that you can esteem as a trusted professional partner, then you can rely on them to connect you with the most appropriate mortgage or insurance products.

I recommend using an insurance broker as an alternative to managing your policies on your own. As soon as you buy your first property, you'll be dealing with multiple insurance policies. There will be landlord insurance, dwelling insurance (protection against fires, floods, hail, and wind), private mortgage insurance (if you paid less than 20 percent for the down payment), and homeowners insurance. Then there are the possible add-ons, such as vandalism, burglary, rental construction, or earthquake policies. All of these policies can lapse, get amended, or be canceled, and it can quickly become confusing and complicated to manage. A good insurance broker simplifies this for you and ensures you have the appropriate insurance for the properties you own. In return for paying the insurance broker a commission or fee, you get the security of knowing you have the best policies on the market, combined with someone who is monitoring those policies on your behalf.

Accountants

In addition to a lawyer, you will need someone who can balance your books. You will quickly come to learn that, as an investor, you are also a business owner. In part IV, we will explore how to turn your rental property investing hobby into a long-term career. A large component of that shift will involve expert organization, books management, and general accounting. A professional accountant can give you income and expenditure reports, offer financial forecasts for your future, and help you prepare for tax season.

Don't wait until you have a large portfolio of properties before hiring a good accountant. I advise that you begin searching for a trusted certified public accountant (CPA) even before you buy your first property. As with the contractor's perspective, the eye of an accountant is a valuable ally. A good accountant may be able to help you home in on the most tax-advantageous properties on your short list.

Personal Partners

Now that I've introduced you to some of the professional partners you will work with, let's discuss the second category of partners: personal partners. These are the members of your team who do not charge you for their services. That does not mean, however, that they are any less valuable to the success of your rental property investments. Personal partners can offer you advice and wisdom and possibly an opportunity or two.

Mentors

I am convinced that the fastest way to advance as a rental property investor is to get a mentor. The word "mentor" comes from the epic poem *The Odyssey*, written by Homer. To catch you up on some classic literature, *The Odyssey* tells the story of Odysseus, a man who left his family to go to battle; on his attempt to return home he encountered a cyclops, sirens, and a witch. While he was at war, Odysseus left his friend Mentor behind to watch over his family. Part of Mentor's role was to raise Odysseus's son, teaching him everything he needed to know. Although it took ten years for Odysseus to journey back to his home, Mentor kept everybody in Odysseus's household safe and well. Over time, Mentor's name was used to refer to a person who had the requisite wisdom to teach and instruct others.

When I first began working in real estate, I was approached by many people asking for wisdom on how they could follow in my footsteps and invest in rental properties. I never begrudged those people but took each request as an opportunity to offer some mentorship. But when the number of people seeking me grew, I had to think of a new way to share my expertise. So I stepped into the educational world, creating courses and providing a pathway for hundreds of thousands of people to benefit from my expertise and advice. This desire to help also led to my writing of this book. I hope it will end up as more than merely a reference tome to be stored, unfinished, on your shelf. On the contrary, I want this book to be the physical embodiment of the mentorship I seek to offer.

One budding rental property investor I knew (we'll call him K) was convinced from an early age that investing in property was the way he would get ahead in life. By the time he turned twenty-one, K had scrimped and saved enough money to buy his first rental property. He was painstakingly careful in choosing the right real estate agent. No matter their experience or number of listings, K always asked each prospective agent the same question: How many rental properties do you own? Many of them said they owned none, but one agent had a personal portfolio of four properties. Knowing that they shared the same interests, K hired that real estate agent to help him make his first purchase. K spent years learning under this agent's mentorship, amassing more properties at a faster rate than he could have had he gone it alone, without the guiding principles of a qualified mentor.

Partner Investors

I completely understand the mindset of the average rental property investor who says, "I want to do this alone." For many investors, owning rental properties allows them to escape the tyranny of the nine-to-five job, where they report to one or several bosses. The allure for many is that, once you become an investor, you report to no one and work on your own, determining your own work–life balance and measures of success. But I want to suggest to you that it's a significant advantage to partner with other investors.

Looking to the highest strata of investors, you'll find that most work with partners, pooling their money to invest in greater opportunities together. One of the main reasons is that with pooled resources, these partnered investors have access to larger properties than they could have operated on their own. Say you have $50,000 to invest. You have the freedom to invest in properties within that budget, but your rental returns will be limited.

Rental yield is the ratio of the rental income we receive to the money we invested.

If you want to make more rental money, you have to invest more capital at the outset. You could simply save up more money, or you could achieve the same result by pooling your $50,000 with two other partners, each contributing the same amount of money, for a total investment capital of $150,000. You could then widen your search to find properties in a significantly higher price range, many of which might offer higher rental yields.

Having a partner investor also allows you to split tasks equally between each member of the partnership. You might be a natural negotiator, good at buying properties or screening tenants, and your partner might be better equipped for the tasks of hiring a reputable contractor or analyzing future profits. A division of labor allows each partner to bring their strengths forward and find accommodation for their weaknesses.

But what if the partnership is financially unbalanced, with one partner having significantly more capital than you do? It's still possible to invest with higher-echelon investors under an incentives-based structure known as the *distribution waterfall framework*. This framework accounts for the inequality of labor and initial capital of each investor and creates an equal and fair distribution of the returns on a rental property. With this method, you can invest a relatively small amount of capital, invest more time and energy than your partners do, and receive a much higher return than you could with a single property in your own price range. Even if you contribute only 5 percent of the total capital within the partnership, you can still find rental property investments through your partnership that are more lucrative than a rental property you operate on your own.

Chapter Recap

» The people you surround yourself with will determine the level of (or lack of) success you have with rental property investing.

» Curating the people in your network should be a conscious decision you make early on, even before you make your first purchase.

» Within your network, there will be people you pay, known as professional partners. These partners are necessary and can provide opportunities and wisdom beyond their job descriptions.

» Personal partners are unpaid members of your team but are just as vital to your network as professional partners.

» Investing with partners opens you up to greater opportunities, resources, and returns.

| 10 |
The Basics of Landlording

Everybody has a plan until they get punched in the mouth.

— MIKE TYSON

Regardless of what you think about musicals, I would highly recommend that you watch *Hamilton*, the smash hit first performed in New York City in 2015. The play, of which a filmed version was recently released, is a surprisingly engaging portrayal of the story of Alexander Hamilton, the first secretary of the US Treasury. It's both entertaining and informative. I've never known any musical that could make a cabinet meeting actually fun to watch. There's one particular moment in the play I want to highlight. After America wins its independence from the British, the character of King George sings a song, basically asking if they are prepared now that they've gotten what they wanted:

What comes next?
You've been freed.
Do you know how hard it is to lead?
You're on your own.
Awesome. Wow.
Do you have a clue what happens now?

In the musical, the character is mockingly asking if the Americans can handle the enormity of running their own country. I feel that King George's words also apply to many first-time landlords. As a rental property owner, you've spent an inordinate amount of time in the preparation phase of your investment. But once you're at the point where you have what you wanted—the property—you may wonder, what comes next?

Up to this point, all your profits are not really profits at all, but merely the potential for profits. Think back to your high school physics lessons: if you pull back on a rubber band to shoot it across the room, that rubber band has stored potential energy. Once you let go of the rubber band, that potential energy transforms into kinetic energy, the motion of the rubber band shooting through the air. Being a landlord is like letting go of that rubber band. You've already accumulated the potential energy—you make money when you buy—and now you're ready to realize your profit potential by running your rental property well.

Throughout the chapter, I will be introducing you to several tools that I've created to assist you in your landlording endeavors, such as the Rental Comparison Worksheet. They are all available for download at **www.clydebankmedia.com/rental-assets**.

I love the quote at the beginning of this chapter because it speaks to the nature of owning rental property. You can plan for how to be an effective landlord, but once real life happens, those plans can, and often do, change. In dealing with tenants, maintaining a property, and protecting your assets, your plans can go awry. I want to share some of my own horror stories in this regard as well as expound on some of the ways you can sidestep those same problems; prevention is by far the best method for avoiding difficult situations.

Things don't always go as planned after you release the rubber band. What's important is that you learn not to panic and to handle the problems as they come. Stay true to the fundamental principles I will share with you in this chapter, and you will establish a solid foundation for success.

Dealing with Tenants

I know of one investor who had a long relationship with a good tenant who occupied one of the units in his apartment complex. The lease agreement specifically stated that the tenant was not to have any other people living in the one-bedroom apartment. Unknown to the landlord, his tenant, a likeable woman in her seventies, was letting her grandson stay with her for a few months.

The landlord eventually found out about the guest while he was on holiday in Hawaii. He received a call saying a SWAT team had surrounded the apartment complex and staged a standoff to capture the grandson.

Although the tenant was lovely, her grandson had a reputation as a wanted drug dealer, which was the reason he was evading the police by living with his grandmother. The capture went smoothly, but the stigma of the sting caused some of the landlord's best tenants to move out. And after all the drama, it was more difficult to get others to move in to fill the vacancies. It took months for the landlord to recover lost income and rebuild a wholesome reputation for the property.

Although these appalling tenant/landlord stories are common, they do not have to be common for you. Throughout this book, I have been preaching the principle of being diligent up front to reap the rewards of that diligence later. The same principle applies to screening and selecting tenants. If you spend the time on the front end of the process, chances are that you will reap the rewards of a smooth, long-lasting, drama-free relationship.

One of the easiest ways to undo all the hard work you put into securing your rental property is by selecting a bad tenant, which can often be more financially ruinous than an extended vacancy. Putting in the effort and time necessary to find a good tenant is worth it in the long run.

Screening Tenants

To minimize the risk of selecting a bad tenant, you need to prequalify the applicants before they move forward in the process. One way I like to do this is by asking my applicants to submit a twenty-dollar fee with each application to cover credit and background checks. If the application is rejected, then I return the fee. Twenty dollars is a nominal amount, but some tenants balk at the idea. If twenty dollars is enough to cause hesitation in an applicant, I know they're not the kind of tenant I want in my property. There are several other ways to create filters. If you're asking for applicants to call you, you can specify that they only call after two p.m. If you're asking for emailed applications, request that they put a specific phrase in the subject line. Any applicant that doesn't go along with these simple requests might not be the ideal tenant for your property.

Just as you can screen out bad tenants, you can create filters that attract good tenants. But what makes a good tenant? As I've already mentioned, you have to determine the kind of tenant that would rent your type of property. What are their goals? What do they value? What makes them attracted to your neighborhood? This is the kind of information you should use when listing a vacancy in your home. Use language in your ads that appeal to the tenant you want. "Landscaped yard" sounds good to families. "Modern amenities" and "within walking distance" appeal to the urban professional. In chapter 7, we used the stories of Emil, Jessica, and Tyson to show you how to view properties through their lenses. The attributes we outlined there should inform you on how to advertise for prospective tenants.

MY TAKE

Good tenants tend to hang out in circles of people who would also make good tenants. As such, I like to offer my tenants a finder's fee as an incentive for a successful referral.

No matter what type of property you're renting, there are certain attributes that make for a good tenant. Look for the following:

» **Good rental history:** I want to know that my tenants have been good tenants previously. I check for evictions or problems with past landlords. I will even straight-up ask them, "Is there anything in your renting history that I should know?" People can change. A mistake made ten years ago does not necessarily disqualify someone from being a good tenant today. And if someone is honest about their past, I am willing to overlook one or two negative marks on their name, if they meet the rest of my criteria.

» **Solid employment records:** It doesn't matter what job a tenant holds; I am only concerned about whether they can pay the rent. For safety's sake, I look for tenants that make a gross monthly income that's four times what I'm asking for rent. For instance, if I'm offering a property with a $750 monthly rent, I want to know my tenants are earning at least $3,000 each month before taxes. Consistent employment also shows me that they are reliable people. Any applicant with a history of several jobs in a short time frame is a big red flag for me.

» **Glowing references:** One of the easiest ways to screen an applicant is to find out what their previous landlords have to say about them. Do they pay their rent on time? Have there been any complaints from neighbors? Are there any unresolved disputes or ongoing mediations? Ask your applicants to provide references to back up their rental history. Honest assessments from other landlords hold tremendous weight in my considerations.

Although screening prospective tenants is important, you must be mindful not to exhibit any form of discrimination. The 1968 Fair Housing Act is designed to protect tenants from being refused a rental property based on certain aspects such as race, gender, or disability. You cannot even indicate a preference for a certain tenant based on any of these qualities. Check your state laws before posting any advertisement for tenants.

I have a handy tenant checklist that will walk you through the standard steps involved in bringing a new tenant onto your property. You can get your copy by visiting **www.clydebankmedia.com/rental-assets**.

Lease Agreements

The goal of a good lease agreement is to set expectations, both yours and the tenant's. This agreement lays out roles and responsibilities and establishes a solid foundation for how the relationship will proceed.

A good lease agreement protects both landlord and tenant. Within the agreement, you can specify the terms of the rental, including dates for rent payment, notifications of maintenance or inspections, and any penalties for late payments. If issues arise, you can always refer to your signed lease agreement to back up any action you take. For instance, if your tenant is habitually late with rent payments, you can refer them to the lease agreement, which states you will charge a late fee or take other punitive action, such as issuing a written warning. The agreement protects the tenant as well. It informs them about your responsibilities and holds you accountable for them, including things such as responding to the need for emergency repairs or providing prior notification to get access to the property.

Most lease agreements are "fixed term," meaning that all aspects of the agreement are locked in place for a set period of time. Although some tenants prefer month-by-month agreements, the fixed-term lease allows you to establish more reliable income projections. Once a fixed-term lease expires, you have the option to renew the agreement, raise the rent, or ask the tenant to vacate the premises.

I have left you a lease agreement template that you can use as the basis for your own contract. Because landlord laws vary from state to state, be sure to have a lawyer look it over. Get your copy of the Simple Lease Agreement Template at **www.clydebankmedia.com/rental-assets**.

Dealing with Problem Tenants

If you were to ask some landlords, they would say rental property investing is great until you get a tenant. I disagree. In all my years of being a rental property owner, I have dealt with only one eviction. Bad tenants and evictions are expensive. One bad tenant can completely ruin years of an investment's profits, so I take care to minimize that risk. But a tenant is a person, and people are notoriously unpredictable. As hard as I try to avoid problem tenants, one occasionally shows up.

Repairs and Maintenance

Obviously, you're going to put in some sweat equity to get your property up to rentable standards before you lease it. Most rental properties have at least some initial repair and maintenance needs, even if they are only cosmetic. Over the life of your investment, however, the property will eventually deteriorate. Things break down. Parts wear out. Stuff gets old. And it can get complicated dealing with repairs in a timely manner without disrupting your tenants' home. It's a balancing act—performing preventative maintenance without disrupting the tenant and also responding to emergencies when they arise.

Repairs and maintenance are not unexpected events. They are necessary to preserve the value of your investment and therefore should be a part of your budget. Each time you collect a rent check, a portion of that check should be set aside in your "repairs and maintenance" fund. For newer properties—those less than five years old—you shouldn't need a large repair budget. Fifty dollars a month could be more than enough. For older properties with a higher likelihood of problems, set aside one hundred dollars a month. These figures might be too conservative, leaving you with more saved than you needed, or you could wind up short. As with most of your planning, time will tell how your assumptions compared to actual repair costs. At the end of the year, adjust your allowance if necessary, so you never have to pay out of pocket when your tenants call to say the plumbing has sprung a leak or the air conditioning is acting up.

Q: Who cares the most about doing repairs on your property?

That question is an easy layup. It's you, of course. Although your tenant lives in the property, you're the owner, ultimately responsible for the home's value. Don't expect that your tenant will always be speedy to let you know when something breaks down. They could be uncertain about how you will react to bad news, thus afraid to let you know when something goes wrong.

Or they might have a relaxed attitude about things breaking down. Or maybe they're uncertain about who is responsible for the cost of a repair or replacement. The ultimate responsibility of checking on the health of your property falls to you. Therefore, establish a regular inspection schedule so you can discover problems, or potential problems, sooner rather than later. Include a clause in your lease agreement stating that twice-yearly inspections are required. The clause should point out that as long as the tenant agrees to those inspections, preventive maintenance costs are your burden. I recommend biannual inspections because, if they are more frequent, tenants can feel like you're intruding on their privacy. But let the intervals stretch out too long and you can miss potential issues.

Please note that not all repairs and maintenance are your obligation. Some of the liability belongs to the tenant. Your job, as the law requires, is to provide a safe and habitable place to live. It must adhere to all relevant local codes and ordinances. Assuming that it does, then you have the freedom to decide what you want to fix beyond that baseline. In return, the tenant has the duty of keeping your property in reasonably good condition. If they flush large foreign objects down the toilet and call you when the plumbing blocks up, you have the right to bill them for the repair costs. Since it is impossible to draw up a comprehensive list of possible repairs in your lease contract, I suggest that you and your tenant make some general agreements. For example, you can encourage your tenant to be responsive by offering to shoulder some of the costs of accidental damages. Let's say the tenant accidentally breaks a window and informs you right away. You might have an agreement stating that you'll pay for the material costs of replacing the window and your tenant is responsible for the labor costs.

NOTE Make sure all communication between you and your tenant is written, never just verbal. A simple email will suffice, but having proof of a notification protects you and your tenant if any future disagreements arise.

Minor Maintenance

Minor maintenance refers to those small repairs and quick patch-ups that occur from time to time. The bathroom tiling starts to chip away. The dishwasher develops a leak. A porch step gets damaged. These minor repairs don't cost much, but neglecting them can get expensive. Your lease agreement should include a clause that specifies how quickly you will respond to minor maintenance calls once a tenant notifies you of the need.

The key to saving money on repairs is prevention. It's easy (and cheap) to regularly replace the filter on your furnace or clean leaves from the gutters. But it could cost you thousands of dollars if the furnace breaks down or an overflowing gutter leaks down the wall. It helps to set up a checklist for your inspections so that you can do preventative maintenance during your scheduled visits. Here are just a few of the items to check on these inspections.

- » Flush the water heater
- » Change the furnace filters
- » Check and replace batteries in smoke and carbon monoxide detectors
- » Clean sediment from shower heads
- » Check for loose handles and knobs
- » Check for mold and mildew
- » Check under sinks for leaks
- » Clear gutters of debris
- » Check water valves (before and after winter)
- » Look for signs of infestation
- » Check roof and siding for wear and tear

It will take only about thirty minutes to cover most of the items on this checklist, and that time could save you thousands of dollars in the long run.

Major Maintenance and Renovations

Major maintenance refers to those once-in-a-while events when something large breaks down or comes due for replacement. Although surprises happen, they will be less frequent if you're proactive with major maintenance rather than reactive. The best way to do that is to keep a record of the expected lifetime of some of the components of your property. That way it won't be a surprise to your tenant or your budget when it's time for a major maintenance call.

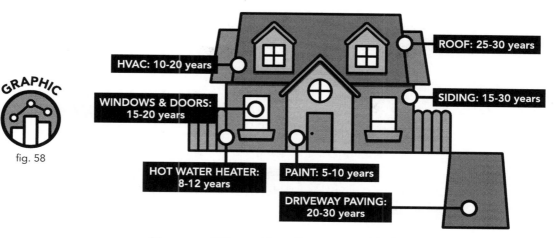

fig. 58

The expected life span (depending on materials) of major components
in and around a typical single-family home

Major repairs can require a few hours or a few days. Talk with your tenant about relocating them if necessary during the time maintenance is underway. Alternatively, consider planning to do major repairs in between tenants. For instance, if you know your roof needs to be replaced in the next five years and your tenant is moving out at the end of this year, schedule your roof replacement during the period of vacancy. No, the roof isn't due for replacement just yet, but because you complete the work while your property is empty, you save the expense and inconvenience of relocating a tenant during the process. Otherwise, if you are forced to make repairs on a component that's critical to maintaining the property's habitable standard (such as a roof), you will be legally obliged to pay for alternative accommodations.

Landlord Insurance

If you invest a lot of money in an asset, it's very upsetting if something happens to that asset. This is why you invest in insurance. Insurance is designed to protect your assets from loss. A central component of your asset protection efforts will be your landlord insurance policy.

Q: As a landlord, what are your assets?

The property you own, of course, is a primary asset. But it is not your only asset. Another asset is the income that results from your property. Landlord insurance is designed to protect both assets, the property itself and the rental income you make from it. Landlord insurance is essential when you have a tenant living in the property, and it's a distinctly different insurance product than a standard homeowners policy.

Protecting Your Property

The reason you get landlord insurance is, first and foremost, to protect your investment property. By this point, you have invested hours of your time and thousands of your dollars into a property that, ideally, you'd like to own for years. The risk is that you're trusting this property to the care of your tenant. Hopefully, you will have practiced diligence in screening and selecting the right tenant, and landlord insurance supports you as you mitigate that risk.

Imagine that your tenant calls one day to report that a loose piece of siding fell and hit him on the head. As a result, he has costly medical bills and is going to be without a paycheck until he can return to work. Are you responsible for those bills and lost income? Unfortunately, you may be. Liability insurance, a key component of your landlord policy, is designed to cover this type of scenario. With this coverage, if your tenant suffers medical or income setbacks as a result of injury on your property, the liability insurance covers lost wages and hospital bills. Be warned that this insurance comes with the stipulation that you must prove that the injury was not a result of negligent maintenance. As long as everything is up to code and in working order, the liability insurance kicks in.

Another section of the landlord insurance policy is dwelling insurance. It protects the property in case of fire, wind, hail, and water damage. But if you plan to store equipment on the property, make sure to list each item on your tenant's lease agreement. This allows these items to be included in your dwelling insurance policy. For example, if you have maintenance tools in a garage, include those tools as part of your tenant's lease contract and they will be covered in the event of burglary, vandalism, or damage.

Your tenants are responsible for securing their own renter's insurance to protect their personal belongings kept in the home.

In chapter 9, I talked about working with a reputable insurance agent as part of your team. There are many optional additions you can include in your insurance policy, not all of which will be applicable to your specific property. A trusted insurance agent can advise you on this. For example, you can get rental construction protection to safeguard you and your income while the property is vacant and undergoing major renovations. Certain policy additions only apply in specific areas. For example, flood insurance is a must in New Orleans but is generally unnecessary in Boulder, Colorado.

Protecting Your Income

A component of landlord insurance is rental income insurance, which protects your rental earnings against excessive vacancies. Given that you can't predict the nature and timing of vacancies in a given market, you can insure your income against this possibility. At the time of this writing during the COVID-19 pandemic, there are moratoriums on evictions and a lessened incentive for tenants to pay their rent in a timely fashion, or at all. I am thus reminded that the loss of rental income is a real and pervasive threat to one's investment.

Although most landlord insurance policies include rental income protection, not all do. So be sure to check that your policy includes a clause that covers you for lost rental income.

Some rental properties are inherently riskier for vacancies, such as an apartment building or a shared home in a college town. Considering that many students want to rent for only a couple of semesters, the turnover rate for your college-town property is likely to be high. Although you can predict the timing of the vacancies, you might not be able to foretell the extent of them. In these types of scenarios, you can fall back on rental income insurance if you need it. But what happens if you have a stable tenant that unexpectedly gets transferred to a new city, or loses their job, or experiences any of the hundreds of reasons that may cause them to leave your property earlier than planned? Or what happens if a natural disaster renders your property uninhabitable for six months while you repair the damage? Your dwelling insurance will cover the cost of the repairs, but what about the six months of rent checks you can't collect? This is another reason for rental income insurance. Although you should set aside a portion of your rental income to get you through the normal expected short vacancy periods, do make a claim with your rental income insurance if you're left without rental income for months at a time.

I talk about insurance from the perspective of my experience with it, not as a licensed agent. Consult with your local insurance broker for the plans and policies that you need in your area.

Chapter Recap

» A successful landlord is defined as someone who realizes the potential profits of a property through effective and responsible management.

» Spend a lot of time screening and qualifying your tenants, as they have the most impact on your expected rental returns.

» An effective tenant agreement provides protection for both the renter and the landlord.

» Create a schedule to keep up to date with minor repairs of your property. Set aside a portion of your rental income to cover expected costs for the year.

» Landlord insurance acts as protection for your assets, both the property you own and the income you derive from it.

| 11 |
Buyers and Sellers

Chapter Overview
- » Steering Sellers to a "Yes"
- » Appealing to the Right Buyers
- » Transitioning Tenants through Change

I love mankind . . . it's people I can't stand!

— LINUS FROM *PEANUTS*

Ryan was panicking. A client in Austin was waiting anxiously for him to show up to sign a lucrative contract that Ryan had spent six months cultivating with the client. And now that the client was ready to sign on the dotted line, the flight Ryan had booked from Baltimore was canceled. As so often happens, the northeastern United States had experienced a terrible storm that left many passengers stranded, unable to make connecting flights or leave the terminal. If Ryan couldn't make his connection in Dallas, the chances of signing that contract could go up in smoke. Desperate to get on the last Dallas flight of the day, Ryan hurried over to the American Airlines ticket counter to see what he could do.

When he arrived, a couple was in front of him in line, and they seemed to be in the same desperate state as he was. They were berating the poor ticketing agent, who was obviously doing her best to keep from replying with equally abusive comments. After five "I'm sorry, I can't do anything, it's all booked" replies by the agent, the couple stormed off. With just thirty minutes left to make the last flight, Ryan knew he had to approach this scenario with a different tack.

"Wow, they sure seemed pretty upset," Ryan remarked as he stepped up to the counter.

"Yeah, they missed a connection and now the weather has delayed them even further," replied the agent.

"Must be a hectic time for you then, dealing with people like that all day."

"It is. And as much as I hate getting yelled at, I get why they're mad. I can't control the weather, and in these conditions, planes are booked solid. Although who knows how many people will actually show up."

This was Ryan's chance. The airline agent had let slip that there would possibly be some no-shows for the flight due to leave. If he played his cards right, he just might be able get himself on that flight.

"Well, it seems like you've handled the situation brilliantly. I'm sure you can already guess that I was also affected by some cancellations, and I'm trying to get to Dallas on this next flight. It's probably booked solid, but there could be someone who won't make the flight because of the weather. Is there a chance that a seat could open up?"

Silence. Ryan waited patiently while the agent tapped on her keyboard. After a few moments, she printed out a boarding pass, handed it to Ryan and said, "There were a few late flights that will likely cause some people to miss this departure. You'd better hurry before they close the gate."

Rental property investing is not just a game of numbers and formulas. Analysis and projections have their place, but there is a human element to this venture as well. Nowhere is this more evident than when it comes to buying and selling your property. There are many books and articles out there that speak about buying and selling homes, but not many of them acknowledge the human side of the transaction. The buyers and sellers of rental properties are people, and you'll need to develop the skills to manage them. You must learn to accommodate them, appeal to them, convince them, negotiate with them, and market to them. So much of your deal hinges on your ability to work with buyers and sellers. Never ignore the human element behind the property in which you are interested. For instance, to buy a property at a price you want, you have to induce the seller to agree to your terms. And when it comes time to sell your property, you must persuade the buyer of the value of your investment. As with Ryan's airline ticketing success, your ability to choose the right approach with the people behind the deal can radically affect the outcome of your investment opportunities.

Working with Sellers

Every listed property's sales price is a combination of two elements. The first is the comparable value of the home—its value compared to similar properties. This is an objective factor, and you have no control over this element of the price. If three-bedroom homes in a neighborhood are selling at an average price of $465,000, there is virtually no chance you can buy a similar home for $250,000. The second element of the sales price is subjective, meaning you can exert some influence on it. The seller of the home has a number in mind, a goal that is often different from the listed price. There are several circumstances that can influence whether seller moves down on the listed price. Typically, the seller needs to pay off the remaining balance of the mortgage on the property and must receive enough money from the sale to do so. As such, the seller may have a very firm minimum amount. The seller could also know there is more demand than supply, making them unlikely to consider lowering the price. Or, Alternatively, the seller's urgent need to get rid of the property can push the price down by a substantial margin.

A common phrase in poker is that you play the man, not the cards. This means that although the cards you hold influence your odds of winning, those cards don't determine how you play. Real estate can be quite similar. The value of a property will influence the seller's price, but it doesn't always need to determine how you make your offer. Because there is a subjective element to a sales price, you can deal with the seller's interests separately from the property you want to buy. Buying and selling a property is commonly done behind the smokescreen of real estate agents, making it easy to forget that there is an actual person accepting or rejecting your offers. Appealing to the seller on their own terms can increase your chances of getting the property you want without paying too much.

You make your money when you buy.

Crafting an Offer

Did you know that seventeenth-century pirates set up a constitutional democracy decades before the American Revolution? It was one of the reasons that formerly honest sailors joined these rogue ships to pillage, plunder, and steal on the high seas. To keep the thieves honest, at least for a short while, pirates had to invent some sort of system that encouraged law and order. Merchant sailors found more freedom in the democracy of a pirate ship than on their own frigates. Not only that, the pay for being a pirate was significantly better, as long as you were willing to accept the risk of death, deceit, and capture. Movies portray pirates as bloodthirsty ravagers, caring only about themselves. As is often the case, Hollywood does not do justice to reality. Pirates had more in common with businessmen than evil villains. These pirates discovered that they needed to present the right incentives for honest sea folk to join their crew. The offer to become a lifelong criminal and face almost certain early death didn't make sense, unless it was paired with the incentives of freedom, a vote, and the ability to get rich.

While I'm not suggesting anything so extreme, this type of mentality is important when crafting an offer for a property. You have to include an incentive for the seller to consider your proposal. Most often, this incentive is a deposit known as *earnest money*. This small deposit is paid to the seller as an act of goodwill, demonstrating your serious intention to buy the property. It distinguishes you from other bidders who are merely testing the waters, and it shows that your bid holds weight. The seller is entitled to keep that deposit if you back out of the deal.

MY TAKE

Typically, an earnest-money deposit is 1-2 percent of the total purchase price. However, in a seller's market with a lot of potential buyers, I would recommend at least a 5 percent earnest-money deposit.

When it's time to pay the down payment, that earnest money offsets the total you owe. For example, if you paid $2,000 in earnest money and the down payment was $30,000, you would be required to come up with only $28,000. If the seller backs out of the deal for any reason, you are entitled to a refund of that earnest money.

Since the earnest deposit is a significant amount of cash you may never get back, you need to protect your offer by including some contingencies. These clauses allow you to legitimately back out of a deal and recoup that earnest money if your conditions are not met. While it's possible to have so many contingencies that the seller becomes wary of dealing with you, a lenient offer without contingencies exposes you to too much risk. Here are some contingencies you should include with your offer.

- **Financing**: Once you have located the property you want to buy, and once you've prequalified with a lender and know that you are able to receive a loan, only then should you seek out the appropriate financing options. That practice, however, leaves you open to the chance your financing will fall through at the last minute. With a financing contingency in place, you will not lose your earnest money deposit if your lending institution suddenly decides it can't offer you a loan.

- **Inspection**: An inspection contingency is a must, especially when paired with an appraisal. Although you (or your proxy if you're investing long distance) have walked through the property, you need to have a trained eye look over every detail of it in order to make an honest and thorough appraisal of its condition. Inspection contingencies often come with time frames, meaning that unless you complete the inspection within the given time, the contingency lapses. In some cases, investors opt not to include this contingency in the interest of saving time and pushing through the deal faster. I do not agree with that sentiment. It's not common to find issues during an inspection, but if you do find a problem and end up saving money because of it, it was worth the time to get the inspection done.

- **Repair costs:** If you are buying a property that requires renovations before you can rent it out, a cost-of-repair contingency allows you to determine if those renovation costs would be too high. The clause specifies the amount of money set aside for repairs. If the inspection report shows that completing all the necessary repairs would exceed that figure, then you can back out of the deal. For example, you have included a cost-of-repair contingency that shows you will allow up to $25,000 to bring the property to current standards. Upon inspection, the contractor informs you of some cracked foundation concerns, for which repair costs would exceed $35,000. With your contingency in place, you can back out of the deal because it was too expensive for you to take on.

Expert Negotiation Skills

In Western culture, we don't often have the opportunity to practice negotiation skills. We pay the sticker price on what we buy, because why wouldn't we? And if you do want to bargain on price, it can feel like speaking a foreign language. It's awkward, uncomfortable, and feels offensive if you're not doing it right. But in many cultures around the world, negotiation is the law of the land. Especially in Asian markets, the price is never listed on the product. It's always an agreement that the buyer and seller come to after a dance, also known as negotiation, is complete. It's expected and normal, and it's never an offense to reject a price.

What is the number one rule when entering a negotiation? Be ready to walk away. The term BATNA, which stands for best alternative to a negotiated agreement, is commonly used in real estate. Your BATNA allows you to demonstrate to the seller that you are prepared to drop your offer if the negotiation is unsatisfactory to you. It's a tool you will use throughout your negotiations to leverage your seller into a lower price.

There's a property you want to buy that's listed at $400,000. You know that similar properties in the neighborhood have recently sold for $350,000. Your BATNA is your ability to purchase other properties in the area for $350,000. And when you make a low offer, you do so confidently and with leverage, because you can quantitatively demonstrate that the value of the home isn't nearly what the seller believes it to be.

MY TAKE

I find that in cases of overpriced homes, the price is usually based on wrong data. If a seller lists their home at a too-high price because that's what their neighbors got a couple of years ago, then the problem is that they aren't using current comps. Unless their real estate agent specifically advised them to list that high, showing them lower comparable prices is an effective negotiating tactic.

When negotiating a purchase, keep in mind that both you and your seller use BATNAs. If the seller has a better offer on the house than what you're willing to put forward, then the seller has a stronger BATNA than you. Alternatively, without any competing offers, your seller has a weaker BATNA than you. Moreover, their BATNA may be not only weak but intolerable. If they urgently need to sell the home and have no other offers, your willingness to exercise your BATNA and walk away further incentivizes the seller to accept your terms.

MY TAKE

I've found that attentive listening is usually the key when you're striving to gain a clearer idea of your negotiating partner's BATNA. In Ryan's story of trying to get a ticket for a fully booked flight, he simply listened to the agent until she provided the clue that ultimately got him what he wanted. In conversation, your seller could mention that they have an impending job offer in another city. That tidbit could be a useful tool in negotiations, especially if you offer a quick purchase to allow them to get to their new job.

Understanding and defining your BATNA can make negotiations—even for less-experienced negotiators—much easier and less stressful. Knowing precisely where you stand and when to walk away is a simple tool that, when applied with commitment and confidence, can create great negotiating outcomes. Here are some other helpful techniques to include when making your offer on a new rental property:

» **Attach a deadline**: Create a sense of urgency with your offers. When you attach a time frame, it puts the pressure on the seller to either agree or counter your offer. Let it be known that if the time frame runs out, you will exercise your BATNA to move on to another property.

» **Make your "no" gentle**: A hard "no" is hard to hear. I like to be gentle but direct when given a counter that I don't like. If your seller comes back with an offer that's too high, instead of closing down conversation with a harsh negative response like "Absolutely not!" encourage the seller to negotiate against themselves. You might say "How am I supposed to do that?" or "I'm not sure that's the best you can do" or "That's not going to work for me." It lets the seller know you are rejecting the offer without shutting down all communication.

» **Be empathetic**: If you can demonstrate that you understand a seller's position, you have the power to introduce your offer without resistance. For instance, if a seller has had the property listed for months, mention that fact as you make your offer, showing that you empathize with their desperation to get the property sold. "It seems like your house hasn't attracted a lot of attention for a while, but I think it's an excellent property. I'd like to offer . . ." In this way, you've subtly demonstrated empathy while also introducing an initial low offer price to begin negotiations.

Negotiations on real estate deals typically transpire through the buyers' and sellers' real estate agents rather than directly between buyers and sellers. Nonetheless, negotiating tactics such as attaching deadlines, giving gentle noes, and being empathetic can readily be deployed through your agent at your request.

Attracting the Right Buyers

Given that your best rental strategy is to find a property you can hold onto for years, you might wonder in what situation it would be an advantage to sell a property. As long as you have a great tenant who pays you rent and your property is appreciating in value, why would you let go of a good thing? If you'll recall from chapter 1, we discussed how the best rental property investment strategy relies heavily on cash flow income as compared to appreciation. Although you (hopefully) make money when you sell the asset, most rental property investors have a goal of creating sustainable, reliable long-term income streams. From time to time, however, usually because you want to trade up to a better property, the best option is to sell.

Your first rental property will likely not be your best income-producing asset. Unless you are very fortunate with your first investment, it's more probable that you will find better opportunities down the road as you accumulate more experience and more capital. To seize those opportunities when they arise, you may need to sell one or more of your current properties. The most crucial factor in maximizing the profit of your sale is attracting the right buyers.

Your first instinct might be to advertise your property to as wide a base as possible. Surely if you have several potential buyers you'll get the best price. Although that makes sense on the surface, you will get a better result if you limit your marketing efforts to the buyers who have the greatest incentive to purchase your property. Let me explain. Imagine that you have a pile of oranges you want to sell. You've listed the price at one dollar per pound and you open the doors of Oranges R Us to the buyers lined up outside. Your store is in Florida, and your customers don't want to pay the exorbitant price of one dollar, since they already have a glut of oranges in their cellars at home. They start to offer you ninety cents per pound, eighty cents, seventy-five cents, but nobody is biting at the price you have set. Now imagine you've set up the same orange store in Alaska in the winter. Oranges, or any fresh produce for that matter, are a hot commodity at that time of year, so your oranges will attract a higher price. You ask the same price, a dollar, but now buyers are eager to get their hands on what you're selling. You have the same number of buyers in Alaska as you had in Florida, but these buyers are motivated and desperate for oranges. You get offers of $1.20, $1.35, even a shout of "$1.50" from the back. Your ability to get the higher price for your product ultimately depends on attracting buyers who really want what you have to sell.

When a small business owner wants to sell her business, she has two different types of prospective buyers. The first type is the buyers who simply want the assets themselves. This happens all the time in the small business world. Large competitors find it cheaper to buy out and absorb their smaller competition. In doing so they obtain the client list, inventory, physical buildings, and market share of the smaller business—in other words, all the assets held by that business. Another type of buyer, however, will not be concerned with the assets themselves, but with the business's ability to generate a stream of income. They value the ability of that business to generate profits, and they buy into the business to take over a ready-made income stream.

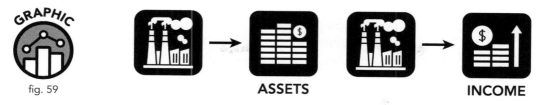

ASSETS   **INCOME**

Buyers of a manufacturing business are interested in either
the physical assets or the income the business generates.

fig. 59

It's no different in real estate. Some buyers will be interested in the asset itself. They have no interest in being a landlord and collecting rents. They want the single-family home, the apartment, or the condo as a new home for themselves, or they want to renovate and flip the property for a profit.

The other kind of buyers are interested in acting as landlords and collecting rent. These buyers want the property for its income potential. As the seller, you've put in the hard work of locating the right property, renovating it, and screening a reputable tenant, and you have years of solid income to prove its sustainability. For this group, buying your income-producing property is a shortcut to their own rental investment.

ASSETS   **INCOME**

Much like the manufacturing business example, home buyers are interested in either the
physical assets or the income the property generates.

fig. 60

How you market the home you're looking to sell depends on the type of buyers you want to attract. To find buyers interested in the asset itself, market the property as the perfect home for the buyer. If your tenant is leaving and you know your best bet is to find a homeowner, highlight the features a homeowner will appreciate. One way to do that is to stage the property, which means outfitting it with furnishings to make it appear neat and inviting. *Staging* is sometimes done just for the listing photos, and sometimes the furnishings remain in the vacant property during showings. Staging is a relatively inexpensive method of helping buyers visualize the property as a functional, welcoming home. Another way to attract the right buyer is to accentuate the features that make your property stand out among the competition. If yours is the only three-bedroom townhouse in an area with one- and two-bedroom townhouses, make sure to mention that in your listing.

If you want to sell your property to another landlord, you'll need to appeal to that buyer in a slightly different way. In this case, you would highlight the rental yield you've been able to achieve, list the renovations and improvements you've made to the home, speak to the forced appreciation of the property that will result from your hard work, and demonstrate the longevity of your tenant, which can be a real selling feature. If you have found the right tenant and have a stable lease agreement, that tenant is an excellent reason for a potential landlord to buy your property, which comes with guaranteed income. However, if a new landlord will be taking over your property, it will be up to you to walk your tenant through the transition.

Long-Term Tenant Transitions

I have bought (and sold) several properties that housed tenants who remained after the sale. It's a common practice among rental property investors, but let's think about it from the tenant's perspective. They have a great home. They know how much the rent will be. They have familiarity with the neighborhood and the area. And nobody really enjoys moving if they don't have to.

When I buy properties with tenants who want to stay, I base my purchase price on the rental income. I underwrite my offer on the expectation that the tenant wants to continue living there under new management of the property.

To make the transition as smooth as possible, I offer to keep rents consistent for at least two years. Tenants often fear the changeover from the old landlord to the new one, particularly in respect to their rent. Although I raise the possibility that I will eventually increase rents, I offer a twenty-four-month grace period to help assuage concerns.

When I'm the seller of a property with an inheritable tenant, I make sure I state honestly the rent I get each month. That sounds basic, but many landlords advertise the fair market rent, not the actual amount they receive. They falsely indicate that they earn an amount equal to what the property *could* attain in ideal market conditions, instead of actual dollars earned. If a renter pays me $800 a month despite the fact that market conditions and comps indicate the property could earn $900, I make sure to report the $800.

In addition to fearing that the rent will increase, tenants are also wary of new leases, new rules, and new requirements. They have become accustomed to how the property was managed and worry that a new landlord will make a lot of changes. To ease this stressor, I make introductions between the tenant and the new landlord during the buying period, making sure that everyone has a chance to say what needs to be said.

As a form of protection for the new landlord and your tenant, ask the tenant to fill out an *estoppel certificate*. This one-page letter is an explanation of the terms and conditions of the current lease, as understood and acknowledged by the tenant. It includes the terms of the lease, the date it was signed, any defaults from either party, and the deposit held in credit by the landlord. Because your current lease still applies when the property is sold to another party, some unscrupulous landlords subvert or even forge clauses on the existing lease. The estoppel certificate protects the tenant from these practices, and it also protects the new landlord from the tenant demanding money or perks that were never agreed to on the original lease. For example, if the tenant claims they don't need to pay rent because the original landlord owed them money, the signed estoppel certificate can prove those claims false.

The rule of thumb is to overcommunicate with your tenants rather than under-communicate. Let them know of your intention to sell the property well before you put up the "For Sale" sign. Inform them of the new landlord's contact details. Assure them of the standing of their current lease, and offer any assistance you can to make the transition easier. If your tenant is happy, you can use that stability and security as leverage to sell your property to the next landlord.

Chapter Recap

» Learning to work with the human element behind your deals is as important as the property itself.

» Understanding why a seller is listing a property helps you present yourself as the perfect buyer.

» Develop a powerful reason to walk away from a deal—your BATNA—and it will give you heightened bargaining power to get the price you want.

» When you are selling your rental property, appealing to the *right* buyers is a better strategy than appealing to *more* buyers.

» To market your property more effectively, ask yourself whether a potential buyer wants your asset or your income.

» Because your tenant and your relationship with them can be part of your negotiations, help ease them through the transition to the new landlord.

PART IV

PLOTTING LONG-TERM SUCCESS

| 12 |
Ongoing Management

It is not the strongest of the species that survive, nor the most intelligent, but the one most responsive to change.

– CHARLES DARWIN

With the reading of these words, you are making a tacit agreement with me and with yourself. You are not going to merely dabble in the world of rental property investing. You're past the stage of learning the introductory information and are ready to learn what it takes to become a successful investor for the long term. This final section of the book, part IV, aims to provide the tools you need to make the final Darwinian adaptation, from student to career rental property investor (assuming that's your goal). However, making that shift from purchasing your first investment property to purchasing your tenth, twentieth, or fiftieth may require greater adaptation than you might think.

In 1971, Southwest Airlines made its inaugural flight out of Dallas, servicing just two Texas cities with three planes. It wasn't until the government deregulated the airline industry in 1978 that the Southwest brand began to really take off. In response to the new freedom in the industry, many airlines tried to rapidly expand into new markets. But as a result, they spread themselves too thin, quickly going bankrupt. Southwest, however, knew that long-term growth would require a different approach.

Many of the practices Southwest adopted were completely foreign to typical airline operations. It seemed that everything Southwest did was different. For instance, the company was militant about having planes spend as little time on the ground as possible, often landing, deboarding, cleaning, and reboarding planes within twenty minutes. They used only one type of aircraft, the Boeing 737, so that all maintenance and parts would be identical from plane to plane. To cut costs, the airline offered no meals and hired no additional cleaning crews, often tasking copilots with cleaning planes between flights. Southwest did not operate out of a hub airport but flew simple routes directly between locations. As a result, their profit margins quickly became higher than those of other airlines in the same market. This strategy is the basis of what has made Southwest profitable for forty-six years in a row. Airline owners from Canada, the UK, Norway, Malaysia, and Australia have visited Southwest's offices in Dallas to learn the unique tactics that have elevated this airline. In an industry where seasonality, oil prices, or a collapsing economy can kill an airline, it's astounding that Southwest has stood the test of time.

Like Southwest, the rental property investor seeking to scale up and dynamically grow his or her business will need to adopt some unique practices, many of which might seem foreign or counterintuitive. I won't sugarcoat this. Longevity in rental property investing is not easy. It takes hard work and the expenditure of a lot of energy to stay profitable. I know many people who can successfully operate one or two properties but who struggle to upgrade to a larger portfolio. Many would-be investors tire quickly after managing only a single property for a few years. If you want to remain a rental property investor for years to come, supplementing or supplanting your income, then you need to be adaptable, attentive, and agile. The lessons you've learned so far will help you get from zero properties to your first, second, and third rental property investments. In the next two chapters I will walk you through the steps that are essential to making the transition from one to ten, twenty, or even a hundred properties.

The following lessons are to be applied *now*, not at some point in the future. Actions like employing property managers and establishing a legal entity can, and should, be done on day one. In this way, you're already preparing for a healthy, enduring future of rental property investing, even before you make your first offer.

Professional Property Managers

When you began your journey as a rental property investor, was it your hope that tenants would call you frequently to complain about one thing or another? Did you plan to drop everything at a moment's notice to fix a leaky pipe? Were you excited about losing your weekends to showings of your vacant property? I doubt it. Your plan, much like that of many other rental property owners, is probably to create a long-lasting, sustainable, and (nearly) passive income. But that dream of a passive income fades away every time you answer another tenant's call, screen applications, or physically collect rent checks. The only way to move toward the goal you have set for yourself is to hire a professional property manager, a service that cares for the daily, weekly, and monthly tasks of operating a successful rental property.

Why might a professional property manager be so important to your investment future? There comes a point when managing your own properties becomes impractical, possibly even costing you money. As an investor, you have a limited supply of time and energy. With just one property, it seems completely feasible to manage the daily operations while also searching for your next deal (see the first image in figure 61). But once you own many more rental properties, your ability to divide your time rapidly diminishes. Self-management as a sustainable investment model has a ceiling, preventing you from scaling up and operating more properties.

fig. 61

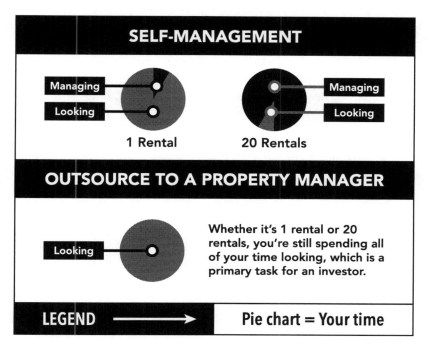

The divisions of your time with both self-managed and professionally managed properties

A property manager, of course, doesn't work for free, a fact that discourages some investors from hiring one. But look at what you get in return. You get time, which is one of your most precious assets and in many cases well worth a property manager's fee.

Q: How can you maximize your limited time for the highest returns?

The best use of your energy is to keep looking for the next investment. This is the trade-off that makes hiring property managers worth every penny, as long as you choose the right one. The property manager collects rent, communicates with tenants, performs inspections, and maintains the property. Their most important task, however, is to free up your time, allowing you to locate and analyze your next property.

The practical wisdom you gain from being your own property manager is invaluable. I can't replace that wisdom with a book. However, you are not a property manager. You are an investor. And hiring a professional property management service is a necessity for any rental property investor looking to scale up.

Q: When should you start to consider a professional property manager for your rental properties?

I get this question a lot from my students, who are eager to know the magic number of properties to own before it's appropriate to use the services of a property manager. Most people believe you have to own and operate several properties before it makes financial sense to bring on a manager, but I see no reason not to start with your first. If you're thinking that a property manager will cost too much, you may need to adapt the approach you take to buying properties.

You make your money when you buy.

Part of your underwriting assumptions when deciding to purchase a property must include the trade-off costs of hiring a professional service to manage it. You will not succeed for long if you craft your deals around your own free labor. You might be able to manage one or two properties in the beginning, but the opportunity cost of madly running through your task list will kill your ability to locate the next profitable property deal. Eventually, the costs of your own sweat equity will overwhelm your revenues and destroy your greater profitability. But all is not lost. If you can account for the costs of a property manager in your analysis, then you can plan for profitable returns while protecting your time and focusing on your next great investment.

MY TAKE

Even if you have only one property, look for a large property management service with several hundred properties on their books. It costs them very little to add one more. If you present yourself as an investor who will buy more properties in the future, they are often willing to include your property for less than what a boutique property manager would charge you.

Experience and History

One of the main reasons rental property owners turn over their properties to a professional management company is because that company has experience. For many of you, this will be your first time owning a rental property. Rather than banking on everything going right the first time, why not turn over that property to a management service with a proven history of good performance?

Professional property managers know how to find the right tenant for your property. They know how to ensure your property is making a profit. They know how to craft airtight lease agreements. They know how to manage everything from the big tasks to the little repairs. This shortcut can be an invaluable way to mitigate the risk of a first-time investment going underwater.

Keep in mind, however, that at the end of the day the property belongs to you. You bought it. You own it. You have the right to the profits it generates. So no one has a bigger stake than you do in making sure your property is managed correctly. Even experienced and reputable property management companies won't have interests that are always perfectly aligned with your own. For example, if the management company fails to find a tenant and you don't collect any rent, the company can simply write off the loss incurred by your property and focus its energies on one of the hundreds of other properties on their books. You, on the other hand, lose everything. They barely notice the dip. After hiring a great property management company, you still need to be involved in the operations. Even if it's just to a small degree, that involvement will help to ensure everything is done correctly.

Interview several companies before making your final decision. Ask to see the past performance of other properties to check for vacancy rates and tenant complaints. Speak to other landlords who have used their services in the past. Interview several companies before making your final decision. And if you do find that your management company isn't performing up to your standards, don't be afraid to let them go and find another one. If you feel that your property isn't being managed as well as you desire, it's your prerogative to find a manager who will measure up.

Hiring Property Managers to Help You Upsize Your Portfolio

As you will soon discover, managing even a single property is time-consuming. Depending on whether you have a vacancy, you could spend as little as two hours a week doing minimal paperwork or as much as fifty hours a week if you're renovating or repairing a property for the next tenant. Do you have that amount of time ready to dedicate to your investment? You might, but what happens if you add a second, a third, or an eighth property? Without a professional management company, the accumulating tasks might threaten to overwhelm you.

Having a property manager enables you to build up your portfolio in a relatively short amount of time; therefore, you would benefit by finding property managers that have the capacity to accommodate your ambition. Regardless of how many properties you have, a good management company will welcome new business and readily scale up alongside your expansion. They will continue to communicate with you, respond to your tenants in a timely fashion, and consistently provide inspection reports on your properties.

When choosing a property manager for one of my properties, I always check to see if they have other properties in my neighborhood. I prefer that my property managers do not represent neighboring properties, because I aim for undiluted advocacy and service.

While receiving complete advocacy and service is my goal, it doesn't always happen. In certain regions, property managers tend to be exceptionally large, with thousands of properties on their books. My handful of rental properties might represent just .01 percent of their total property load. And as such, these large national chain property managers are willing to afford me just .01 percent of their time. I have no sway in asking for my properties to supersede any others they manage. But, though they may not be the most personally attentive, the big players do bring several benefits to the table. I take comfort in knowing that with thousands of properties, these large operations have the requisite experience and resources to handle almost any situation, any property, and any tenant that comes under their substantial purview. I know that they can easily slot my properties into their established organizational systems, making the whole operation a smooth ride.

Nevertheless, there are also distinct advantages that come from doing business with a smaller, regional property manager. If I can bring five to ten properties to a small property manager with only a few hundred properties, my investments give me negotiating leverage. In those cases, our partnership opens doors to discussions about reduced fees, higher prioritization for filling vacancies, and more. When choosing regional property management services, I might forgo the established, streamlined, headache-free systems, but I know that my properties are being handled with a more personal, attentive touch.

Fees and Costs

Nearly everything associated with professional property management is a trade-off. You trade the cost of hiring a manager for the time saved to devote to higher-value tasks. You trade the price of services for the ability to quickly scale up to more properties. You trade the fees you must pay for the experience and network they have.

Q: In real terms, how much does a property manager actually cost?

A standard professional management company will charge an annual fee equal to one or one and a half months' rent. That's around 10 percent of your annual cash flow. It sounds steep, but remember, you need to account for these fees when you buy the property. As you pursue your negotiations and make your buying decisions, you should always keep the property management expense in mind. Property management costs have a way of appearing much more feasible to investors once they're factored into the overall path to profitability.

For instance, let's say that a property manager charges 10 percent of your rental income for their services. If you charge $1,500 in rent each month, you would pay your property manager $150 that month, or $1,800 for the year. If that $1,800 payment frees up your time to find another property that makes $6,000 in net profits, you have earned $4,200 more that year

($6,000 - $1,800). It would be in your best interests to happily pay that 10 percent fee because it enables you to increase your profits.

Make sure your property managers are charging fees based on actual rents collected, not pro forma rents. ***Pro forma rent*** is the money your property could potentially make, so even if it sits vacant, you still get charged. Unfortunately, I see many newbie investors getting lured into bad deals like these.

Management companies also offer bulk discounts, meaning that the more properties you have under their management, the cheaper it is for you. While most property managers base their fee structure on rent collected, they make money in other ways as well. For example, some management companies charge an up-front leasing fee every time the property is rented to a new tenant. This fee can be the equivalent of a month's rent, which can be devastating. If you operate a rental property in a college town with high turnover every year, this "one-time" leasing fee can quickly eat into your profit margins. Always read the fine print carefully before signing on the dotted line with any service. Here are a few other fees to keep in mind as you search for your ideal property management company (figure 62).

fig. 62

FEE	HOW IT'S CALCULATED	WHEN IT'S APPLICABLE	PAYMENT FREQUENCY
Management Fee	Percentage of rent	Receiving rent from tenant	Monthly
Leasing Fee	Flat fee	Upon signing the lease agreement	Once (per each new lease)
Advertising Fee	Flat fee	While vacant	Monthly
Lease Renewal Fee	Flat fee	Upon lease agreement renewal	Yearly
Setup Fee	Flat fee	When creating account with company	Once
Vacancy Fee	Flat fee	While no rent collected	Monthly
Eviction Fee	Flat fee	If tenant is evicted	Once (per eviction)
Early Termination Fee	Remaining contract balance	If ending contract early	Once
Nonresident Fee	Flat fee	Payable if investing outside of the country	Monthly

Some common fee structures for property managers

If it makes financial sense, a property manager can be worth every penny you pay. However, without your due diligence, management fees can quickly make a tight profit margin evaporate into thin air.

Turnkey Providers

Turnkey providers are quickly becoming a popular option as a professional property management service for long-distance investors. Turnkey providers handle the market analysis for a busy investor. They locate and analyze dozens of potential properties and offer a complete management service, from renovations to tenants to rent collection. The selling point for these turnkey providers is that you simply need to turn the key to get in, and they will handle the rest. Sounds like a good deal, and it can be.

For investors who want to find profitable properties across the country, the lure of the turnkey provider saves them an enormous amount of time. As long as you know the market, these providers can offer lucrative investments. Many of my students have successfully used turnkey providers to their benefit.

However, these deals can, and often do, go wrong. The immediate problem is that turnkey providers prey on inexperienced investors. For example, if you live in a coastal city, the prices of properties inland can seem cheap. A turnkey provider might advertise inland properties with prices that are well below what you as a first-time investor are used to seeing in your coastal neighborhood. But as you'll remember from chapter 7, a property does not exist as an island. Every property price must be compared against the backdrop of the market where it sits. A three-bedroom home for $150,000 might sound cheap to you as a San Francisco resident, where house values regularly exceed $1,000,000. But if that house is in a market where three-bedroom homes are valued at $90,000, it's a bad deal!

There are many, many less-than-reputable turnkey providers who unwittingly (or knowingly) don't provide enough context for the property they are advertising. The pictures on the website might look nice, but they fail to include the dilapidated properties down the road. Properties often get "overrepresented," appearing to have more value than they actually do, making it easy for you to get suckered into a deal that isn't worth what you initially thought it was.

If you find yourself intrigued by a prospective turnkey deal, proceed with caution. Get an independent inspection done and make sure you get a complete report. Compare that turnkey deal to other comps in the market. Check vacancy rates and rental prices in the neighborhood. Do the math on expected returns. I have faith that with the analysis tools I've provided for you already, you can spot the pitfall properties and avoid the bad deals.

From Hobby to Business

The ABC TV show *Shark Tank* gives aspiring entrepreneurs the opportunity to pitch their business to wealthy experienced investors, the "Sharks." The entrepreneurs are offering a percentage of their startup in exchange for cash. These businesses come in all shapes and sizes and have varying degrees of success before their owners ever set foot in front of the Sharks. Throughout the pitch, investors pepper the people seeking cash with questions about their track record, their target audience, their projections, and their performance. There is one sure way to lose a deal with the Sharks: if the investors find out that an entrepreneur hasn't been completely committed to working on their business, then they run—er, swim—the other way. If the entrepreneurs treat their cupcake shop, their woodworking tool kit, or their smoked rib sauce company like a hobby to be pursued in their spare time, the Sharks lose interest.

Why do these experienced investors sniff out hobbyists and leave them high and dry? They want to know that their potential business partner has the hunger, the drive, to succeed. They trust the ambition of a committed business owner more than someone who works part time on their dreams. The Sharks also know that people who think of their endeavor as a business, not just a time-filling hobby, will likely see greater success in the future.

As you'll discover, rental properties are time-intensive and will demand much of your money and energy when you're getting started. Success will be found by those who adopt the mentality of the business owner. The business owner understands where the money is coming in and where it's going out and must make the adjustments necessary to maximize profits.

Operating your rental properties through a formal business entity can afford you certain protections and freedoms. It might not sound like a whole lot of fun to set up an LLC (*limited liability company*) and meticulously track income and expenditures, save your receipts, file your taxes, etc., but the payoffs are substantial.

A lot of new rental property investors make the mistake of adopting the following attitude: *I'm going to wait until I get some momentum and money coming in, and then I'll set up my LLC and make it official.* My advice is that you should take these measures immediately; set up a formal business entity even before you make your first investment.

Creating an LLC

The most commonly used business structure for a rental property owner is a limited liability company (LLC). An LLC is a simple legal entity that shelters your personal assets from the operations of your business. Unfortunately, we live in a litigious society with no deterrents against frivolous lawsuits. You should prepare for the reality that you will face a lawsuit at one point or another in your investing career. You can be sued by tenants, business partners, former homeowners ... the list goes on. If you want to protect your personal assets such as your home, your salary, and your vehicle from lawsuits, then setting up an LLC is the way to go. If you are sued, the LLC, not you, is named in the lawsuit, and it is the LLC's assets, not your personal assets, that are subject to seizure.

Consider the following scenario. A tenant in an apartment leaves her bedroom window open on a 15-degree day, and the cold wind coming in causes the radiator pipe to burst. The burst pipe kills the tenant's two pets, who were locked in the room. Subsequently, the tenant files a lawsuit against the landlord seeking $25,000 in recompense for the loss of her cat and dog. The landlord barely escapes having to pay the damages claim, and only because he's able to prove the negligence of the tenant. Since the landlord was operating as a sole proprietor (not as an LLC), had he been unable to prove negligence, he may have been personally liable for the damages claimed.

Q: If you operate your investments under an LLC, does that mean you pay corporate tax on your profits?

Fair question, but no. The significant tax advantages of an LLC allow you to claim all income on your personal tax returns. This tax advantage enables you to escape double taxation of your profits—the profit you make from your investment under an LLC is not subject to corporate taxation. It's simply reported (and therefore taxed) as your personal income. But because you will be asked to provide accurate records to claim these tax benefits, be diligent about keeping LLC and personal expenditures separate.

When established with the help of an experienced lawyer and adhering to all corporate formalities, a dutifully created LLC can be a very valuable tool, but it does not come with an ironclad guarantee of personal asset protection. There are occasions when a poorly insured LLC, or even negligent or criminal actions, ultimately expose the personal liability of the owners behind the LLC shell. This, in legalese, is known as "piercing the corporate veil." Typically, this happens when an LLC is used as a holding company for a property investment but does not have the proper landlord insurance. It can also occur if the LLC doesn't make repairs or address safety issues in the property. In those circumstances, the LLC may not provide the corporate shield necessary to protect your personal assets from liability.

MY TAKE

Because LLCs operate differently from state to state, it might be worth it to consider setting up an LLC outside of your home state. Ask your lawyer to help you establish an LLC in Wyoming, Delaware, or Nevada. These states have excellent privacy laws and landlord-friendly tax laws.

Although it might not be on your short-term horizon, in the future you may consider taking on investing partners. Having an LLC can help with that, too. Ownership of an LLC is easily modified. There is much less hassle in adding a partner to an LLC than in splitting up ownership when you've started as a sole proprietorship.

Automating the Process

In the year 2000, Howard Schultz stepped down from his role as chief executive officer of Starbucks. Under his leadership, the famous coffee brand had flourished. And under new leadership, Starbucks shifted its focus toward aggressively rapid expansion. A large part of the strategy was to speed up the customer experience by installing automatic espresso machines, removing the handmade coffee experience that took too much time. Over the course of just seven years, the number of stores more than quadrupled, to 15,000 locations around the globe. At its peak, Starbucks was opening a brand-new store somewhere in the world every three hours. During this time, revenue jumped from $2 billion to $9.4 billion.

But then the global financial crisis hit in 2007. People suddenly found that a four-dollar latte was a luxury they didn't want to pay for. Sales became stagnant. Starbucks was struggling, losing 50 percent of its stock price as a result. They rehired Howard Schultz as the CEO. He released a memo about the direction of the company, which said in part, "In order to achieve the growth, development, and scale necessary . . . we have watered down the Starbucks experience. When we went to automatic espresso machines, we solved the problem of speed and efficiency, but we overlooked . . . the romance and theatre that was in play." Schultz had the automatic espresso machines removed, reminding the Starbucks board and the world that, at its heart, Starbucks is still about the experience of a handmade coffee. This decision may have slowed down the transactions, but it brought back the glamour of making coffee that was Schultz's inspiration for the brand all those years ago.

Although Howard Schultz didn't particularly like the idea, even he couldn't deny that automation had paved the way for Starbucks' rapid expansion and growth in profit. Though it came, in Schultz's view, at the expense of the brand's ambience, automation removed human error and improved the speed of the transaction. It streamlined business and prompted incredible expansion around the world. I doubt that dense global expansion is your immediate goal as a rental property investor, but even with more modest objectives—perhaps your goal is to acquire and run three profitable properties within five years' time—you'll find that, unlike with Starbucks, automation *is* your friend.

Q: How do you identify the parts of your business that are primed for automation?

The answer is to look for any aspect of your business where your touch is not adding value and/or is increasing costs, uncertainty, or risk. Consider, for example, the payment of bills and the collection of rents. Why take the chance that a busy investor like you might forget to pay a bill on time? By automating your bill payments, you remove that risk. Similarly, you can ask your tenants to pay rent with automated clearing house (ACH) transactions or other online payment systems. This removes the uncertainty of mailed checks getting lost or delayed.

Also, consider using a template for all your communications. From late payment reminders to automatic lease renewals, the template keeps all your language consistent and professional no matter how many properties you operate.

As technology rapidly improves, so does your ability to outsource various processes and procedures of your rental investment. Here are a few more considerations for automating investing tasks:

- » **Market research**: Tools and websites like PropStream automatically scour for and identify properties that are suitable for investments. You can set up filters and receive alerts when any listed property goes online in your selected markets.

- » **Tenant relations**: Apps like Tellus make rent collection and tenant communications even easier, streamlining all the work for you.

- » **Applications**: Using simple Google Forms software, you can automatically screen tenants as they apply for your vacant rental positions.

- » **Repairs and maintenance**: Services like UpKeep automatically remind you of upcoming scheduled maintenance and generate work orders for contractors doing repairs on the property.

- » **Time management**: There are a number of apps and sites, such as Calendly, that can schedule showings, coordinate calls, and arrange all your meetings.

- » **Financials**: Free apps like Stessa, designed for rental property management, can make financial tracking easy.

Achieving Financial Freedom

Let's return to one of my favorite guilty-pleasure television shows, *Shark Tank*. If you have even an oblique knowledge of the show, then you are familiar with the persona of Mr. Wonderful, aka Kevin O'Leary. In an article on Business Insider, Kevin talked about a formative experience in his early years. When he was just a teenager, he got a job at an ice cream shop in a mall near his home. On his first day of work, he quickly learned how to talk to customers and serve ice cream, and he generally enjoyed himself. But on day two, his manager asked him to clean the floor. He was taken aback by the manager's request.

"Kevin, I need you to scrape that gum off the floor before our next customers come in," the manager repeated. Burning with indignation, Kevin stood his ground and refused to do so, claiming his job was to serve ice cream, not to scrape someone else's gum off the ground. And as you can imagine, Kevin was promptly fired and asked to leave the store for good. His eyes brimmed with tears as he pedaled his bike home, furious that someone had been able to speak to him that way. From that day forward, Kevin vowed that no one would ever hold that kind of power over him, which is what eventually steered him down the path to becoming a wealthy, independent business owner and TV personality. This would be how he defined personal freedom: the ability to say no to whoever and whatever he was asked to do. As long as he retained that freedom, he knew he was successful.

Q: What does freedom look like to you?

Before you embark on your journey to become a rental property investor, you must ask yourself what you want to achieve. What are your goals? How do you define personal freedom? Once you know this, it will help you with the next question I'm about to pose.

We've talked about the "how" of achieving passive income, but many of my students want to know "how many." How many properties will it take until I can quit my job (or replace my income, or retire with security)? The answer is "it depends." You need to know what *you* define as success in order to know how many properties it will take to reach it. Maybe your own personal financial goal is to have just what you need to live on. Maybe you're replacing your nine-to-five job. You may seek to reach new levels of wealth. Or you may want only to cultivate a modest but reliable source of income for the next forty years. Don't be unduly swayed by how many properties other investors have in their portfolios. Your desired personal freedom determines the number of investment properties it will take to achieve your personal benchmark of success.

I have created a calculator that will help you determine how many rental properties you should operate in order to meet your financial goals. You can get your copy of the Rental Calculator for Up to 10 Rentals in your Digital Asset Vault at **www.clydebankmedia.com/rental-assets**.

Chapter Recap

» There are actions you can take before investing in your first property that will increase your chances of maintaining the practice of rental property investing for the long term.

» If you want to grow and maintain a thriving portfolio of properties, you must employ a professional property manager.

» Account for the costs of a property manager before you buy a property. If you do, you can turn over even your first property to a management service and still remain profitable.

» Be cautious of turnkey providers who claim to offer a complete package without providing sufficient context for the deal. Always conduct your own analysis on any deal offered.

» A legal entity such as an LLC shelters you from lawsuits and offers significant tax advantages. Begin operating your rental property endeavor as a business from day one.

| 13 |
Long-Term Rental Income

If you can meet with Triumph and Disaster, and treat those two impostors just the same ...

— RUDYARD KIPLING

If you look at a map, you'll see that the nation of Bangladesh is one big delta of the Brahmaputra River. This enormous river circles southward around the Himalayan mountains before it reaches the flatlands of Bangladesh and empties out into the Bay of Bengal. Because of this massive delta, Bangladesh is one of the nations most affected by climate change, with erosion, floods, and storms often leaving millions of people stranded and displaced. Farmers in the area have responded by altering the way they do business. At one point, these paddy farmers earned a living by raising thousands of chickens. Now, those same farmers throughout the interior are raising ducks rather than chickens. Why? Because ducks can swim.

When any part of Bangladesh's upriver region receives more than the expected amount of rainfall, the flatlands in Bangladesh get a deluge of water, flooding out the chicken farms and killing the farmers' investments. But in the duck trade, flood waters are a boon to the flock. Despite the yearly floods, a farmer knows that he can still make a living from his ducks. And as a result of this transition, a growing number of restaurants and cafes in Dhaka have started serving duck as their featured dish. Duck has even replaced chicken as a favorite Bengali meal. This ability to adapt from chickens to ducks has meant that hundreds of thousands of poor farmers can withstand the floods of the future. They are hedging their bets on ducks, and that bet is paying off in the long term.

In my opinion, rental property investors can learn from these Bengali duck farmers. Calamities will happen. Things will go wrong. Economies will crash. You can choose to move forward, hoping to survive. Or you can adapt to the changing times, targeting your efforts toward rental properties that can withstand calamities. If you want to future-proof your plans to earn a rental income, you need to consciously invest in properties that safeguard you from the expected bumps in the road. Noah built his ark before it was even raining. As an investor, you need to prepare for a future economic collapse and have a plan in place for when (not if) that reality occurs. Through diversified portfolios, good insurance policies, and avoidance of overleveraging, you can safely remain profitable throughout the lifetime of your investments.

Building a Resilient Portfolio

Even though I invest in some commercial properties, my first choice is residential real estate. I am convinced that savvy investors can create wealth and sustain their incomes—even in the hard times—with residential properties. Consider a comparison between residential properties and other common real estate investments, namely, agricultural and commercial properties. The value of the residential real estate market looms over these other types of assets by a five to one margin (see figure 63). That higher total market value correlates with a much higher volume of properties available to purchase, which means more options for investors.

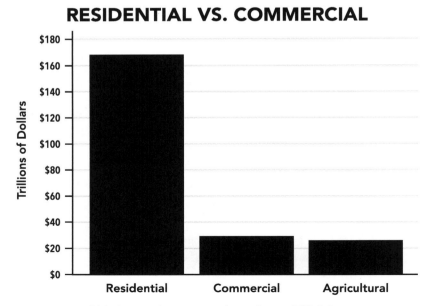

GRAPHIC

fig. 63

RESIDENTIAL VS. COMMERCIAL

Global asset values, measured in trillions of US dollars

With residential rental properties as the backbone of your investment portfolio, you can endure the bumps and dips of any economic condition. Many real estate investors share the dream of building and owning the next billion-dollar skyscraper in New York or San Francisco. While that sounds appealing, the reality is that residential rental properties, in the right proportions and markets, can create a more resilient portfolio than a huge office building.

I know many investors who sing the praises of mixed-use properties, buildings that have both residential and commercial purposes, like downtown apartment complexes with some shops or office space on the ground floor. These properties are commonly seen as resilient investments. They generate profits by combining the need for housing with the needs of commercial space, but a mixed-use property is still not as resilient as a wisely curated portfolio of residential rental properties.

Resilience isn't a defense when things go wrong. It's an offensive strategy that plans and prepares for any outcome. If everything works out, fantastic. But if the economy faces a rough patch, then it is your resilience that will help you weather the storm and still come out profitable. The key to resilience is **diversification**. This is Investing 101. A diverse portfolio of rental properties allows you to be agile, to mitigate and manage risk, and to deliver consistent results no matter the external conditions. Diversification with rental properties occurs on two fronts. You need to have properties in several markets and of several types. Let's discuss a few practical ways to build a resilient portfolio from the very onset of your investing journey.

Buying in Multiple Markets

There is a curious anomaly in marketing known as a "harbinger zip code." The term refers to a neighborhood, town, or county where typical buying patterns do not apply. In fact, the differences between people living in these harbinger areas and those in neighboring zip codes is so stark that it's possible to predict the success or failure of a new product based on how residents in the harbinger zip codes react. One study analyzed the purchasing patterns of failed products like Crystal Pepsi, Cheetos lip balm, and Watermelon Oreos. A remarkable motif emerged, showing that if certain products did well in harbinger zip codes, they were doomed from the start. The more of these products this subgroup of consumers purchased, the higher the likelihood that they would perform horribly nationwide. Harbinger zip codes have also been used to determine how successful a political candidate will be on the national stage. When candidates receive disproportionately large numbers of donations from residents of harbinger zip codes, their chances of winning the election drop dramatically. In addition to new-issue consumer products and political candidates, property values in these neighborhoods were shown to perform anomalously below the national rate of appreciation.

There are vast differences in market conditions, varying even from neighborhood to neighborhood, as the harbinger zip code study shows. Where you buy your rental property counts. As we discussed in chapter 3, real estate cycles throughout the country don't move at the same pace. The cycle for coastal cities is delayed by twelve to eighteen months in the inland markets. But as a rental property investor, you can use this variance between markets to your advantage, hedging your portfolio and offsetting the performance of one market with the performance of another. Let's use the Case-Shiller data of four unique metropolitan markets to demonstrate the point (figure 64):

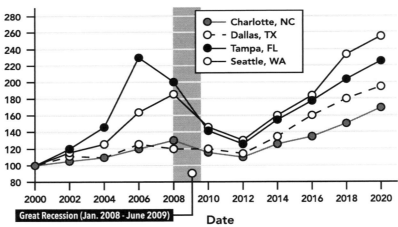

DIFFERENT STROKES FOR DIFFERENT METROPOLITAN MARKETS
Index Jan 2000 = 100

fig. 64

Source: Federal Reserve Economic Data

Four of the markets used in the Case-Shiller Home Price Index

Imagine it's the year 2004. Everyone is quoting the new movie *Anchorman*. *Mr. Brightside* has been playing nonstop on the radio. We're all watching newcomer Michael Phelps win six gold Olympic medals in swimming in Greece. And you have just bought four single-family three-bedroom homes as rental property investments, one each in Tampa, Charlotte, Seattle, and Dallas.

You don't know it yet, but the looming global financial crisis is going to test the resiliency of your portfolio to its limit. At first, you're a bit disheartened by the performance in Dallas. Rent hasn't changed much in the last five years, and house values haven't done well, at least not as well as in Tampa, where your property seems to increase in value every day. You are easily outperforming your rental return projections in this hot Florida market. Maybe you should buy another Tampa home? Charlotte and Seattle make modest returns and provide consistent income, helping to balance out your portfolio.

Just four years later, it's a different story. Florida, which was hit hardest in the 2008 recession, sees property values plummet. All those gains you made over the last four years in Tampa are wiped out, and you have to lower rents to keep the tenants you've got. You thank your lucky stars that you hadn't yet generated enough capital to buy a second home there. Home values in Seattle and Charlotte also drop, but not as severely as in Tampa. Surprisingly, your Dallas property continues to churn out a consistent income. Property values don't decline as dramatically there, and your rent returns prove to hold steady.

Over the next ten years, your portfolio's performance continues to improve. Seattle and Charlotte, although on opposite sides of the country, show promising growth. You have long-term tenants who are happy with a gentle rent increase in line with property value rises. Tampa's recovery is slower at first, but who doesn't want to live in Tampa? Your rent quickly recovers to pre-recession levels, and you show strong growth in appreciated value. Dallas, however, is in a league of its own. Through a combination of factors, Dallas hits a growth spurt and people flock to live in the city. You outperform your rental return projections, more than making up for any losses incurred from your other investments. In fact, the returns have spurred you to buy another two properties in Dallas, capitalizing on the growth rate and surge of tenants in the area.

Although this example is fictitious, the numbers are not. You can see the dramatic changes as different markets react to the same economic conditions. Some properties are hit hard while others simply hit a bump in the road. And then, some properties temper their recoveries while others shoot up dramatically in value. In the example, your rent in pre-recession Tampa covers your lack of rent increases in Dallas. Post-recession, the pattern is reversed. Dallas performs very well, with rent returns that make up for the slow recovery of Tampa's housing values.

Practically, you diversify your portfolio not only in different cities but in different neighborhoods as well. As an example, you can hedge your investments by buying properties in blue-collar working-class neighborhoods while also buying properties in more white-collar areas. White-collar and blue-collar job markets rarely react in equal measure to the same economic forces. Depending on the nature of the economic factors in play, times of change will often bring about winners and losers. It is therefore wise to diversify your property investments to include both white- and blue-collar neighborhoods—one to provide more resiliency for your portfolio and the other to provide more profit potential.

During the COVID-19 lockdowns, job numbers changed dramatically. Low-income workers without the option to work from home lost their jobs by the tens of millions, while many white-collar workers had the luxury of working remotely. Landlords felt the pinch as well, with several regions extending eviction bans that lasted for months. In times like this, a portfolio with rental properties in blue-collar areas would suffer, and rental properties in white-collar markets would be more resilient.

Multiple Asset Types in a Residential Real Estate Portfolio

In the previous section, I used the Case-Shiller Home Price Index to illustrate the power of investing in different markets. The strength of that index as a guide for investors is due to its reliance on one asset type: the single-family home. But within the residential real estate market, single-family homes aren't the only option. In a large residential real estate portfolio, you should aim to have several different rental asset types to further diversify your investments.

Part of the diversification strategy is covering your bases, making sure that in the event of a catastrophic failure you aren't left underwater with your rental properties. Part of your strategy is also to make some assumptions about the future. In your area, will residential housing trends change over time? Will there be an increase in inner-city living? Will the shifting market move people out into the suburbs? Will emerging job markets see an influx of families looking for single-family homes? These are the kinds of hedges that shelter your portfolio throughout its lifetime.

Although time will eventually prove me right or wrong, I am making some assumptions about how people will react to the COVID-19 pandemic and its aftermath. I believe that lower- and middle-income groups will trade down in their living arrangements, choosing smaller homes with less square footage, renting cheaper alternatives in less expensive neighborhoods, or living in larger, often multigenerational households. With increased job and income insecurity due to the economic fallout from the pandemic, it's impractical for many to continue paying more to live in large homes with empty rooms.

I believe part of the response to this shift will be an increase in density, with many cities and states relaxing restrictions on accessory dwelling units (ADUs). ADUs are small additional dwelling units built within an existing property that weren't, by design, intended to be rented out for residential use. If you convert and rent out your garage, basement, or an add-on unit on your property, it's considered an ADU. Once the rules surrounding these secondary suites are loosened, opportunistic investors can capitalize by looking for properties on large plots in supply-constrained markets with the goal of adding on ADUs. This move can dramatically increase the profitability of a given plot of land, because ADUs can command higher rent in relation to the cost to build them than traditional units can.

At the same time, however, high-income earners may do just the opposite and move out of urban centers for more space in rural neighborhoods, especially if we see a permanent shift toward remote work. As such, I would advise that you include larger properties in rural/suburban markets as well as smaller properties in dense urban markets as a part of your diversification plan. As I've mentioned, single-family homes can be a solid start for the early investor, but for the long run, including different-sized properties in the right markets for the right audiences can increase the overall resilience of your portfolio.

People who invest exclusively in shared accommodations in college towns have typically had good returns. That is, until the lockdown pushed all learning online. In many locations, student housing has been left vacant as entire student bodies are pursuing their degrees remotely, without the need to be on campus. Many investors who primarily hold these shared accommodation properties in college towns have been left high and dry. A similar story applies to tourism-driven short-term rental markets.

Generating a Thriving Rental Income

Many investors, even those investing outside of the real estate asset class, put too much emphasis on portfolio size and net worth rather than on income. Let me ask you a question: would you rather have a $1 million stock portfolio or $100,000 in rental income every year? The answer is not immediately intuitive. Many would take the big portfolio without a second thought. But that portfolio is more susceptible to market volatility, and if you have no other source of income, you'll draw it down to zero within twenty years. But with rental properties generating consistent rental income, you'll live off your rent rather than selling off your properties to pay your expenses. To achieve the same level of income security with a $100,000-per-year spend rate from a stock portfolio alone, you would need at least $2.5 million, assuming a 4 percent drawdown. Although your rental properties may also lose value in an economic downturn, people still, through good times and bad, need a place to live, and most will continue to pay their rent. One's net worth can crash alongside the economy, asset prices can be volatile, but long-term rental income security, I find, is the best hedge and insurance against an unpredictable economy.

In her book *The Biggest Bluff*, Maria Konnikova, a writer and psychologist, tells the amazing story of her journey from never having played poker to winning over $300,000 in a year as a professional poker player. To accomplish this feat, Maria teamed up with poker legend Erik Seidel, who has been a professional poker player for nearly forty years. At one point in the book, Maria tells the story of her first experience playing a live game. Her hand was exceptional, but another player at the table lucked out and beat her, kicking her out of the tournament in which she was playing. When she told Seidel about the losing hand, his reaction astounded her.

"Are you asking me what you should have done?" he probed.

"No, I played my cards right," said Maria. "But with my set of—"

"Stop, I don't want to hear it."

Seidel then chastised Maria, saying that every poker player in the world will tell you about the time they lost big with the best hand. That isn't what he wanted her to do. Poker is part skill and part luck. You can't focus on the luck, said Seidel. Doing that makes you the victim, because luck happens to you.

"Whenever you tell me about a hand," Seidel explained, "I don't want you to tell me the result at all. I only want to hear about your strategy. That way, you are focused on what *you* can control, the skill of your game, not the luck of the draw."

To continue the analogy, poker players use a term to describe the ups and downs of a poker game: variance. Variance is deviation from the expected results. Poker, much like rental real estate, is not a guarantee. There are externalities, elements outside of your control that affect your returns. The distinguishing mark of a professional poker player is choosing a profitable, smart game plan and executing it with consistency despite the wild swings of the game. When bad beats (losses) happen, when opponents luck out even when the odds were in their favor, the pros maintain a consistent strategy that they know, over the long term, will eventually win. If you look at a typical poker player's winnings, as exhibited in figure 65, you'll see that the path to success is not a straight line but full of ups and downs. Big wins are soon followed by steep losses. Instead of reacting to the bad times, the professional poker player continues making the plays they know will eventually earn them the big bucks. Substitute "poker player" with "basketball player," "boxer," or "rental property investor" and you'll see virtually no difference in the outcome in their respective fields.

GRAPHIC

fig. 65

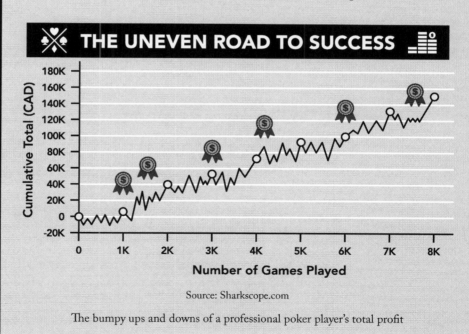

Source: Sharkscope.com

The bumpy ups and downs of a professional poker player's total profit

Erik Seidel's advice, while geared toward playing cards, is sound. There are forces in the economy and the real estate market that are beyond your control. There are countless examples of investors who will tell you about their bad properties, their horror stories, their lost investments. These investors will rant to you about their bad breaks, about what happened to them. They play the victim. They focus on external forces beyond their control, and it makes for a riveting story. But that's not your story. Your job is to focus on what *you* can control, the internal forces within your investment. Focus your energy on your actions, so that when those external forces happen, you can play with the right strategy.

Adding Value to Your Properties

The idea of adding value to your property should not be an afterthought but part of your plan from the beginning. One way to ensure a sustainable income is to add more value to your property (and therefore earn higher rent). Let's take a look at some actions you can take to achieve that.

» **Increase desirability**: Short of buying and bulldozing every single home in a neighborhood, I can't affect the economic demand for my own property there. But I can take small yet meaningful steps to improve the desirability of the property. How I choose to advertise makes a big difference in who applies for my vacancy. If my area is rich with other rental options, I can increase the desirability of my property with incentives, such as waiving the security deposit or partnering with a local landscaping company to offer free lawn mowing services.

» **Decrease expenses**: The equation for calculating profit is simple. Your income less your expenses is the value you get out of a property. Therefore, if you can decrease your expenses, your net profit will increase. Some suggestions would be negotiating cheaper professional property management fees, buying newer properties to cut down on maintenance costs, or refinancing your property for lower debt service repayments.

» **Make improvements**: If you buy a property at a discount, often the reason for that discount is that the property doesn't meet the same standards as other properties in the area. Making renovations to bring it up to current standards can drastically add to its value. A common strategy is to buy a property that is smaller than comparable properties and add more square footage. If you can add a second floor to the home or even just enlarge the kitchen, the value of the property shoots up. Higher value then translates into higher rent for you.

Building Up Reserves

After the oil crisis of 1973, the US government decided it would never again allow an oil embargo to threaten the economy. The Department of Energy built what would become the world's largest emergency oil reserve, the Strategic Petroleum Reserve. Massive underground tanks were installed deep below Texas and Louisiana, with the capacity for almost 800 million barrels of petroleum. This emergency reserve is ready to deploy in regions affected by floods, hurricanes, or any other catastrophe that disrupts normal distribution channels. Although the reserve is designed to cover temporary needs of a region, there is enough fuel in these tanks to meet the entire country's oil needs for several weeks.

The US controls 2.9 percent of the world's oil, with fifty billion barrels still untapped, placing this country ninth on the list of the world's oil producers. Even with all that local oil production, it was still necessary for the government to create a reserve, an emergency supply to assure availability. I don't say this often, but I'll say it now: I think the US government model is worth replicating. Rental property investors should build up a reserve of cash to have on hand in the event of an emergency. Even if your rental returns are high, your cash reserves protect you from an emergency that could quickly deplete your income.

Healthy cash reserves help with more than just buffering your income. They can also prevent you and your property from becoming bogged down by unexpected big expenses. A leaky roof, for example, will cost you thousands to repair. You don't want your property to remain uninhabitable while you scramble to find the cash to make necessary repairs.

A Texan rental property investor was forced to evict his tenant. The eviction was slow, dragging out for three months before the court had the tenant removed. That was three months without rent, and the landlord had to pay the loan repayment costs out of pocket. On top of that, the property had to be renovated and cleaned to make it suitable to rent again, costing another month in lost income. Without the cash reserves to cover these costs, this investor would have been thousands of dollars in debt.

How much cash should you have? It depends on your portfolio. How old is the property? How many properties do you have? What are your future projects going to cost? Let's say you have one older property that you know will require some maintenance. You would be wise to set aside 15 percent of your monthly rent as a reserve for that eventuality. However, if you own several properties, you don't need that same 15 percent for each one, especially if some are newer. For one thing, it's not likely that all your rentals will require emergency funding at once. And one of the advantages of scaling up your portfolio is that you can "borrow" the emergency reserve from one property to cover any costs from another.

I save a portion of my rent checks every month to build up reserves. My goal is to have six months' worth of expenses for each property. I have seen different figures from different investors, but as for me, I prefer having a suitable cushion if the world begins to cave in around me.

Chapter Recap

» Dig your well before you're thirsty. Take action now that will prepare you to weather the inevitable bumps and dips of your rental income.

» Limiting risk to your investment portfolio always means diversifying what you hold.

» Buy investment properties in several markets that respond differently to economic conditions. Hedge with different types of properties (assets) that react differently to economic forces.

» To improve your income in the long term, add value to your property and increase its desirability.

» Don't depend on a large income to protect you from catastrophic collapse. Build up cash reserves and establish an emergency fund for each property you own.

Conclusion

For me, rental property checks all the boxes on my list of requirements for an ideal long-term investment strategy. It is also, relatively speaking, easier than many other wealth-building pursuits. Throughout my fifteen-year history of real estate investing, I have become more convinced than ever that generating wealth and finding financial freedom through rental properties is achievable for nearly everyone.

I ask myself the same questions whenever I consider any investment opportunity:

» What are the most accessible ways in which I can create wealth?
» How can my investments earn stronger returns sooner?
» How do I maintain control over my investments?
» How do I create income stability in a world that is anything but stable?

Some real estate investments favor long-term forecasts. Perhaps you buy land and hold on to it for years, hoping that market conditions will allow you to sell it for a profit in a decade. Other real estate investments favor short-term returns. Fix-and-flip properties can be lucrative investments, but they only provide a one-time profit windfall. You earn a sizable return quickly, but it's not long before you have to find your next suitable fix-and-flip property. Rental property investments have features of both worlds. Rental properties appreciate in value over time while also providing sustainable income on an ongoing basis. By learning and pursuing this endeavor, you are putting yourself in a position to be paid both now and later; how fun!

For those intent on building wealth through investing, the paths before you are many. From cryptocurrencies to startups to the stock market, the aspiring entrepreneur will not lack for options. It's obvious by now that I'm both a staunch advocate and an avid practitioner of rental property investing. And I do wonder sometimes how I came to be involved with real estate as opposed to pursuing other financial routes. At the end of the day, I think that, for me, and probably for a lot of investor entrepreneurs, rental real estate is accessible, simple, and a proven way to build wealth.

Looking Ahead

If you look back over the last fifteen years, it becomes clear that no one can predict the future of the real estate market. Economic depressions, global pandemics, and unforeseen downturns have all wreaked havoc on the tidy plans of most investors. Your goal, however, is not to predict the patterns of real estate, but to be adequately prepared for what's ahead.

Risks are inevitable, but you can make your best guess about the types of risks that could affect you. As you look to the future, you can manage your own strategy and straddle the risks and opportunities that come your way. Be vigilant. Tomorrow's most profitable property investments might look nothing like today's.

What might be some of the disruptions and trends in store for the next generation of rental property investors?

» **Urbanization**: According to the majority of demographic predictions, cities will continue to grow. Large urban centers will grow at different rates, with megacities emerging in unexpected markets. Investors can seek out likely growth spots for increasing home values and rents.

» **Household composition**: As culture shifts away from an individualistic mentality, multigenerational households will become more common. This will likely lower homeownership rates as more people live in the same house.

» **Postponed adulthood**: Millennials are but the first wave of a generational shift away from homeownership and traditional families. As cities grow, these generations will look for rental properties that cater to their desire for vibrant social lives and robust employment opportunities.

» **Aging population**: What happens when the fastest-growing population sector is the sixty-five-plus community? An aging demographic has drastically different needs regarding consumption, amenities, employment, and housing size. This generation will seek out homes with access to state-of-the-art medical facilities and senior-friendly transportation and amenities.

» **Climate change**: As the world's population anxiously observes the effect climate has on their lives, the value of homes outside of danger zones will increase. Coastal cities like Miami could see mass migration as people choose to live in cities at higher elevations or with more temperate climates.

I can offer no predictions about when, or if, these disruptions might occur. I only want to prepare you as best I can with the principles in this book. I paraphrase Charles Darwin when I say the investor who is most adaptable and responsive to change is the investor who is most likely to thrive in any circumstance. I have given you every tool at my disposal to prepare you to respond to any and all shifts. Think of this book as a toolbox. The actionable knowledge and lessons contained in these chapters are your tools for the work ahead, the blueprint that will allow you to construct the financial freedom you desire. But just as owning a toolbox does not a master craftsman make, your study of the concepts presented in this book, in and of itself, does not guarantee a profitable future.

fig. 66

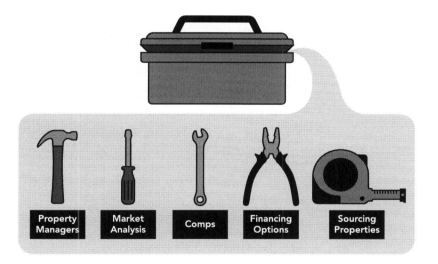

Your rental property investor toolbox. Use it wisely!

The next step is putting these lessons, these tools, into practice, and it's a step that no one can take for you. My goal in writing this book was to show you what you didn't know that you didn't know. My second goal was to give you enough information so you can decide where you want to go next. For instance, if you are now ready to find a suitable single-family rental home, I encourage you to begin the analysis process in your own town or city. Examine the data and identify key neighborhoods, beginning in your own backyard—before expanding to other regions—in search of the most profitable properties. Examine comparable properties to get a sense of prices and discounts in areas that show promise. Conduct your own "back of the envelope" analyses to determine costs and potential returns.

Next, consider how you'll finance those properties. Set aside a budget within your price range for a small property with low risk to minimize the chance of failure when you're just getting out of the gate. Remember that the goal of your first rental investment is to get you to your second rental investment. If you don't currently have the finances for your first property, look for creative options like seller financing or hard money loans.

Finally, take a step forward in the direction you want to go. You could identify and shadow an experienced rental property investor, watching how they operate and learning all you can from direct experience. You could grab a copy of my other book, *Real Estate Investing QuickStart Guide*, to gain a better grasp of other real estate investing plays beyond just rental properties. You could even invest with a partner, pooling your capital to quickly advance to the next level of investing.

I want to congratulate you on making your way this far in your journey, but as you can tell, there is a long way to go. Every rental property investor, including me, was once at the same point where you now stand. Be sure to reread and study the lessons in this book. Even as you take action and make your first rental property investment, return to this book often as a reference tool to refresh your knowledge. You'll be glad you did.

The road ahead is exciting, challenging, and rewarding, all at the same time. Put one foot in front of the other and keep walking. I hope to see you along the way.

REMEMBER TO DOWNLOAD YOUR FREE DIGITAL ASSETS!

 Tenant Templates

 Various Types of Rental Calculators

 Rental Comparison Worksheet

 Market Analysis Tool

TWO WAYS TO ACCESS YOUR FREE DIGITAL ASSETS

Use the camera app on your mobile phone to take a picture of the QR code or visit the link below and instantly access your digital assets.

 SCAN ME

or

www.clydebankmedia.com/rental-assets

VISIT URL

Appendix I

BRRR(R) Case Study

I touched on the subject of the BRRR(R) investment strategy in chapter 1. To refresh your memory, BRRR(R) stands for buy, rehab, rent, refinance (and repeat). You buy a property with the intention of renovating it and increasing its value. You then rent the property to tenants and refinance it, repaying the original loan and pocketing the difference. The BRRR(R) strategy shares some similarities with the fix-and-flip model of investing, with one huge distinction. While the intent of fix-and-flip is to grab a property, fix it up, and make a quick sale, the BRRR(R) strategy calls for holding a property for a longer period of time. That distinction makes all the difference in how you should approach a BRRR(R) investment property, as the following case study will illustrate.

The first step of the BRRR(R) strategy is to locate a property with significant potential for improvement that can be acquired for well below its market value. Though the target property will initially be valued at less than comparable properties, the improvements you make will bring its value up to par with, if not slightly above, the market value of other homes in the neighborhood.

I have included a Rental Calculator for BRRR(R) as a downloadable resource. Get your copy at **www.clydebankmedia.com/rental-assets** and use it to follow along, plugging in the numbers on your spreadsheet to get a sense of how this BRRR(R) model works.

Next Stop, Vegas

Consider the following scenario: you want to find a good three-bedroom home near the University of Nevada, Las Vegas, to use as a shared student accommodation. You search the neighborhoods and find many homes priced around $150,000, with some higher and some lower. After some looking, you find a home on East Rochelle Avenue, within walking distance of the university, that's listed for $90,000.

The home is a pre-foreclosure, and the previous tenants left it in a terrible state of disrepair. The kitchen is old. The cupboards are broken and visibly hanging off the walls. The appliances look like they were original to the home, which was built in 1962. Throughout, the carpet is stained and threadbare. The walls are paneled and dated, creating a dark, dingy environment. The bathroom is in need of major attention, with a cracked tub and loose tiles throughout. Outside, the concrete patio has patches of grass and the yard is overgrown and weedy. It's obvious why the property is being sold so cheaply, and you recognize it will take a considerable amount of work to restore it to the level of the other homes in the area and to make it suitable and attractive enough for student accommodations.

Let's add up the costs of the Rochelle Avenue property. With the help of your trusted contractor, you work through the necessary renovations. The kitchen and bathroom alone will take $19,000 to fix up. The basement, as you discover upon inspection, has some leaks that need to be repaired, adding another $4,000 to the total. When you calculate the paint, carpet, a couple of extra windows, new appliances, lighting, flooring, and landscaping, you have a $32,000 bill looming. Add up the purchase price, closing costs, advertising costs, and the time it will take to acquire tenants, and you get a total project cost of $125,000 (figure 67).

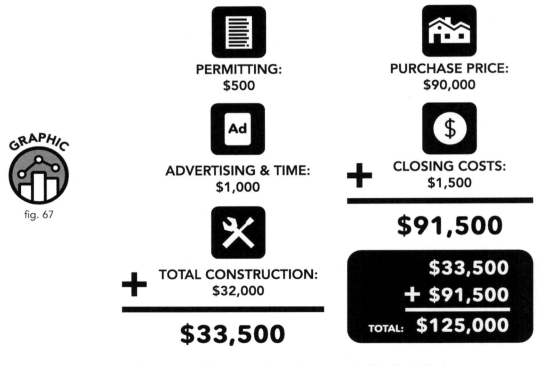

An estimate of the costs to buy and renovate the East Rochelle Avenue property

Success! You've just accomplished your first BRRR(R) strategy win by finding a house that needs major renovations at a steep discount. Even after all the repair costs, you're still coming in at $25,000 under the average comparable house cost in the neighborhood ($150,000), making this property a great candidate for your portfolio. If you haven't already decided to buy the house, it's time to pull the trigger and secure financing for the project.

Investors who have built up a good cash reserve appreciate the BRRR(R) strategy because it allows them to buy a property for cash before refinancing with a lending institution. But let's assume that you're not yet at the point where you can pay cash and you have to finance the entire project with a loan. You will have to cover the loan repayments until you have paying tenants in the property. You estimate it will take a total of four months to complete renovations, advertise the property, and procure good tenants. Assuming you can secure a loan for the total project ($125,000) with a 20 percent down payment ($25,000), and that you're going to spend four months on the hook for your loan service costs at $600 per month, your total personal capital outlay needed to kick off the deal will be $27,400. That's the amount of cash you'll need on hand. The bank will supply the remaining balance ($100,000) of your total project costs (figure 68).

GRAPHIC
fig. 68

FINANCING:

**EQUITY %
OF TOTAL:**
20% - $25,000

**DEBT SERVICE
COSTS:**
$600 - 4 Months

**TOTAL CASH
IN HAND:**
$27,400

LOAN BALANCE:

[$100,000]
$125,000 - $25,000
Down Payment

The financing costs to invest in this property

With your loan in hand, you put in a bid for the East Rochelle Avenue home and get to work. The weeks of renovation are long and arduous, but in time the property shows itself to be worth the investment. With a modern kitchen, two completely revamped bathrooms, a fresh coat of paint, new carpet, and a lot of work on the yard, the property's value has increased immensely. As soon as the work is done, you list it with the university, some local real estate agents, and a good property manager. A modern three-bedroom home is alluring, especially one so close to the university. In no time you have three tenants, sophomore students who don't want to live on campus.

You're now collecting rent, but that's only half of the equation. The real benefit of the BRRR(R) plan is about to become apparent. It's time to refinance the property with the bank, forcing the lender to appraise it at a higher value, which enables you to secure a larger loan. You manage to find a lender offering 80 percent LTV, meaning that the bank will refinance the property and give you a loan that is equivalent to 80 percent of the appraised value. After the appraisal, your property is valued at $155,000, allowing you to borrow $124,000 (80 percent of the value) against the property. Your rental income will easily cover the repayments of the new loan. And now you can pay off your previous loan and pocket the difference.

fig. 69

REFINANCED LOAN (LTV of 80%):

$124,000

INITIAL LOAN (Total Costs):

$100,000

REMAINING CASH IN HAND:

$24,000

The resulting profits of your BRRR(R) strategy

Congrats! This is exactly what you hoped for. You now have $24,000 cash, which you can save as an emergency cash reserve for the property or use to replenish most of your initial capital expenditure. Yes, you started with $27,400, meaning $3,400 is locked up in your new property. Which is a steal considering you are now the proud owner of a positive-cash-flowing rental property and you've increased your net worth by $25,000.

Getting back to the BRRR(R) model, the last R in the strategy stands for repeat. You could take that $24,000 and, using the experience you just gained, repeat the process. Maybe you learned which renovations didn't add much value to the home, which will save you some time and money in the next go-round. Maybe you discovered a better market with more suitable properties—steeply discounted homes with room for massive gains in value.

Or maybe you can use the BRRR(R) strategy to quickly buy a second, a third, and a fourth property. That's the advantage of this investing strategy, and if done correctly it can work remarkably well to help you build your skills, your portfolio, and your investment income.

As a companion to this book, I've created a course where I explain the concepts of the BRRR(R) using real-life examples. This free course is available to all my readers at **www.clydebankmedia.com/rental-assets**.

Appendix II

A "Back of the Envelope" Analysis Case Study

In part II of this book, you learned about the principle of narrowing down your search for the right property, beginning at the regional level, then looking at neighborhoods within that region, and finally looking at individual properties. I want to show you what this looks like as I do my own analysis on a property. You can follow along with me as I take a likely candidate for an investment property and put it through a "back of the envelope" (BOE) analysis. This relatively simple and quick analysis allows me to quantify some of the assumptions I make about a property and calculate the returns I expect to earn throughout the lifetime of the investment.

I have built a spreadsheet for you to play around with as you follow along. It's called the BOE Rental Property Calculator and you can get your copy at **www.clydebankmedia.com/rental-assets**. Substitute your own property's numbers as you get used to how this spreadsheet works.

Let's imagine I've done my market analysis and narrowed my search to the Denver region, based on favorable trends I see in this city. Growth is strong in both rental income and housing prices (figures 70 and 71). I see Denver as boasting steady, consistent numbers, not subject to wild swings in either direction. That sort of trend is encouraging to me, as I plan to buy a property I will operate for several years.

The *Wall Street Journal* recently ranked Denver as having the third-hottest job market for cities with more than one million people. Big tech companies are making the move to Colorado, and I fully expect an explosion in Denver real estate prices, similar to what's happened in Austin, Texas, which received an influx from the tech sector over the last several years. Based on these assumptions, I want to find a suitable three-bedroom home for a family. When the jobs come to Denver, more families will move here, looking for safe, convenient accommodations in a good neighborhood. One of the neighborhoods I've identified is Parker. It's a bedroom community on the outskirts of Denver, but it's rapidly becoming a family favorite with plenty of amenities. It's already a hot destination for those working in the tech industry, with plenty of affordable housing options. Because of these trends, I expect Parker to undergo tremendous growth in housing prices over the next few years.

fig. 70

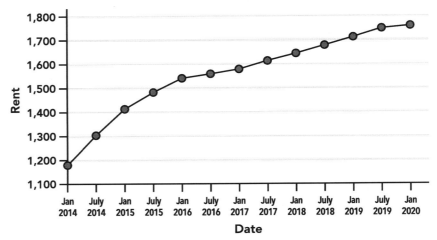

AVERAGE RENTS:
DENVER, CO

Source: Federal Reserve Economic Data

fig. 71

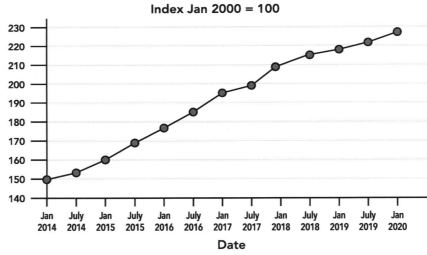

GROWTH IN HOME PRICES:
DENVER, CO
Index Jan 2000 = 100

Source: Zillow Research

After some searching, I find my property candidate for the BOE analysis. It's a lovely, well-kept three-bedroom house, built about twenty years ago on a street called Ironstone Place. If anything, the only work needed would be minor repairs and some cosmetic touchups, like painting and landscaping. And the unfinished basement gives me some room in the future to add value to the property by finishing it up, adding more living space and another bedroom and bathroom. But that can come later. The modern furnishings, fenced yard, and good school district will allow me to attract higher-income families who want long-term leases.

Now to pull out the BOE spreadsheet and fill in some of the details. The figures that I input are partially drawn from the comparable properties in the area, and some are basic assumptions about the health of the real estate market in the neighborhood.

NOTE

If you're having trouble finding data to make comparisons, a local real estate agent can easily provide context and figures to fill in the missing numbers.

First, I'll enter the expected purchase price of the home. I can check out sales in the area in the last ninety days to see how homes have sold in the past. Using a site like Zillow or RedFin, I see if comparable properties have sold at their asking price or if there have been reductions. In this case, assuming the asking prices weren't too high, homes in Parker have sold quickly and often without any discount. So if I make a bid on this home, I have to assume that I'll end up paying the full asking price or close to it, which in this case is $420,000. Now, I don't live in Parker, nor have I ever been there, so again, I have to rely on comps to determine the rent I can charge for a property like this. I can use the same site (RedFin, Zillow, etc.) to pull up rental properties in the area, and I see that most properties this size are charging around $2,600 a month. Knowing that the home is in good shape, I can reasonably expect to charge that rate. The market seems very healthy at the moment, so I allow for four weeks of vacancy annually to find and retain the right tenants.

IMAGE

fig. 72

Assumptions		
Monthly Rents	$	2,600
Vacancy		4 Weeks Per Year
Property Taxes	$	2,520 Per Year
Repair & Maintenance	$	150 Monthly
Insurance		$450 Year
Utilities	$	75.0 Monthly
HOA	$	- Monthly
OTHER	$	- Monthly
OTHER	$	- Monthly
Purchase Price	$	420,000
Closing Costs	$	4,200

Ironstone Place assumptions for costs and rent

As you can see in figure 72, I have included some assumptions about utility costs, insurance, and how much I will set aside each month for repairs and maintenance costs. I looked up the effective property tax rate for Colorado and accounted for that expense as well. I have also made allowances on this BOE model for any other costs that may be incurred, such as an HOA fee or other monthly expenses like property management services.

Now, let's factor in the debt costs. For this property, I'm prepared to put 25 percent down and borrow the rest. I'll base my figures on a long-term twenty-five-year mortgage and set the interest rate at 3 percent. In the fallout of the great COVID-19 lockdown, I'm confident I can find low-interest-rate loans as the Fed tries to spur economic growth again. The Ironstone property is in fantastic shape, so I'm going to allow just $2,500 for some cosmetic upgrades to enhance its curb appeal. I also set my assumptions at holding this property for the next twenty years.

fig. 73

Total Equity Investment		25%	$	106,675
Loan Amount	$	320,025		
Interest Rate		3.0%		
Loan Term (Up to 30 years)		25	Years	
Length of Hold (Up to 50 years)		20	Years	
Renovations @ Purchase	$	2,500		
Renovations @ Exit	$	-		
Rental Growth Rate		3%	Annual Rate	
Expense Growth Rate		3%	Annual Rate	

Ironstone Place assumptions for debt costs

If you look at figure 73, you'll see that I allowed for a conservative 3 percent growth rate for rent. Personally, I think it could go much higher, but for the purposes of a BOE analysis, it's wise to remain conservative.

These are all the assumptions I need for this simple BOE model. It's basic, but using what I've gleaned from real estate sites, I have enough here to figure out if I want to say yes to this investment. In this scenario, I look at my standard metrics, IRR, average yield, and cash multiple. These are the same apples-to-apples comparison metrics that help me make the best decision when considering an investment in any particular property, anywhere in the world.

IMAGE

fig. 74

	Unlevered	Levered
IRR	7.4%	12.9%
Yield	5.4%	12.7%
Cash Multiple	2.71	6.34

Ironstone Place investment metrics

REMEMBER

IRR is a measure of the efficiency of your returns. Yield is a measure of the money you earn after expenses compared against the money you invest. Cash multiple is how much of each dollar you invest will return to you.

You can see that I've included metrics that are specific to a full cash purchase (unlevered) as well as metrics that account for the use of debt to leverage my investment (levered). In this case, I am intent on borrowing money, so I pay the closest attention to my levered metrics fare. I'm ecstatic with the numbers. This property has both an IRR and a yield of more than 12 percent. This shows me the rental returns are efficient and timely. My yield percentage tells me the average rent I will earn after expenses is high enough to justify the initial capital I invest ($106,675). In fact, taking into account the conservative projections on rental increases and allowing for potential vacancies, I will still earn back all my capital after eleven years. And all the while I will build up my equity and earn a steady income that grows over time.

For me, with fifteen years of experience as a real estate investor, I've come to see these metrics with the same revelatory clarity as the characters in *The Matrix* came to see the green screen of scrolling symbols. For pure beginners, without the context of broad experience and practice, these data may not be intuitively revealing, but those numbers tell me everything. Interpreting data like this simply takes time. Be patient, because once you have gone through this analysis process dozens of times, you too will be able to intuit the best investments from just a cursory glance at the numbers.

At the bottom of the BOE spreadsheet you will find several projections that provide a clearer picture of your investment's anticipated returns. These projections include gross rental revenue, net rents, and levered cash flow (see figure 75). Here, I see how much rent I will collect, what I will pay in expenses and debt service costs, and how much I will net after all is said and done.

fig. 75

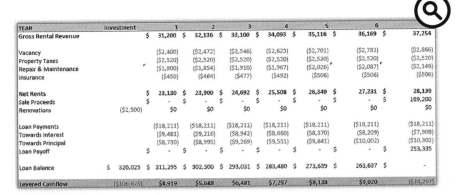

YEAR	Investment	1	2	3	4	5	6	
Gross Rental Revenue		$ 31,200	$ 32,136	$ 33,100	$ 34,093	$ 35,116	$ 36,169	$ 37,254
Vacancy		($2,400)	($2,472)	($2,546)	($2,623)	($2,701)	($2,782)	($2,866)
Property Taxes		($2,520)	($2,520)	($2,520)	($2,520)	($2,520)	($2,520)	($2,520)
Repair & Maintenance		($1,800)	($1,854)	($1,910)	($1,967)	($2,026)	($2,087)	($2,149)
Insurance		($490)	($464)	($477)	($492)	($506)	($506)	($506)
Net Rents		$ 23,130	$ 23,900	$ 24,692	$ 25,508	$ 26,349	$ 27,231	$ 28,139
Sale Proceeds		$ -	$ -	$ -	$ -	$ -	$ -	$ 169,200
Renovations	($2,500)	$0	$0	$0	$0	$0	$0	$0
Loan Payments		($18,211)	($18,211)	($18,211)	($18,211)	($18,211)	($18,211)	($18,211)
Towards Interest		($9,481)	($9,216)	($8,942)	($8,660)	($8,370)	($8,209)	($7,909)
Towards Principal		($8,730)	($8,995)	($9,269)	($9,551)	($9,841)	($10,002)	($10,302)
Loan Payoff		$ -	$ -	$ -	$ -	$ -	$ -	$ 253,335
Loan Balance	$ 320,025	$ 311,295	$ 302,300	$ 293,031	$ 283,480	$ 273,639	$ 263,637	$ -
Levered Cashflow	($106,675)	$4,919	$5,688	$6,481	$7,297	$8,138	$9,020	($74,207)

The first five years of my Ironstone Place investment (projections)

By looking at these figures, I can see that in my first year I will make $31,200 in rent before expenses. Once I cover vacancy costs, taxes, expenses, and the debt repayments, I will net $4,919 as my first-year profit. As rent increases over time, I will net more and more profit each year. In this analysis, I can see I will be making more than $8,000 in year five. And during those five years, I will have built up nearly $50,000 in equity from the principal repayments on the loan ($320,025 - $273,639).

Within a matter of minutes, this BOE analysis allows me to do serious market research on an individual property. I'm reasonably confident about the assumptions I've used (rent price, vacancy, taxes, etc.), so I can expect that this model is an accurate representation of my real-world returns. But those returns are only possible, of course, if I act now and buy the property.

Appendix III

A Short-Term Rental Case Study

In chapter 6, we talked about the advantages (and disadvantages) of buying a short-term rental (STR) property as an investment model. This type of property isn't fundamentally different than a property you would use for a standard long-term rental with tenants and year-long contracts. It could be the same condo, single-family home, or apartment. The key distinction is in how you operate it. The question on your mind should be, "How do I know that a short-term rental property would be a better investment with higher returns than a traditional rental?" At the time of this writing, it's a legitimate question due to the fact that many prime rental markets have recently dropped 10, 20, or even 30 percent in total listings. That's the problem with the STR market. Once the tourism industry dries up (thanks to an economic downturn or a global pandemic), the owners of these STR properties are among the first to feel the brunt of it. That makes it even more crucial to analyze and determine if a short-term rental property is a good investment model.

Watch over my shoulder as I analyze the short-term rental market of Austin, Texas. Austin is a particularly prime market for STRs. It has been named America's fastest-growing city, with one hundred people moving there every single day. Every year, 70,000 students descend on the city to attend Texas A&M University, creating an entire side market of visiting parents and relatives. Austin also hosts the immensely popular South by Southwest (SXSW), a tech, film, and music conference that has become a destination for up to 100,000 guests. The city has an exceptional climate, welcoming thousands of tourists each year to play, relax, and enjoy what Austin has to offer. All of this has resulted in a booming STR market, one that has lured investors by the droves. Because of these factors, Austin is a city in which it's likely that a short-term rental property can perform better than a standard rental operation. And now you're here to see if you can't catch just a bit of that hot STR action.

NOTE

I'm going to be conducting this analysis as if I were doing it today, in the middle of the pandemic with a depressed rental market. Some of the assumptions I'm making won't be applicable a few years from now, but the principles will not change. Bear that in mind as you make your own analysis, no matter what the economy is like in the future.

Let's look at a reasonably standard three-bedroom, two-bathroom condo, an ideal property type for the Austin region. Tourists can book this condo and bring the whole family to vacation in the Texas sun. Parents of college students can use the condo while visiting to attend an awards night or an important game. The condo has a broad enough appeal to cater to many visitors of this fine city. It is priced at $400,000, without any extra capital needed for the repairs. Assuming we make a $100,000 down payment (inclusive of all closing costs), we can secure financing of $300,000 at 3.25 percent over a thirty-year term, leaving $1,306 for the monthly mortgage repayment (figure 76).

fig. 76

Purchase Price	$	420,000	
Closing Costs	$	-	
Total Equity Investment	25%	$	100,000
Loan Amount	$	300,000	
Interest Rate		3.25%	
Loan Term		30	Years
Loan Repayments	$	1,305.62	
Renovations @ Purchase	$	-	
Renovations @ Exit	$	-	

The purchase and financing costs of the Austin condo

Before we determine whether the property will be profitable as a short-term rental, we must create a control figure. For this, we'll use what we could reasonably expect to earn with a traditional long-term rental in the current market (figure 77). Using the comparables from the neighborhood (see chapter 4), we know that this condo can support $2,000 a month in rent. This will easily cover our mortgage repayments, and we might even be able to break even on the total costs. If we include all our property taxes, insurance costs, and other expenses, we'll make a $54 net profit at the end of each month. At least we're in the black!

fig. 77

Monthly Rents	$	2,000	
Vacancy		4	Weeks
Property Taxes	$	5,400	
Repair & Maintenance	$	-	Monthly
Insurance		$400	Year
Utilities	$	-	Monthly
Net Profits		54.00	

The assumed monthly cash flow of our Austin condo

Now that we have our control figure based on a standard rental model, we can look at how much profit we could make as a short-term rental property. Austin was once a prime tourist market, attracting thousands of visitors every year, but the current circumstances and economic climate have severely weakened that industry. Based on data we can glean from short-term rental analytic sites like AllTheRooms.com, we can see current and historical trends for Austin's STR market (figure 78).

GRAPHIC

fig. 78

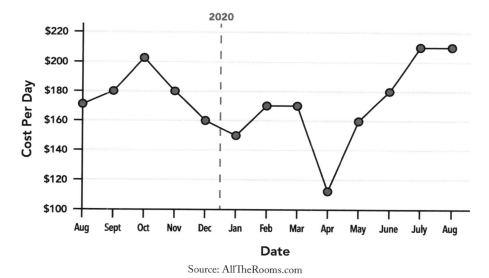

AVERAGE DAILY ROOM RENTS
AUSTIN, TX

Source: AllTheRooms.com

The monthly average of a daily room rate across all Austin short-term rentals

Although the global pandemic put a dip in the average room rates, they've recovered quickly and even risen to a year-long high. But that room rate tells only part of the story. As with all short-term rentals, the key analytic is the occupancy rate. It's all good and well to charge $212 a day, but if you don't have a high enough occupancy rate, you won't make money. Austin's once-prime market has fallen, with the average occupancy rate hovering around 32 percent as of January 2021. Before the pandemic, it was over 45 percent, and the top quartile listings did well over 65 percent.

Let's apply these current averages to our three-bedroom Austin condo. Would it be a smart move to enter the STR market right now? Based on occupancy and room rates, we would expect to make $2,100 a month. We must consider, however, that there are additional expenses involved with listing and hosting a short-term rental. Our property taxes and insurance costs remain the same, but now a portion of our booking fees are paid to the platform or property manager. We also have to pay for cleaning and repairs with a higher turnover in guests. After adding an additional $456 a month for those expenses, we're left with a net loss of $152 each month. Obviously this is not the right move, at least not at the moment.

That net result figure is only half the equation. I have purposely left out a variable from our calculations: the time it takes to operate each investment. When we include the variable of time spent on each investment model, the results become even clearer. With our traditional rental model, we're making a net profit of $54, and we're only spending up to one hour each month to monitor and maintain the property. But a short-term rental property with this number of bookings would require up to eight hours of our time per month— time spent responding to guests, optimizing our listing, and coordinating cleaning and repairs. With a net loss of $152 each month, that means that for every hour we spend on the property, we lose $19 (figure 79). More time. Less money. Not a good deal.

fig. 79

	AS LONG-TERM RENTAL	32% occupancy $212/night AS SHORT-TERM RENTAL (7/20)
MORTGAGE	$1,306	$1,306
GROSS RENTAL REVENUE	$2,000	$2,100
NET RENTS	$694	$794
EST. PROPERTY TAX + INSURANCE	$490	$490
OTHER EXPENSES	$150	$456
EST. PROFITS	**$54**	**($152)**
EST. HOURS OF WORK	1 hour	8 hours
EST. PROFIT/HR	$54	($19)

The traditional/short-term rental comparison in the current market conditions

The good news is that the short-term rental market isn't going to remain as stagnant as it is right now. Even if it takes a couple of years, the tourism industry will eventually return to Austin. In light of that hopeful future, let's analyze that same property as if two years have passed and the occupancy rates have doubled (a reliable yet conservative prediction). If in two years we double our occupancy rate from 32 percent to 65 percent, we can assume we would make $4,200 a month from bookings. Less our mortgage repayment and tax/insurance/listing expenses, we'd have a net profit of $1,672 each month (figure 80).

fig. 80

	AS LONG-TERM RENTAL	32% occupancy $212/night AS SHORT-TERM RENTAL (7/20)	65% occupancy $212/night AS SHORT-TERM RENTAL (7/22)
MORTGAGE	$1,306	$1,306	$1,306
GROSS RENTAL REVENUE	$2,000	$2,100	$4,200
NET RENTS	$694	$794	$2,894
EST. PROPERTY TAX + INSURANCE	$490	$490	$490
OTHER EXPENSES	$150	$456	$732
EST. PROFITS	$54	($152)	$1,672
EST. HOURS OF WORK	1 hour	8 hours	16 hours
EST. PROFIT/HR	$54	($19)	$105

The current and future cash flow of our short-term rental condo

But, as you can imagine, increased listings demand more of our time. We now have to spend twice as long maintaining the property and dealing with guests. Requiring sixteen hours each month, the upkeep is much more intensive than for a traditional rental model (one hour a month). But have a look at figure 80, especially noting the profit per hour. We're busier, yes, but that time is twice as profitable. Whereas we were making $54 an hour in the long-term rental, in two years we'll be making $105 for every hour we spend on the short-term rental. That makes for an easy decision.

According to our analysis, our best bet presently would be to buy and hold the condo with a long-term tenant, sacrificing any expectation of good returns right now in hopes of a much larger payoff when the future short-term rental market explodes. When you read this, you may find that the tourism industry in your area is booming, making the comparison much easier than speculating about what may happen in the future. In that case, you may want to include a short-term rental property as a way to boost the earnings of your portfolio. I know of some apartment owners who set aside 10 to 20 percent of their units to operate as short-term rentals. Those STR units cover up to 80 percent of the operating costs of the entire building. I would caution you not to overburden your portfolio with short-term rentals because of the potential volatility of the tourism industry. But as a way to juice your returns, I wholly endorse STR properties as part of a balanced and healthy real estate portfolio.

Appendix IV

Rental Property Resources

Analysis Tools

Although I have my preferences for websites here in the United States that I use to perform analysis, my students from 180 different countries have informed me of recommended sites in their respective markets.

Real Estate Sites for the USA

» Zillow.com
» Trulia.com
» Redfin.com
» Remax.com
» Craigslist.org
» Loopnet.com (commercial property)
» Rentometer.com (rent estimates)

Real Estate Sites for Canada

» Realtor.ca
» Rew.ca
» Remax.ca
» Craigslist.ca

Real Estate Sites for the UK

» Rightmove.co.uk
» Zoopla.co.uk

Real Estate Sites for Latin America

» Zapimoveis.com.br
» Vivareal.com.br
» Pisofincasa.com

Real Estate Sites for the UAE

» Dubizzle.com
» Propertyfinder.ae

Real Estate Sites for India

» Indiaproperty.com
» 99acres.com
» Housing.com/in
» Magicbricks.com

Real Estate Sites for China

» Fang.com
» Dichan.com
» Juwai.com

Real Estate Sites for South Africa

» PrivateProperty.co.za
» Property24.com

Other Real Estate Markets

» Realtor.com/international
» Europeanproperty.com
» Suumo.jp

Calculators

Everybody seems to offer some version of a mortgage calculator. Here are some of my online favorites. I've also included an amortization schedule calculator as a downloadable resource for you.

» Mortgagecalculator.org

» Zillow.com/mortgage-calculator (This is convenient when using Zillow for your Back of the Envelope analysis. It also includes current interest rates for accurate calculations.)

» USBank.com/home-loans/mortgage/mortgage-calculators

GET YOUR NEXT
QuickStart Guide™
FOR FREE

Leave us a quick video testimonial on our website and we will give you a **FREE *QuickStart Guide*** of your choice!

RECORD TESTIMONIAL

SUBMIT TO OUR WEBSITE

GET A FREE BOOK

About
the Author

SYMON HE, MBA

Symon He, MBA, is an author, best-selling online business and real estate investing course instructor, licensed real estate investor, and consultant based in Los Angeles. His training courses in real estate investing, deal structuring, and financial modeling have reached over 300,000 students in nearly 180 countries. His real estate investing expertise has been cited in numerous prominent media outlets including the *Wall Street Journal*, *Reuters*, *Forbes*, *CNBC*, and Skift. He has previously partnered with prominent finance companies such as RichDad.com.

Mr. He's consulting services help private real estate investors make smart acquisitions and profitably structure their deals. Previous to this line of work, he was the head of marketing analytics at the Panda Restaurant Group. Before that, he worked as a manager in the global M&A unit for Ingram Micro, a Fortune 80 company. Going even further back in his professional career, he worked on commercial real estate acquisitions at a private equity real estate fund, covering a wide range of asset classes across the western United States. Symon received degrees in computer engineering (magna cum laude) and economics (summa cum laude) from UC Irvine and received his MBA from Stanford University.

Symon is a cofounder of LearnBNB, a boutique consultancy and education blog that specializes in the home-sharing economy. Connect with Symon at www.learnbnb.com, explore the world of real estate investing on his blog at symonhe.com, or find Symon on LinkedIn.

About ClydeBank Media

We create simplified educational tools that allow our customers to successfully learn new skills in order to navigate this constantly changing world.

The success of ClydeBank Media's value-driven approach starts with beginner-friendly high-quality information. We work with subject matter experts who are leaders in their fields. These experts are supported by our team of professional researchers, writers, and educators.

Our team at ClydeBank Media works with these industry leaders to break down their wealth of knowledge, their wisdom, and their years of experience into small and concise building blocks. We piece together these building blocks to create a clearly defined learning path that a beginner can follow for successful mastery.

At ClydeBank Media, we see a new world of possibility. Simplified learning doesn't have to be bound by four walls; instead, it's driven by you.

Glossary

1031 exchange

A strategy that allows investors to defer paying capital gains taxes on the sale of one property when they use the proceeds to buy a similar, often larger property. Named after Section 1031 of the Internal Revenue Code.

Asset class

A group of investment properties that behave in a similar way under identical market conditions. Within an asset class, there can be several types of investment options.

Capital

The money provided by an investor, either through debt or paid out of pocket, to secure an investment.

Case-Shiller Index

An index based on single-family homes that tracks sales prices in nine divisions of the US. The index is standardized and set to January 2000 = 100.

Cash Flow Schedule

The measurement of the flow of money in and out of an investment.

Cash Multiple

A measurement of the money each dollar invested is expected to return. Cash flow income is divided by the cash invested to derive a ratio that determines profits per dollar.

Commercial Property

Any real estate property that is intended to be used to generate a profit. Any residential property with five or more units is considered a commercial property.

Comparable

Properties similar to a given property in the same market that are used as comparisons to help determine fair market value of the given property.

Consumption

The resources spent on goods and services.

Conventional Mortgage

A loan offered by a private lender, such as a bank, for use by a borrower to buy property. Conventional loans are not secured by a government entity.

Core Investment

An investment that requires minimal effort from an investor in order to return profits. Often considered to pose low risk for failure.

Creative Financing

Securing the funding to purchase property outside of the traditional loans offered by private lenders and government entities.

Debt Service Coverage Ratio (DSCR)

A metric used by lenders to assess the risk of a borrower. In real estate, the metric is calculated by dividing the cash flow income of a property (before expenses) by the debt payment costs of the loan.

Discount Rate

A risk-adjusted rate measurement used by an investor to calculate present rates from future earnings.

Diversification

A risk management strategy of spreading investments across a variety of assets and types.

Earnest Money

A deposit made to a seller in conjunction with a buyer's offer, intended to represent the authenticity of the offer.

Equities

A type of investment comprised of ownership shares in a business or real property.

Equity

The degree of one's ownership, represented as a dollar amount.

Estoppel Certificate

A signed statement provided by a tenant certifying the conditions of a lease agreement such as rent, security deposit, and term of lease.

Financing

Procuring funding for the purchase of a property.

Geographic Arbitrage

Taking advantage of the disparity between low-cost-of-living areas and high-income areas, often through remote working arrangements.

Hard Money Lenders

Individual money lenders that offer private equity as a loan for an investment.

Homeowners Association

An organization populated by the residents of a community for the purpose of enforcing rules within that community.

Internal Rate of Return

A measurement used to analyze the efficiency of an investment's returns.

Leverage

Using debt to finance a property, increasing the potential returns of the investment.

Limited Liability Company

A business structure that separates the assets and liabilities of a business from those of the owner.

Market

A defined system where commodities are bought and sold. The term "real estate market" can also refer to the properties within a specific city or region.

Months of Inventory

The measurement of time, in months, that it would take to sell all listed properties in a certain area. Assumes no additional listings and a consistent rate of sale.

Multiple Listing Service (MLS)

A network of active listings in a certain market..

Negative Leverage

A situation in which the cost of the debt used to buy a property exceeds the profits made by that property.

Net Present Value (NPV)

An investing metric used to assess and compare risks of an investment. Calculates all future returns as if paid in one lump sum today.

Opportunistic Investment

An investment that requires maximum effort from an investor in order to return profits. These investments are often considered to pose high risk for failure.

Overleveraged

Having too much debt owing on an investment. Can also refer to having zero equity in an investment.

Passive Income

Cash flow earned without the active involvement of the investor.

Portfolio Lenders

Lending institutions that do not sell existing loans to new lenders but keep the debt on their own books.

Positive Leverage

Debt used to finance an investment that allows the investor to earn higher profits than with a cash-only investment.

Principal

The borrowed money portion of a loan upon which interest owing is calculated.

Pro Forma Rent
The potential rent a property could earn when operating at peak efficiency in ideal market conditions.

Property Manager
A professional service that manages the daily operations of a rental property, including locating tenants, collecting rent, and maintaining the property.

Real Estate Owned (REO)
Repossessed property held by the lender that has not sold at a foreclosure auction.

Refinance
The replacement of one mortgage with another mortgage, often at a better interest rate or with a different appraised property value.

Residential Property
Property designed exclusively to serve as a domicile for residents.

Return
Cash flow income due to an investor from an investment. In real estate, returns come in the form of rent and as lump sum payments from the sale of property.

Risk Tolerance
The ability of an investor to withstand the potential failure of an investment and loss of capital.

Short-Term Rental
Property designed to house tenants, often refered to as guests, for short periods of time. Although legal definitions vary by region, the term often refers to any stay of less than six months.

Staging
The act of dressing up a vacant property with tasteful furnishings to boost its appearance in order to attract buyers.

Tenant
The occupant of a property who pays rent to the property's owner, or landlord.

Turnkey Providers
Professional services that offer renovated properties that need no additional work before being put up for rent.

Underwriting
The agreement of an individual to accept the risk of an investment or deal.

Vacancy
A period of time during which a property is without a tenant paying rent.

Value-Added Investment
An investment that requires moderate effort from an investor in order to return profits. These investments are often considered to pose low-to-medium risk for failure.

Distribution Waterfall Framework
A structure of equitable assignment of the profits from an investment that accounts for the capital and time invested by each contributor in a partnership investment.

Yield
The earnings due to an investor over the life of an investment. Can also be calculated as the cash flow income divided by the capital spent by the investor.

References

Anderson, Eric, Song Lin, Duncan Simester. 2015. "Harbingers of Failure." *Journal of Marketing Research*.

Barrero, Jose Maria, Nick Bloom, Steven J. Davis. 2020. "COVID-19 Is Also a Reallocation Shock." Working paper, Becker Friedman Institute of Economics at the University of Chicago.

Cross, Bettie. 2019. "Austin Leads Nation in Population Growth for 8 Consecutive Years." *CBS Austin*. April 18. Accessed March 30, 2021. https://cbsaustin.com/news/local/austin-leads-nation-in-population-growth-for-8-consecutive-years .

Feloni, Richard. 2015. "How Getting Fired from an Ice Cream Shop Changed 'Shark Tank' Investor Kevin O'Leary's Life." *Business Insider*. February 12. https://www.businessinsider.com/kevin-oleary-fired-from-ice-cream-shop-2015-2.

Foldvary, Fred. 1998. "Will There Be a Recession?" *Progress Report*. Accessed June 2020. https://web.archive.org/web/20011123103024/http://www.progress.org/archive/fold19.htm.

Foldvary, Fred E. 2007. "The Depression of 2008." Berkeley: The Gutenberg Press.

Gawande, Atul. 2009. *The Checklist Manifesto: How to Get Things Right*. Metropolitan Books.

George, Henry. 1879. *Progress and Poverty: An Inquiry into the Cause of Industrial Depressions and of Increase of Want with Increase of Wealth: The Remedy*. New York: Cosimo Books.

Gladwell, Malcolm. 2000. *The Tipping Point*. Little Brown.

Kolbert, Elizabeth. 2019. "Louisiana's Disappearing Coast." *The New Yorker*. March 25. https://www.newyorker.com/magazine/2019/04/01/louisianas-disappearing-coast.

Konnikova, Maria. 2020. *The Biggest Bluff: How I Learned to Pay Attention, Master Myself, and Win*. Penguin Press.

Long, Heather. 2016. "The New Normal: 4 Job Changes By the Time You're 32." *CNN Business*. April 12. https://money.cnn.com/2016/04/12/news/economy/millennials-change-jobs-frequently.

Molina, Kimberley. 2019. "Couple Sues Landlord After Pets 'Boiled to Death' When Radiator Pipe Bursts." *CBC News*. October 1. https://www.cbc.ca/news/canada/ottawa/couple-blames-minto-pets-death-1.5294572.

Oh, Soo. 2020. "Austin, Nashville Rank at Top of Hottest U.S. Job Markets." *The Wall Street Journal*. February 24. https://www.wsj.com/articles/austin-nashville-rank-at-top-of-hottest-u-s-job-markets-11582545600.

Savage, Susannah. 2019. "To Survive in a Wetter World, Raise Ducks, Not Chickens." *The Atlantic*, July 13.

Shilling, Gary. 2019. "Millennials Should Be Happy They Are Stuck Renting." *Bloomberg*. November 4. https://www.bloomberg.com/opinion/articles/2019-11-04/millennials-should-be-happy-they-are-stuck-renting.

Voss, Chris. 2016. *Never Split The Difference: Negotiating As If Your Life Depended On It*. HarperCollins.

Yates, Tyler. 2020. "How Much Are People Making From the Sharing Economy?" *Earnest*. March 31. https://www.earnest.com/blog/sharing-economy-income-data.

Index

Spike TV, 155
Staging, 181–182
Starbucks, 198–199
Stock market, Kuwaiti, 142
Stock market, U.S.
    average return for, 8
    real estate investing versus, 8–9, 37
Storage, 129
Students, as tenants, 130–132
Subdividing of rental property, 31–32
"Subject-to" deals, 49
Suburban markets, 209
Subway, 97–98
Supply and demand
    description of, 54
    mobile home market affected by, 109
    rental prices affected by, 65
Svetec, James, 113–114

T

Taleb, Nassim Nicholas, 52
Tampa, 206*f*, 207
Taxes
    corporate, 197
    occupancy, 112
    property, 126–127
Tenants
    apartment, 105, 131–132
    background checks on, 163
    bad, 166
    as buyers, 91
    with children, 129
    in co-living facilities, 31
    communication with, 167
    dealing with, 162–166
    description of, 17
    discrimination considerations, 165
    employment records for, 164
    families as, 128–130
    good, 163–164
    injuries in, liability insurance for, 170
    lease agreements for, 92, 162, 165
    long-term transitions, 182–183
    new rental properties and, 25
    niches, 118, 127–133
    privacy law considerations, 92
    problem, 166
    professionals as, 132–133
    references of, 164
    referrals from, 164
    relationships with, 162–163
    rental history of, 92, 164
    rent collection from, 9
    screening of, 163–165
    during selling of rental property, 91–92
    short-term rentals, 109
    students as, 130–132

templates for, 92, 162, 165
    written communication with, 167
Tipping Point, The, 154
Tokyo Stock Exchange, 142
Townhouses, 101–102, 102*f*, 133
"Trailer parks," 108. *See also* Mobile home parks
Turnkey providers, 195–196

U

"Underwater," 38–39
Underwriting, 61–63, 190
Unemployment, 58
United Arab Emirates, real estate sites for, 239
United Kingdom, real estate sites for, 239
United States
    real estate sites for, 239
    rental market recovery in, 6*f*
    urbanization of population in, 5, 5*f*
Upgrades, 28
"Upside down," 61
Urbanization, 5, 5*f*, 216

V

Vacancy
    costs of, 21
    rental income insurance protection for, 171
Vacancy rates
    for apartments, 105, 132
    in California, 55*f*
    housing starts and, 57, 58*f*
Vacation homes, 109–114
Valuation, 23
Value(s)
    appreciated, 75
    loan-to-value ratio, 44*f*, 44–45
    net present, 81–84
    rental property, 23, 120–123, 212–213
Value-added investments, 24
Variance, 211
Voss, Chris, 91

W

Walkscore.com, 124, 131
Wall Street Journal, The, 227
Waterfall framework, distribution, 159–160
Weather, 89–90
Websites
    global, 239–240
    government, 140
    neighborhood evaluations using, 124
    recommended, 239–240
West Virginia, 127*f*
Wholesalers, 144
Written communication, 167
Wyoming, 127*f*

Notes

EXPLORE MORE BEST-SELLING
QuickStart Guides®

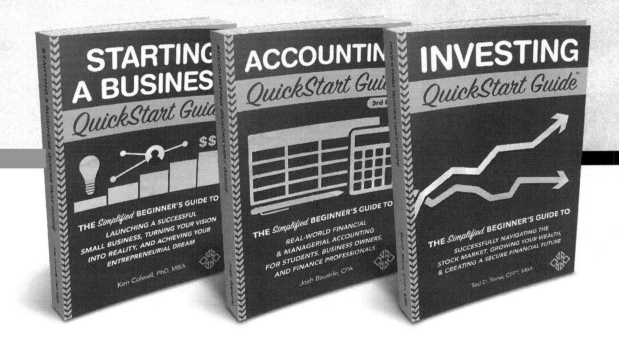

TO EXPLORE ALL TITLES, VISIT:

www.clydebankmedia.com/shop

CLYDEBANK MEDIA

QuickStart Guides®

PROUDLY SUPPORT ONE TREE PLANTED

One Tree Planted is a 501(c)(3) nonprofit organization focused on global reforestation, with millions of trees planted every year. ClydeBank Media is proud to support One Tree Planted as a reforestation partner.

Every dollar donated plants one tree and every tree makes a difference!

Made in the USA
Middletown, DE
28 September 2021